Honda
XR50/70/80/100R
CRF50/70/80/100F
Owners Workshop Manual

by Alan Ahlstrand
and John H Haynes
Member of the Guild of Motoring Writers

Models covered:
XR50R, 2000 through 2003
XR70R, 1997 through 2003
XR80R, 1985 through 2003
XR100R, 1985 through 2003
CRF50F, 2004 through 2016
CRF70F, 2004 through 2012
CRF80F, 2004 through 2013
CRF100F, 2004 through 2013

(2218 - 4U4)

ABCDE
FGHIJ
KLMN

Haynes Publishing
Sparkford Nr Yeovil
Somerset BA22 7JJ England

Haynes North America, Inc
859 Lawrence Drive
Newbury Park
California 91320 USA
www.haynes.com

Acknowledgments

For the 80/100 models, our thanks to Honda of Milpitas, Milpitas, California, for providing the facilities used for the chassis photographs; to Pete Sirett, service manager, for arranging the facilities and fitting the mechanical work into his shop's busy schedule; and to Steve Van Horn, service technician, for doing the mechanical work and providing valuable technical information. Thanks also to Denny Jewell, service technician, for providing the engine used in the overhaul photographs, performing the teardown, and offering the technical insight that comes from his years of experience as a motorcycle mechanic and racer. For the 50 and 70 models, our thanks to Grand Prix, Santa Clara, California, for providing the facilities used for the photgraphs; to Mark Zueger, service manager, for arranging the mechanical work and fitting the teardown into his shop's busy schedule, and to Craig Wardner, service technican, for performing the teardown and giving us the benefit of his many years experience as a racing engine builder.

© **Haynes North America, Inc. 1996, 2004, 2007, 2016**
With permission from J.H. Haynes & Co. Ltd.

A book in the Haynes Owners Workshop Manual Series

Printed in Malaysia

ISBN-13: 978-1-62092-239-2
ISBN-10: 1-62092-239-8

Library of Congress Control Number: 2016938760

We take great pride in the accuracy of information given in this manual, but motorcycle manufacturers make alterations and design changes during the production run of a particular motorcycle of which they do not inform us. No liability can be accepted by the authors or publishers for loss, damage or injury caused by any errors in, or omissions from, the information given.

Contents

1996 Honda XR100R

About this manual

Its purpose

The purpose of this manual is to help you get the best value from your motorcycle. It can do so in several ways. It can help you decide what work must be done, even if you choose to have it done by a dealer service department or a repair shop; it provides information and procedures for routine maintenance and servicing; and it offers diagnostic and repair procedures to follow when trouble occurs.

We hope you use the manual to tackle the work yourself. For many simpler jobs, doing it yourself may be quicker than arranging an appointment to get the vehicle into a shop and making the trips to leave it and pick it up. More importantly, a lot of money can be saved by avoiding the expense the shop must pass on to you to cover its labor and overhead costs. An added benefit is the sense of satisfaction and accomplishment that you feel after doing the job yourself.

Using the manual

The manual is divided into Chapters. Each Chapter is divided into numbered Sections, which are headed in bold type between horizontal lines. Each Section consists of consecutively numbered paragraphs or steps.

At the beginning of each numbered Section you will be referred to any illustrations which apply to the procedures in that Section. The reference numbers used in illustration captions pinpoint the pertinent Section and the Step within that Section. That is, illustration 3.2 means the illustration refers to Section 3 and Step (or paragraph) 2 within that Section.

Procedures, once described in the text, are not normally repeated. When it's necessary to refer to another Chapter, the reference will be given as Chapter and Section number. Cross references given without use of the word `Chapter' apply to Sections and/or paragraphs in the same Chapter. For example, `see Section 8' means in the same Chapter.

References to the left or right side of the vehicle assume you are sitting on the seat, facing forward.

Motorcycle manufacturers continually make changes to specifications and recommendations, and these, when notified, are incorporated into our manuals at the earliest opportunity.

Even though we have prepared this manual with extreme care, neither the publisher nor the authors can accept responsibility for any errors in, or omissions from, the information given.

NOTE

A **Note** provides information necessary to properly complete a procedure or information which will make the procedure easier to understand.

CAUTION

A **Caution** provides a special procedure or special steps which must be taken while completing the procedure where the Caution is found. Not heeding a Caution can result in damage to the assembly being worked on.

WARNING

A **Warning** provides a special procedure or special steps which must be taken while completing the procedure where the Warning is found. Not heeding a Warning can result in personal injury.

Introduction to the Honda XR50/70/80/100R and CRF50/70/80/100F

The Honda XR50/70/80/100F and CRF50/70/80/100F are highly successful and popular lightweight trail bikes.

The engine on all models is an air-cooled single with an overhead camshaft. Power is transmitted through a three-speed transmission (50 and 70 models) or a five-speed transmission (80 and 100 models), wet multi-plate clutch and chain final drive. The clutch on 50 and 70 models disengages automatically when the shift pedal is moved.

Identification numbers

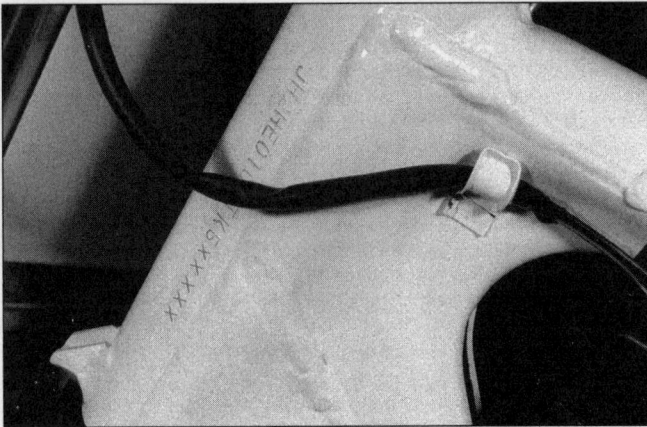

The frame serial number is located at the front of the frame, on the steering tube

The engine serial number is located on the left side of the crankcase

The frame serial number is stamped into the front of the frame (see illustration) and printed on a label affixed to the frame. The engine number is stamped into the left side of the crankcase (see illustration). Both of these numbers should be recorded and kept in a safe place so they can be furnished to law enforcement officials in the event of a theft.

The frame serial number, engine serial number and carburetor identification number should also be kept in a handy place (such as with your driver's license) so they are always available when purchasing or ordering parts for your machine.

The models covered by this manual are as follows:

XR50R, 2000 through 2003

XR70R, 1997 through 2003
XR80R, 1985 through 2003
XR100R, 1985 through 2003
CRF50F, 2004 through 2016
CRF70F, 2004 through 2012
CRF80F, 2004 through 2013
CRF100F, 2004 through 2013

Identifying models and years

The procedures in this manual identify the bikes by model year. The model year is included in a decal on the frame.

Buying parts

Once you have found all the identification numbers, record them for reference when buying parts. Since the manufacturers change specifications, parts and vendors (companies that manufacture various components on the machine), providing the ID numbers is the only way to be reasonably sure that you are buying the correct parts.

Whenever possible, take the worn part to the dealer so direct comparison with the new component can be made. Along the trail from the manufacturer to the parts shelf, there are numerous places that the part can end up with the wrong number or be listed incorrectly.

The two places to purchase new parts for your motorcycle - the accessory store and the franchised dealer - differ in the type of parts they carry. While dealers can obtain virtually every part for your motorcycle, the accessory dealer is usually limited to normal high wear items such as shock absorbers, tune-up parts, various engine gaskets, cables, chains, brake parts, etc. Rarely will an accessory outlet have major suspension components, cylinders, transmission gears, or cases.

Used parts can be obtained for roughly half the price of new ones, but you can't always be sure of what you're getting. Once again, take your worn part to the wrecking yard (breaker) for direct comparison.

Whether buying new, used or rebuilt parts, the best course is to deal directly with someone who specializes in parts for your particular make.

General specifications

XR80R, CRF80F

Bore	47.5 mm (1.87 inches)
Stroke	45.0 mm (1.77 inches)
Compression ratio	9.7 to 1
Wheelbase	
1985 through 1997	1195 mm (47.1 inches)
1998 through 2000	1210 mm (47.6 inches)
2001 through 2003	1208 mm (47.6 inches)
2004 and later	1209 mm (47.6 inches)
Overall length	
1985 through 1997	1730 mm (68.1 inches)
1998 through 2000	1740 mm (68.5 inches)
2001 through 2003	1743 mm (68.6 inches)
2004 and later	1749 mm(68.9 inches)
Overall width	
1985 through 2000	755 mm (29.7 inches)
2001 through 2003	778 mm (30.6 inches)
2004 and later	727 mm (28.6 inches)
Overall height	
1985 through 1997	955 mm (37.6 inches)
1998 through 2000	980 mm (38.6 inches)
2001 through 2003	1030 mm (40.6 inches)
2004 and later	995 mm (39.2 inches)
Seat height	
1985 through 2000	725 mm (28.6 inches)
2001 through 2003	727 mm (28.6 inches)
2004 and later	734 mm (28.9 inches)
Ground clearance	
1985 through 1997	210 mm (8.3 inches)
1998 through 2000	220 mm (8.7 inches)
2001 through 2003	206 mm (8.1 inches)
2004 and later	218 mm (8.6 inches)
Dry weight	
1985 through 2000	64 kg (141.1 lbs)
2001 and later	70 kg (154 lbs)

XR100R, CRF100F

Bore	53.0 mm (2.09 inches)
Stroke	45.0 mm (1.77 inches)
Compression ratio	9.4 to 1
Wheelbase	
1985 through 2000	1255 mm (49.4 inches)
2001 through 2003	1264 mm (49.8 inches)
2004 and later	1249 mm (49.2 inches)
Overall length	
1985 through 2000	1855 mm (73.0 inches)
2001 through 2003	1869 mm (73.6 inches)
2004 and later	1853 mm (73.0 inches)
Overall width	
1985 through 2000	800 mm (31.5 inches)
2001 through 2003	816 mm (32.1 inches)
2004 and later	786 mm (30.9 inches)
Overall height	
1985 through 1997	1030 mm (40.6 inches)
1998 through 2000	1050 mm (41.3 inches)
2001 through 2003	1102 mm (43.4 inches)
2004 and later	1046 mm (4.12 inches)
Seat height	
1985 through 2000	770 mm (30.3 inches)
2001 through 2003	775 mm (30.5 inches)
2004 and later	621 mm (24.4 inches))

General Specifications

XR100R, CRF100F (continued)

Ground clearance
 1985 through 2000 .... 265 mm (10.4 inches)
 2001 through 2003 .... 253 mm (10.0 inches)
 2004 and later .... 252 mm (9.9 inches)
Dry weight
 1985 through 2000 .... 68 kg (149.9 lbs)
 2001 and later .... 75 kg (165 lbs)

XR50R, CRF50F

Bore .... 39.0 mm (1.54 inches)
Stroke .... 41.4 mm (1.63 inches)
Compression ratio .... 10.0 to 1
Wheelbase
 XR50R .... 915 mm (36.0 inches)
 CRF50F .... 911 mm (35.9 inches)
Overall length
 XR50R .... 1305 mm (51.4 inches)
 CRF50F .... 1302 mm (51.2 inches)
Overall width
 XR50R .... 583 mm (23.0 inches)
 CRF50F .... 581 mm (22.9 inches)
Overall height
 XR50R .... 780 mm (30.7 inches)
 CRF50F .... 774 mm (30.5 inches)
Seat height
 XR50R .... 550 mm (21.7 inches)
 CRF50F .... 548 mm (21.6 inches)
Ground clearance
 XR50R .... 150 mm (5.9 inches)
 CRF50F
  2004 through 2012 .... 146 mm (5.8 inches)
  2013 and later .... 150 mm (5.9 inches)
Dry weight .... 47 kg (104 lbs)

XR70R

Bore .... 47.0 mm (1.85 inches)
Stroke .... 41.4 mm (1.63 inches)
Compression ratio .... 9.1 to 1
Wheelbase
 1997 through 2000 .... 1055 mm (41.5 inches)
 2001 and later .... 1067 mm (42.0 inches)
Overall length
 1997 through 2000 .... 1543 mm (60.7 inches)
 2001 and later .... 1565 mm (61.6 inches)
Overall width .... 694 mm (27.3 inches)
Overall height
 1997 through 2000 .... 877 mm (34.5 inches)
 2001 and later .... 881 mm (34.7 inches)
Seat height
 1997 through 2000 .... 648 mm (25.5 inches)
 2001 and later .... 655 mm (25.8 inches)
Ground clearance
 1997 through 2000 .... 163 mm (6.42 inches)
 2001 and later .... 162 mm (6.37 inches)
Dry weight
 1997 through 2000 .... 57 kg (126 lbs)
 2001 and later .... 58 kg (128 lbs)

CRF70F

Bore .... 47.0 mm (1.85 inches)
Stroke .... 41.4 mm (1.63 inches)
Compression ratio .... 9.1 to 1
Wheelbase .... 1063 mm (41.9 inches)
Overall length .... 1569 mm (61.8 inches)
Overall width .... 694 mm (27.3 inches)
Overall height .... 885 mm (34.8 inches)
Seat height .... 655 mm (25.8 inches)
Ground clearance .... 178 mm (7.0 inches)
Dry weight .... 58 kg (128 lbs)

Maintenance techniques, tools and working facilities

Basic maintenance techniques

There are a number of techniques involved in maintenance and repair that will be referred to throughout this manual. Application of these techniques will enable the amateur mechanic to be more efficient, better organized and capable of performing the various tasks properly, which will ensure that the repair job is thorough and complete.

Fastening systems

Fasteners, basically, are nuts, bolts and screws used to hold two or more parts together. There are a few things to keep in mind when working with fasteners. Almost all of them use a locking device of some type (either a lock washer, locknut, locking tab or thread adhesive). All threaded fasteners should be clean, straight, have undamaged threads and undamaged corners on the hex head where the wrench fits. Develop the habit of replacing all damaged nuts and bolts with new ones.

Rusted nuts and bolts should be treated with a penetrating oil to ease removal and prevent breakage. Some mechanics use turpentine in a spout type oil can, which works quite well. After applying the rust penetrant, let it work for a few minutes before trying to loosen the nut or bolt. Badly rusted fasteners may have to be chiseled off or removed with a special nut breaker, available at tool stores.

If a bolt or stud breaks off in an assembly, it can be drilled out and removed with a special tool called an E-Z out (or screw extractor). Most dealer service departments and motorcycle repair shops can perform this task, as well as others (such as the repair of threaded holes that have been stripped out).

Flat washers and lock washers, when removed from an assembly, should always be replaced exactly as removed. Replace any damaged washers with new ones. Always use a flat washer between a lock washer and any soft metal surface (such as aluminum), thin sheet metal or plastic. Special locknuts can only be used once or twice before they lose their locking ability and must be replaced.

Tightening sequences and procedures

When threaded fasteners are tightened, they are often tightened to a specific torque value (torque is basically a twisting force). Over-tightening the fastener can weaken it and cause it to break, while under-tightening can cause it to eventually come loose. Each bolt, depending on the material it's made of, the diameter of its shank and the material it is threaded into, has a specific torque value, which is noted in the Specifications. Be sure to follow the torque recommendations closely.

Fasteners laid out in a pattern (i.e., cylinder head bolts, engine case bolts, etc.) must be loosened or tightened in a sequence to avoid warping the component. Initially, the bolts/nuts should go on finger-tight only. Next, they should be tightened one full turn each, in a criss-cross or diagonal pattern. After each one has been tightened one full turn, return to the first one tightened and tighten them all one half turn, following the same pattern. Finally, tighten each of them one quarter turn at a time until each fastener has been tightened to the proper torque. To loosen and remove the fasteners the procedure would be reversed.

Disassembly sequence

Component disassembly should be done with care and purpose to help ensure that the parts go back together properly during reassembly. Always keep track of the sequence in which parts are removed. Take note of special characteristics or marks on parts that can be installed more than one way (such as a grooved thrust washer on a shaft). It's a good idea to lay the disassembled parts out on a clean surface in the order that they were removed. It may also be helpful to make sketches or take instant photos of components before removal.

When removing fasteners from a component, keep track of their locations. Sometimes threading a bolt back in a part, or putting the washers and nut back on a stud, can prevent mix-ups later. If nuts and bolts can't be returned to their original locations, they should be kept in a compartmented box or a series of small boxes. A cupcake or muffin tin is ideal for this purpose, since each cavity can hold the bolts and nuts from a particular area (i.e., engine case bolts, valve cover bolts, engine mount bolts, etc.). A pan of this type is especially helpful when working on assemblies with very small parts (such as the carburetors and the valve train). The cavities can be marked with paint or tape to identify the contents.

Whenever wiring looms, harnesses or connectors are separated, it's a good idea to identify the two halves with numbered pieces of masking tape so they can be easily reconnected.

Gasket sealing surfaces

Throughout any motorcycle, gaskets are used to seal the mating surfaces between components and keep lubricants, fluids, vacuum or pressure contained in an assembly.

Many times these gaskets are coated with a liquid or paste type gasket sealing compound before assembly. Age, heat and pressure can sometimes cause the two parts to stick together so tightly that they are very difficult to separate. In most cases, the part can be loosened by striking it with a soft-faced hammer near the mating surfaces. A regular hammer can be used if a block of wood is placed between the hammer and the part. Do not hammer on cast parts or parts that could be easily damaged. With any particularly stubborn part, always recheck to make sure that every fastener has been removed.

Avoid using a screwdriver or bar to pry apart components, as they can easily mar the gasket sealing surfaces of the parts (which must remain smooth). If prying is absolutely necessary, use a piece of wood, but keep in mind that extra clean-up will be necessary if the wood splinters.

After the parts are separated, the old gasket must be carefully scraped off and the gasket surfaces cleaned. Stubborn gasket material can be soaked with a gasket remover (available in aerosol cans) to soften it so it can be easily scraped off. A scraper can be fashioned from a piece of copper tubing by flattening and sharpening one end. Copper is recommended because it is usually softer than the surfaces to be scraped, which reduces the chance of gouging the part. Some gaskets can be removed with a wire brush, but regardless of the method used, the mating surfaces must be left clean and smooth. If for some reason the gasket surface is gouged, then a gasket sealer thick enough to fill scratches will have to be used during reassembly of the components. For most applications, a non-drying (or semi-drying) gasket sealer is best.

Hose removal tips

Hose removal precautions closely parallel gasket removal precautions. Avoid scratching or gouging the surface that the hose mates against or the connection may leak. Because of various chemical reactions, the rubber in hoses can bond itself to the metal spigot that the hose fits over. To remove a hose, first loosen the hose clamps that secure it to the spigot. Then, with slip joint pliers, grab the hose at the clamp and rotate it around the spigot. Work it back and forth until it is completely free, then pull it off (silicone or other lubricants will ease removal if they can be applied between the hose and the outside of the spigot). Apply the same lubricant to the inside of the hose and the outside of the spigot to simplify installation.

If a hose clamp is broken or damaged, do not reuse it. Also, do not reuse hoses that are cracked, split or torn.

Spark plug gap adjusting tool

Feeler gauge set

Control cable pressure luber

Hand impact screwdriver and bits

Tools

A selection of good tools is a basic requirement for anyone who plans to maintain and repair a motorcycle. For the owner who has few tools, if any, the initial investment might seem high, but when compared to the spiraling costs of routine maintenance and repair, it is a wise one.

To help the owner decide which tools are needed to perform the tasks detailed in this manual, the following tool lists are offered: *Maintenance and minor repair, Repair and overhaul* and *Special*. The newcomer to practical mechanics should start off with the *Maintenance and minor repair* tool kit, which is adequate for the simpler jobs. Then, as confidence and experience grow, the owner can tackle more difficult tasks, buying additional tools as they are needed. Eventually the basic kit will be built into the *Repair and overhaul* tool set. Over a period of time, the experienced do-it-yourselfer will assemble a tool set complete enough for most repair and overhaul procedures and will add tools from the *Special* category when it is felt that the expense is justified by the frequency of use.

Maintenance and minor repair tool kit

The tools in this list should be considered the minimum required for performance of routine maintenance, servicing and minor repair work. We recommend the purchase of combination wrenches (box end and open end combined in one wrench); while more expensive than

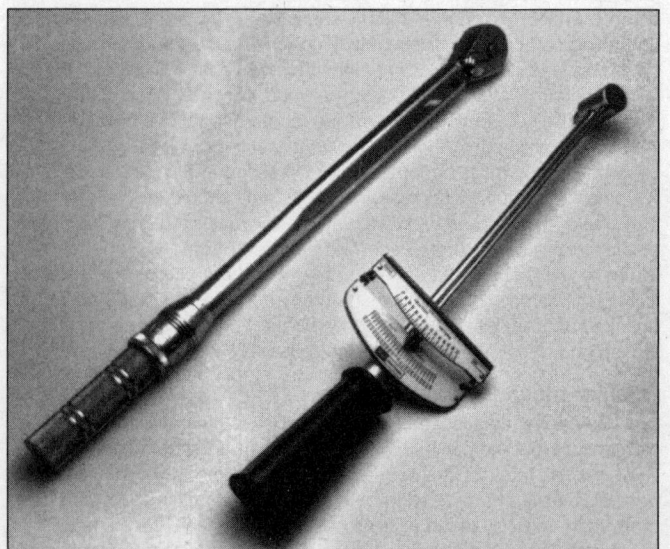

Torque wrenches (left - click; right - beam type)

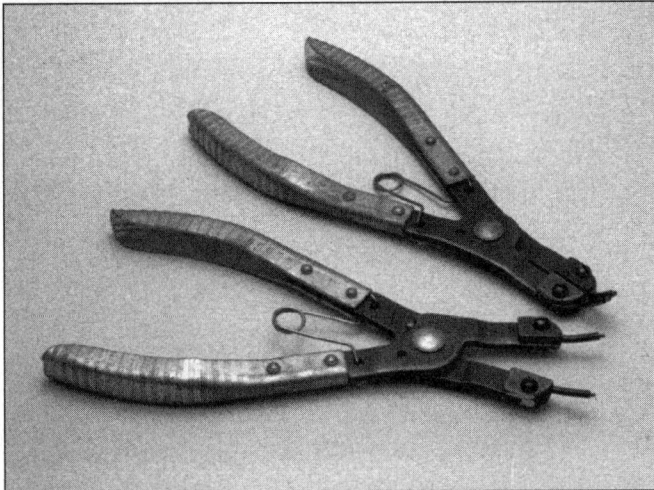

Snap-ring pliers (top - external; bottom - internal)

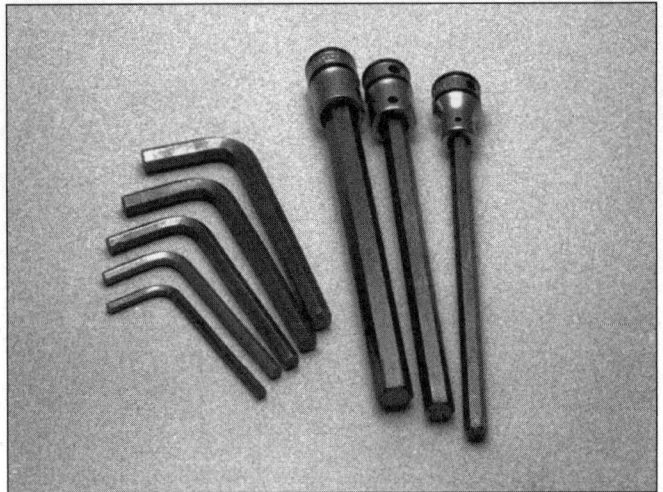

Allen wrenches (left), and Allen head sockets (right)

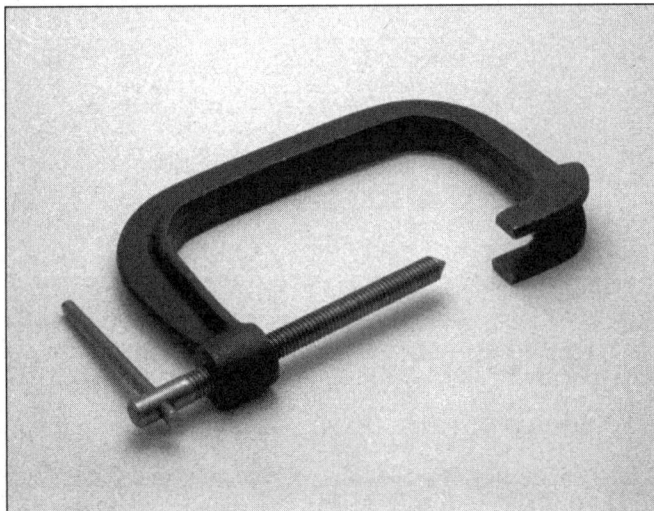

Valve spring compressor

Piston ring removal/installation tool

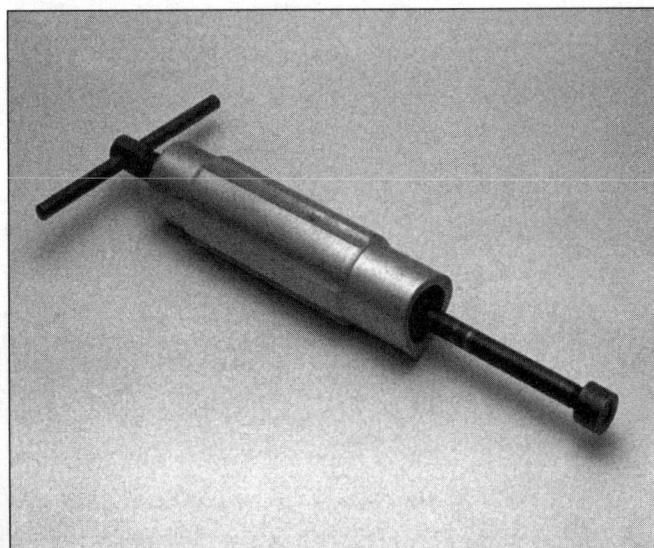

Piston pin puller

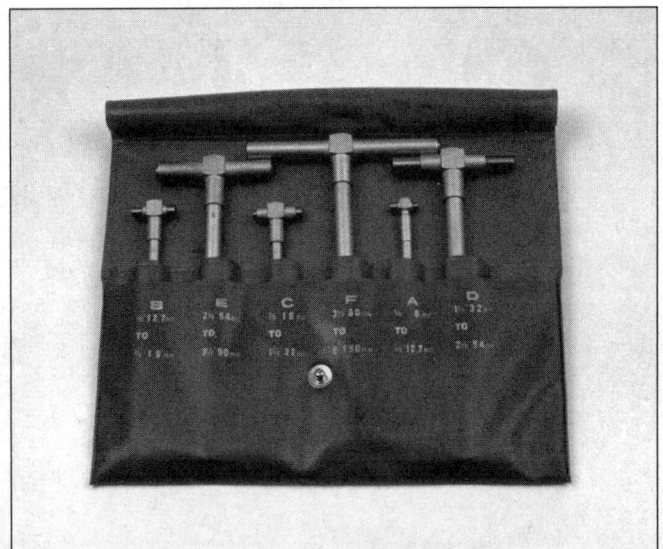

Telescoping gauges

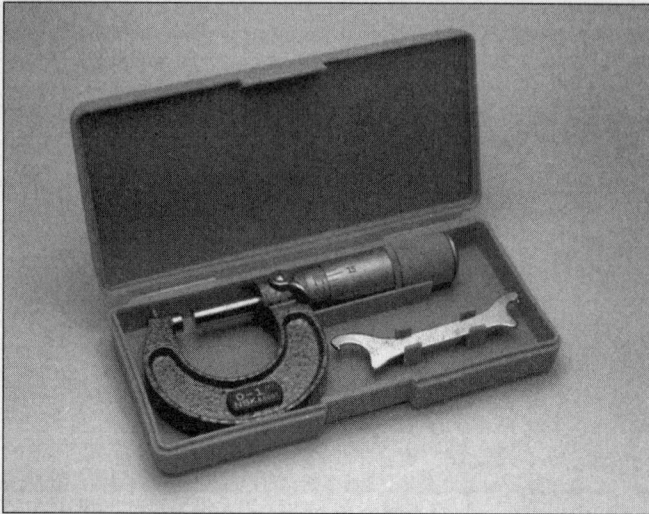

0-to-1 inch micrometer

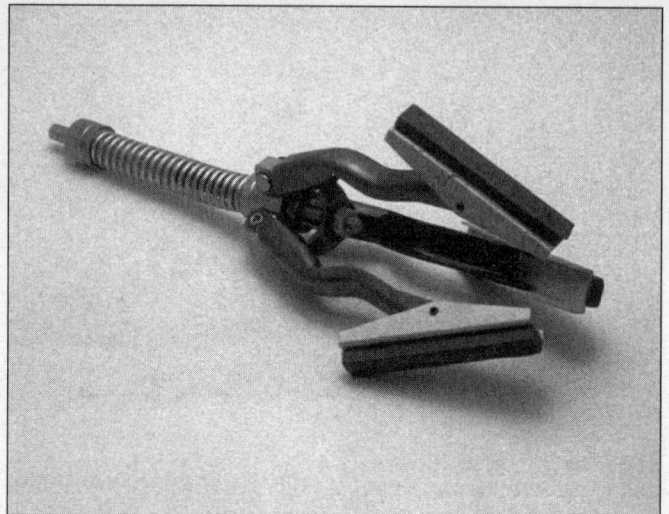

Cylinder surfacing hone

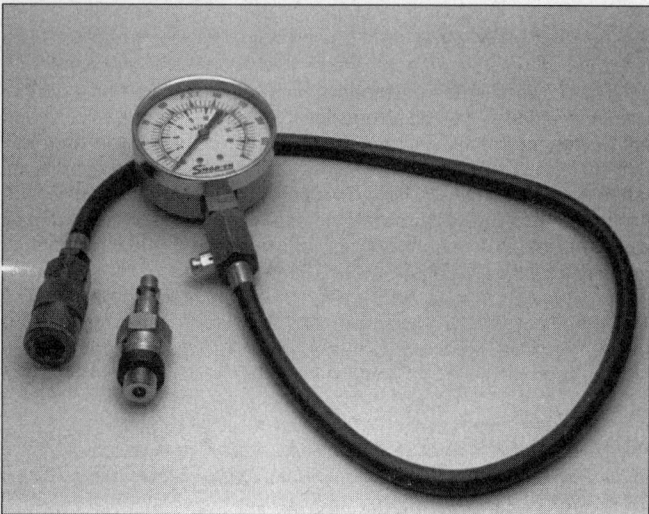

Cylinder compression gauge

Dial indicator set

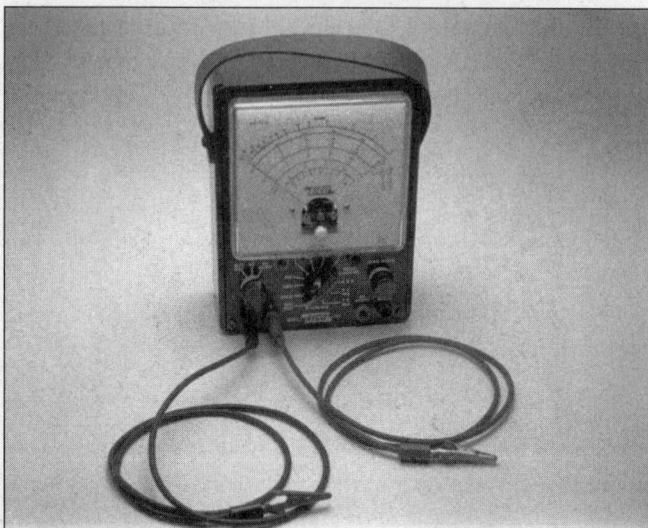

Multimeter (volt/ohm/ammeter)

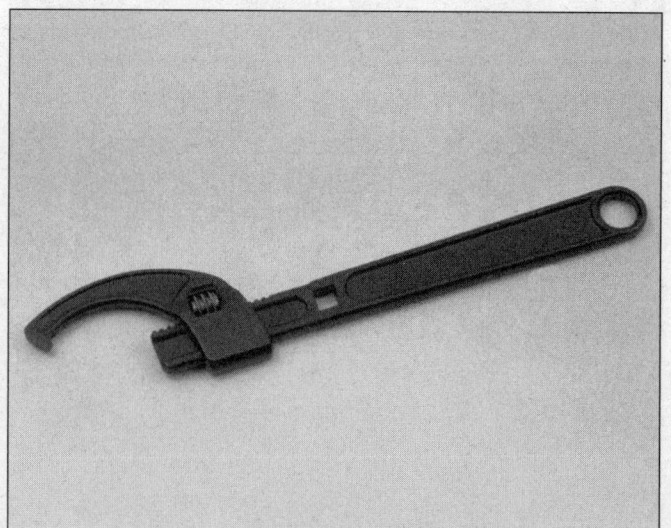

Adjustable spanner

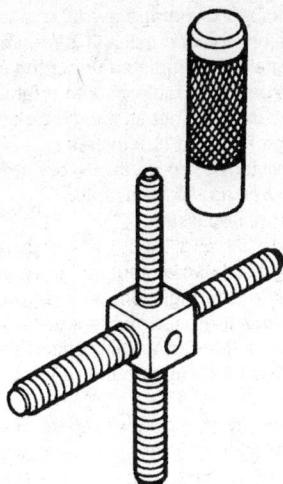

Alternator rotor puller

open-ended ones, they offer the advantages of both types of wrench.

Combination wrench set (6 mm to 22 mm)
Adjustable wrench - 8 in
Spark plug socket (with rubber insert)
Spark plug gap adjusting tool
Feeler gauge set
Standard screwdriver (5/16 in x 6 in)
Phillips screwdriver (No. 2 x 6 in)
Allen (hex) wrench set (4 mm to 12 mm)
Combination (slip-joint) pliers - 6 in
Hacksaw and assortment of blades
Tire pressure gauge
Control cable pressure luber
Grease gun
Oil can
Fine emery cloth
Wire brush
Hand impact screwdriver and bits
Funnel (medium size)
Safety goggles
Drain pan
Work light with extension cord

Repair and overhaul tool set

These tools are essential for anyone who plans to perform major repairs and are intended to supplement those in the *Maintenance and minor repair* tool kit. Included is a comprehensive set of sockets which, though expensive, are invaluable because of their versatility (especially when various extensions and drives are available). We recommend the 3/8 inch drive over the 1/2 inch drive for general motorcycle maintenance and repair (ideally, the mechanic would have a 3/8 inch drive set and a 1/2 inch drive set).

Alternator rotor removal tool
Socket set(s)
Reversible ratchet
Extension - 6 in
Universal joint
Torque wrench (same size drive as sockets)
Ball pein hammer - 8 oz
Soft-faced hammer (plastic/rubber)
Standard screwdriver (1/4 in x 6 in)
Standard screwdriver (stubby - 5/16 in)
Phillips screwdriver (No. 3 x 8 in)
Phillips screwdriver (stubby - No. 2)
Pliers - locking
Pliers - lineman's

Pliers - needle nose
Pliers - snap-ring (internal and external)
Cold chisel - 1/2 in
Scriber
Scraper (made from flattened copper tubing)
Center punch
Pin punches (1/16, 1/8, 3/16 in)
Steel rule/straightedge - 12 in
Pin-type spanner wrench
A selection of files
Wire brush (large)

Note: *Another tool which is often useful is an electric drill with a chuck capacity of 3/8 inch (and a set of good quality drill bits).*

Special tools

The tools in this list include those which are not used regularly, are expensive to buy, or which need to be used in accordance with their manufacturer's instructions. Unless these tools will be used frequently, it is not very economical to purchase many of them. A consideration would be to split the cost and use between yourself and a friend or friends (i.e., members of a motorcycle club).

This list primarily contains tools and instruments widely available to the public, as well as some special tools produced by the vehicle manufacturer for distribution to dealer service departments. As a result, references to the manufacturer's special tools are occasionally included in the text of this manual. Generally, an alternative method of doing the job without the special tool is offered. However, sometimes there is no alternative to their use. Where this is the case, and the tool can't be purchased or borrowed, the work should be turned over to the dealer service department or a motorcycle repair shop.

Paddock stand (for models not fitted with a centerstand)
Valve spring compressor
Piston ring removal and installation tool
Piston pin puller
Telescoping gauges
Micrometer(s) and/or dial/Vernier calipers
Cylinder surfacing hone
Cylinder compression gauge
Dial indicator set
Multimeter
Adjustable spanner
Manometer or vacuum gauge set
Small air compressor with blow gun and tire chuck

Buying tools

For the do-it-yourselfer who is just starting to get involved in motorcycle maintenance and repair, there are a number of options available when purchasing tools. If maintenance and minor repair is the extent of the work to be done, the purchase of individual tools is satisfactory. If, on the other hand, extensive work is planned, it would be a good idea to purchase a modest tool set from one of the large retail chain stores. A set can usually be bought at a substantial savings over the individual tool prices (and they often come with a tool box). As additional tools are needed, add-on sets, individual tools and a larger tool box can be purchased to expand the tool selection. Building a tool set gradually allows the cost of the tools to be spread over a longer period of time and gives the mechanic the freedom to choose only those tools that will actually be used.

Tool stores and motorcycle dealers will often be the only source of some of the special tools that are needed, but regardless of where tools are bought, try to avoid cheap ones (especially when buying screwdrivers and sockets) because they won't last very long. There are plenty of tools around at reasonable prices, but always aim to purchase items which meet the relevant national safety standards. The expense involved in replacing cheap tools will eventually be greater than the initial cost of quality tools.

It is obviously not possible to cover the subject of tools fully here. For those who wish to learn more about tools and their use, there is a book entitled *Motorcycle Workshop Practice Manual* (Book no. 1454) available from the publishers of this manual. It also provides an introduction to basic workshop practice which will be of interest to a home mechanic working on any type of motorcycle.

Care and maintenance of tools

Good tools are expensive, so it makes sense to treat them with respect. Keep them clean and in usable condition and store them properly when not in use. Always wipe off any dirt, grease or metal chips before putting them away. Never leave tools lying around in the work area.

Some tools, such as screwdrivers, pliers, wrenches and sockets, can be hung on a panel mounted on the garage or workshop wall, while others should be kept in a tool box or tray. Measuring instruments, gauges, meters, etc., must be carefully stored where they can't be damaged by weather or impact from other tools.

When tools are used with care and stored properly, they will last a very long time. Even with the best of care, tools will wear out if used frequently. When a tool is damaged or worn out, replace it; subsequent jobs will be safer and more enjoyable if you do.

Working facilities

Not to be overlooked when discussing tools is the workshop. If anything more than routine maintenance is to be carried out, some sort of suitable work area is essential.

It is understood, and appreciated, that many home mechanics do not have a good workshop or garage available and end up removing an engine or doing major repairs outside (it is recommended, however, that the overhaul or repair be completed under the cover of a roof).

A clean, flat workbench or table of comfortable working height is an absolute necessity. The workbench should be equipped with a vise that has a jaw opening of at least four inches.

As mentioned previously, some clean, dry storage space is also required for tools, as well as the lubricants, fluids, cleaning solvents, etc., which soon become necessary.

Sometimes waste oil and fluids, drained from the engine or cooling system during normal maintenance or repairs, present a disposal problem. To avoid pouring them on the ground or into a sewage system, simply pour the used fluids into large containers, seal them with caps and take them to an authorized disposal site or service station. Plastic jugs (such as old antifreeze containers) are ideal for this purpose.

Always keep a supply of old newspapers and clean rags available. Old towels are excellent for mopping up spills. Many mechanics use rolls of paper towels for most work because they are readily available and disposable. To help keep the area under the motorcycle clean, a large cardboard box can be cut open and flattened to protect the garage or shop floor.

Whenever working over a painted surface (such as the fuel tank) cover it with an old blanket or bedspread to protect the finish.

Safety first

Professional mechanics are trained in safe working procedures. However enthusiastic you may be about getting on with the job at hand, take the time to ensure that your safety is not put at risk. A moment's lack of attention can result in an accident, as can failure to observe simple precautions.

There will always be new ways of having accidents, and the following is not a comprehensive list of all dangers; it is intended rather to make you aware of the risks and to encourage a safe approach to all work you carry out on your bike.

Essential DOs and DON'Ts

DON'T start the engine without first ascertaining that the transmission is in neutral.

DON'T suddenly remove the pressure cap from a hot cooling system - cover it with a cloth and release the pressure gradually first, or you may get scalded by escaping coolant.

DON'T attempt to drain oil until you are sure it has cooled sufficiently to avoid scalding you.

DON'T grasp any part of the engine or exhaust system without first ascertaining that it is cool enough not to burn you.

DON'T allow brake fluid or antifreeze to contact the machine's paint work or plastic components.

DON'T siphon toxic liquids such as fuel, hydraulic fluid or antifreeze by mouth, or allow them to remain on your skin.

DON'T inhale dust - it may be injurious to health (see *Asbestos* heading).

DON'T allow any spilled oil or grease to remain on the floor - wipe it up right away, before someone slips on it.

DON'T use ill fitting wrenches or other tools which may slip and cause injury.

DON'T attempt to lift a heavy component which may be beyond your capability - get assistance.

DON'T rush to finish a job or take unverified short cuts.

DON'T allow children or animals in or around an unattended vehicle.

DON'T inflate a tire to a pressure above the recommended maximum. Apart from over stressing the carcase and wheel rim, in extreme cases the tire may blow off forcibly.

DO ensure that the machine is supported securely at all times. This is especially important when the machine is blocked up to aid wheel or fork removal.

DO take care when attempting to loosen a stubborn nut or bolt. It is generally better to pull on a wrench, rather than push, so that if you slip, you fall away from the machine rather than onto it.

DO wear eye protection when using power tools such as drill, sander, bench grinder, etc.

DO use a barrier cream on your hands prior to undertaking dirty jobs - it will protect your skin from infection as well as making the dirt easier to remove afterwards; but make sure your hands aren't left slippery. Note that long-term contact with used engine oil can be a health hazard.

DO keep loose clothing (cuffs, ties, etc., and long hair) well out of the way of moving mechanical parts.

DO remove rings, wristwatch, etc., before working on the vehicle - especially the electrical system.

DO keep your work area tidy - it is only too easy to fall over articles left lying around.

DO exercise caution when compressing springs for removal or installation. Ensure that the tension is applied and released in a controlled manner, using suitable tools which preclude the possibility of the spring escaping violently.

DO ensure that any lifting tackle used has a safe working load rating adequate for the job.

DO get someone to check periodically that all is well, when working alone on the vehicle.

DO carry out work in a logical sequence and check that everything is correctly assembled and tightened afterwards.

DO remember that your vehicle's safety affects that of yourself and others. If in doubt on any point, get professional advice.

IF, in spite of following these precautions, you are unfortunate enough to injure yourself, seek medical attention as soon as possible.

Asbestos

Certain friction, insulating, sealing and other products - such as brake pads, clutch linings, gaskets, etc. - contain asbestos. *Extreme care must be taken to avoid inhalation of dust from such products since it is hazardous to health*. If in doubt, assume that they *do* contain asbestos.

Fire

Remember at all times that gasoline (petrol) is highly flammable. Never smoke or have any kind of naked flame around, when working on the vehicle. But the risk does not end there - a spark caused by an electrical short-circuit, by two metal surfaces contacting each other, by careless use of tools, or even by static electricity built up in your body under certain conditions, can ignite gasoline (petrol) vapor, which in a confined space is highly explosive. Never use gasoline (petrol) as a cleaning solvent. Use an approved safety solvent.

Always disconnect the battery ground (earth) terminal before working on any part of the fuel or electrical system, and never risk spilling fuel on to a hot engine or exhaust.

It is recommended that a fire extinguisher of a type suitable for fuel and electrical fires is kept handy in the garage or workplace at all times. Never try to extinguish a fuel or electrical fire with water.

Fumes

Certain fumes are highly toxic and can quickly cause unconsciousness and even death if inhaled to any extent. Gasoline (petrol) vapor comes into this category, as do the vapors from certain solvents such as trichloroethylene. Any draining or pouring of such volatile fluids should be done in a well ventilated area.

When using cleaning fluids and solvents, read the instructions carefully. Never use materials from unmarked containers - they may give off poisonous vapors.

Never run the engine of a motor vehicle in an enclosed space such as a garage. Exhaust fumes contain carbon monoxide which is extremely poisonous; if you need to run the engine, always do so in the open air or at least have the rear of the vehicle outside the workplace.

Electricity

When using an electric power tool, inspection light, etc., always ensure that the appliance is correctly connected to its plug and that, where necessary, it is properly grounded (earthed). Do not use such appliances in damp conditions and, again, beware of creating a spark or applying excessive heat in the vicinity of fuel or fuel vapor. Also ensure that the appliances meet national safety standards.

A severe electric shock can result from touching certain parts of the electrical system, such as the spark plug wires (HT leads), when the engine is running or being cranked, particularly if components are damp or the insulation is defective. Where an electronic ignition system is used, the secondary voltage is much higher and could prove fatal.

Motorcycle chemicals and lubricants

A number of chemicals and lubricants are available for use in motorcycle maintenance and repair. They include a wide variety of products ranging from cleaning solvents and degreasers to lubricants and protective sprays for rubber, plastic and vinyl.

Contact point/spark plug cleaner is a solvent used to clean oily film and dirt from points, grime from electrical connectors and oil deposits from spark plugs. It is oil free and leaves no residue. It can also be used to remove gum and varnish from carburetor jets and other orifices.

Carburetor cleaner is similar to contact point/spark plug cleaner but it usually has a stronger solvent and may leave a slight oily reside. It is not recommended for cleaning electrical components or connections.

Brake system cleaner is used to remove grease or brake fluid from brake system components (where clean surfaces are absolutely necessary and petroleum-based solvents cannot be used); it also leaves no residue.

Silicone-based lubricants are used to protect rubber parts such as hoses and grommets, and are used as lubricants for hinges and locks.

Multi-purpose grease is an all purpose lubricant used wherever grease is more practical than a liquid lubricant such as oil. Some multi-purpose grease is colored white and specially formulated to be more resistant to water than ordinary grease.

Gear oil (sometimes called gear lube) is a specially designed oil used in transmissions and final drive units, a s well as other areas where high friction, high temperature lubrication is required. It is available in a number of viscosities (weights) for various applications.

Motor oil, of course, is the lubricant specially formulated for use in the engine. It normally contains a wide variety of additives to prevent corrosion and reduce foaming and wear. Motor oil comes in various weights (viscosity ratings) of from 5 to 80. The recommended weight of the oil depends on the seasonal temperature and the demands on the engine. Light oil is used in cold climates and under light load conditions; heavy oil is used in hot climates and where high loads are encountered. Multi-viscosity oils are designed to have characteristics of both light and heavy oils and are available in a number of weights from 5W-20 to 20W-50.

Gas (petrol) additives perform several functions, depending on their chemical makeup. They usually contain solvents that help dissolve gum and varnish that build up on carburetor and intake parts. They also serve to break down carbon deposits that form on the inside surfaces of the combustion chambers. Some additives contain upper cylinder lubricants for valves and piston rings.

Brake fluid is a specially formulated hydraulic fluid that can withstand the heat and pressure encountered in brake systems. Care must be taken that this fluid does not come in contact with painted surfaces or plastics. An opened container should always be resealed to prevent contamination by water or dirt.

Chain lubricants are formulated especially for use on motorcycle final drive chains. A good chain lube should adhere well and have good penetrating qualities to be effective as a lubricant inside the chain and on the side plates, pins and rollers. Most chain lubes are either the foaming type or quick drying type and are usually marketed as sprays.

Degreasers are heavy duty solvents used to remove grease and grime that may accumulate on engine and frame components. They can be sprayed or brushed on and, depending on the type, are rinsed with either water or solvent.

Solvents are used alone or in combination with degreasers to clean parts and assemblies during repair and overhaul. The home mechanic should use only solvents that are non-flammable and that do not produce irritating fumes.

Gasket sealing compounds may be used in conjunction with gaskets, to improve their sealing capabilities, or alone, to seal metal-to-metal joints. Many gasket sealers can withstand extreme heat, some are impervious to gasoline and lubricants, while others are capable of filling and sealing large cavities. Depending on the intended use, gasket sealers either dry hard or stay relatively soft and pliable. They are usually applied by hand, with a brush, or are sprayed on the gasket sealing surfaces.

Thread cement is an adhesive locking compound that prevents threaded fasteners from loosening because of vibration. It is available in a variety of types for different applications.

Moisture dispersants are usually sprays that can be used to dry out electrical components such as the fuse block and wiring connectors. Some types can also be used as treatment for rubber and as a lubricant for hinges, cables and locks.

Waxes and polishes are used to help protect painted and plated surfaces from the weather. Different types of paint may require the use of different types of wax polish. Some polishes utilize a chemical or abrasive cleaner to help remove the top layer of oxidized (dull) paint on older vehicles. In recent years, many non-wax polishes (that contain a wide variety of chemicals such as polymers and silicones) have been introduced. These non-wax polishes are usually easier to apply and last longer than conventional waxes and polishes.

Troubleshooting

Contents

Engine doesn't start or is difficult to start

1   Kickstarter moves but engine won't start

1   Engine kill switch Off.
2   Wiring open or shorted. Check all wiring connections and harnesses to make sure that they are dry, tight and not corroded. Also check for broken or frayed wires that can cause a short to ground (see wiring diagram, Chapter 8).
3   Engine kill switch defective. Check for wet, dirty or corroded contacts. Clean or replace the switch as necessary (Chapter 4).

2   Kickstarter moves but engine does not turn over

1   Kickstarter mechanism damaged. Inspect and repair or replace (Chapter 2).
2   Damaged kickstarter pinion gears. Inspect and replace the damaged parts (Chapter 2).

3   Kickstarter won't turn engine over (seized)

Seized engine caused by one or more internally damaged components. Failure due to wear, abuse or lack of lubrication. Damage can include seized valves, rocker arms, camshaft, piston, crankshaft, connecting rod bearings, or transmission gears or bearings. Refer to Chapter 2 for engine disassembly.

4   No fuel flow

1   No fuel in tank.
2   Tank cap air vent obstructed. Usually caused by dirt or water. Remove it and clean the cap vent hole.
3   Clogged strainer in fuel tap. Remove and clean the strainer (Chapter 1).
4   Fuel line clogged. Pull the fuel line loose and carefully blow through it.
5   Inlet needle valve clogged. A very bad batch of fuel with an unusual additive may have been used, or some other foreign material has entered the tank. Many times after a machine has been stored for many months without running, the fuel turns to a varnish-like liquid and forms deposits on the inlet needle valve and jets. The carburetor should be removed and overhauled if draining the float chamber does not solve the problem.

5   Engine flooded

1   Float level too high. Check as described in Chapter 3 and replace the float if necessary.
2   Inlet needle valve worn or stuck open. A piece of dirt, rust or other debris can cause the inlet needle to seat improperly, causing excess fuel to be admitted to the float bowl. In this case, the float chamber should be cleaned and the needle and seat inspected. If the needle and seat are worn, then the leaking will persist and the parts should be replaced with new ones (Chapter 3).
3   Starting technique incorrect. Under normal circumstances (i.e., if all the carburetor functions are sound) the machine should start with little or no throttle. When the engine is cold, the choke should be operated and the engine started without opening the throttle. When the engine is at operating temperature, only a very slight amount of throttle should be necessary. If the engine is flooded, turn the fuel tap off and hold the throttle open while cranking the engine. This will allow additional air to reach the cylinder. Remember to turn the fuel tap back on after the engine starts.

6   No spark or weak spark

1   Spark plug dirty, defective or worn out. Locate reason for fouled plug using spark plug condition chart and follow the plug maintenance procedures in Chapter 1.
2   Spark plug cap or secondary wiring faulty. Check condition. Replace either or both components if cracks or deterioration are evident (Chapter 4).
3   Spark plug cap not making good contact. Make sure that the plug cap fits snugly over the plug end.
4   Defective alternator (see Chapter 4).
5   Breaker point models: Points worn, burned, or gapped incorrectly (see Chapter 1). Condenser defective (see Chapter 4).
6   CDI models: Defective CDI unit (see Chapter 4).
7   Ignition coil defective. Check the coil, referring to Chapter 4.
8   Kill switch shorted. This is usually caused by water, corrosion, damage or excessive wear.
9   Wiring shorted or broken between:

a) *CDI unit (or breaker points) and engine kill switch*
b) *CDI unit (or breaker points) and ignition coil*
c) *CDI unit and alternator*
d) *Ignition coil and plug*

Make sure that all wiring connections are clean, dry and tight. Look for chafed and broken wires (Chapter 4).

7   Compression low

1   Spark plug loose. Remove the plug and inspect the threads. Reinstall and tighten to the specified torque (Chapter 1).
2   Cylinder head not sufficiently tightened down. If the cylinder head is suspected of being loose, then there's a chance that the gasket or head is damaged if the problem has persisted for any length of time. The head nuts and bolts should be tightened to the proper torque in the correct sequence (Chapter 2).
3   Improper valve clearance. This means that the valve is not closing completely and compression pressure is leaking past the valve. Check and adjust the valve clearances (Chapter 1).
4   Cylinder and/or piston worn. Excessive wear will cause compression pressure to leak past the rings. This is usually accompanied by worn rings as well. A top end overhaul is necessary (Chapter 2).
5   Piston rings worn, weak, broken, or sticking. Broken or sticking piston rings usually indicate a lubrication or carburetion problem that causes excess carbon deposits or seizures to form on the pistons and rings. Top end overhaul is necessary (Chapter 2).
6   Piston ring-to-groove clearance excessive. This is caused by excessive wear of the piston ring lands. Piston replacement is necessary (Chapter 2).
7   Cylinder head gasket damaged. If the head is allowed to become loose, or if excessive carbon build-up on a piston crown and combustion chamber causes extremely high compression, the head gasket may leak. Retorquing the head is not always sufficient to restore the seal, so gasket replacement is necessary (Chapter 2).
8   Cylinder head warped. This is caused by overheating or improperly tightened head nuts and bolts. Machine shop resurfacing or head replacement is necessary (Chapter 2).
9   Valve spring broken or weak. Caused by component failure or wear; the spring(s) must be replaced (Chapter 2).
10 Valve not seating properly. This is caused by a bent valve (from over-revving or improper valve adjustment), burned valve or seat (improper carburetion) or an accumulation of carbon deposits on the seat (from carburetion or lubrication problems). The valves must be cleaned and/or replaced and the seats serviced if possible (Chapter 2).

8   Stalls after starting

1   Improper choke action. Make sure the choke lever is getting a full stroke and staying in the out position.
2   Ignition malfunction. See Chapter 4.
3   Carburetor malfunction. See Chapter 3.
4   Fuel contaminated. The fuel can be contaminated with either dirt or water, or can change chemically if the machine is allowed to sit for several months or more. Drain the tank and float bowl and refill with fresh fuel (Chapter 3).
5   Intake air leak. Check for loose carburetor-to-intake joint connections or loose carburetor top (Chapter 3).
6   Engine idle speed incorrect. Turn throttle stop screw until the engine idles at the specified rpm (Chapter 1).

9   Rough idle

1   Ignition malfunction. See Chapter 4.
2   Idle speed incorrect. See Chapter 1.
3   Carburetor malfunction. See Chapter 3.
4   Idle fuel/air mixture incorrect. See Chapter 3.
5   Fuel contaminated. The fuel can be contaminated with either dirt or water, or can change chemically if the machine is allowed to sit for several months or more. Drain the tank and float bowls (Chapter 3).
6   Intake air leak. Check for loose carburetor-to-intake joint connections, loose or missing vacuum gauge access port cap or hose, or loose carburetor top (Chapter 3).
7   Air cleaner clogged. Service or replace air cleaner element (Chapter 1).

Poor running at low speed

10   Spark weak

1   Spark plug fouled, defective or worn out. Refer to Chapter 1 for spark plug maintenance.
2   Spark plug cap or secondary wiring defective. Refer to Chapters 1 and 4 for details on the ignition system.
3   Spark plug cap not making contact.
4   Incorrect spark plug. Wrong type, heat range or cap configuration. Check and install correct plug listed in Chapter 1. A cold plug or one with a recessed firing electrode will not operate at low speeds without fouling.
5   Breaker point models: Points worn, burned or gapped incorrectly (see Chapter 1).
6   CDI models: CDI unit defective. See Chapter 4.
7   Alternator defective. See Chapter 4.
8   Ignition coil defective. See Chapter 4.

11   Fuel/air mixture incorrect

1   Pilot screw out of adjustment (Chapter 3).
2   Pilot jet or air passage clogged. Remove and overhaul the carburetor (Chapter 3).
3   Air bleed holes clogged. Remove carburetor and blow out all passages (Chapter 3).
4   Air cleaner clogged, poorly sealed or missing.
5   Air cleaner-to-carburetor boot poorly sealed. Look for cracks, holes or loose clamps and replace or repair defective parts.
6   Float level too high or too low. Check and replace the float if necessary (Chapter 3).
7   Fuel tank air vent obstructed. Make sure that the air vent passage in the filler cap is open.
8   Carburetor intake joint loose. Check for cracks, breaks, tears or loose clamps or bolts. Repair or replace the rubber boot and its O-ring.

12   Compression low

1   Spark plug loose. Remove the plug and inspect the threads. Reinstall and tighten to the specified torque (Chapter 1).
2   Cylinder head not sufficiently tightened down. If the cylinder head is suspected of being loose, then there's a chance that the gasket and head are damaged if the problem has persisted for any length of time. The head nuts should be tightened to the proper torque in the correct sequence (Chapter 2).
3   Improper valve clearance. This means that the valve is not closing completely and compression pressure is leaking past the valve. Check and adjust the valve clearances (Chapter 1).
4   Cylinder and/or piston worn. Excessive wear will cause compression pressure to leak past the rings. This is usually accompanied by worn rings as well. A top end overhaul is necessary (Chapter 2).
5   Piston rings worn, weak, broken, or sticking. Broken or sticking piston rings usually indicate a lubrication or carburetion problem that causes excess carbon deposits or seizures to form on the piston and rings. Top end overhaul is necessary (Chapter 2).
6   Piston ring-to-groove clearance excessive. This is caused by excessive wear of the piston ring lands. Piston replacement is necessary (Chapter 2).
7   Cylinder head gasket damaged. If the head is allowed to become loose, or if excessive carbon build-up on the piston crown and combustion chamber causes extremely high compression, the head gasket may leak. Retorquing the head is not always sufficient to restore the seal, so gasket replacement is necessary (Chapter 2).
8   Cylinder head warped. This is caused by overheating or improperly tightened head nuts and bolts. Machine shop resurfacing or head replacement is necessary (Chapter 2).
9   Valve spring broken or weak. Caused by component failure or wear; the spring(s) must be replaced (Chapter 2).
10   Valve not seating properly. This is caused by a bent valve (from over-revving or improper valve adjustment), burned valve or seat (improper carburetion) or an accumulation of carbon deposits on the seat (from carburetion, lubrication problems). The valves must be cleaned and/or replaced and the seats serviced if possible (Chapter 2).

13   Poor acceleration

1   Carburetor leaking or dirty. Overhaul the carburetor (Chapter 3).
2   Timing not advancing. The spark advancer (breaker point models) or CDI unit (CDI models) may be defective. If so, they must be replaced with new ones, as they can't be repaired.
3   Engine oil viscosity too high. Using a heavier oil than that recommended in Chapter 1 can cause drag on the engine.
4   Brakes dragging. Usually caused by a sticking brake cam or from a warped drum or bent axle. Repair as necessary (Chapter 6).

Poor running or no power at high speed

14   Firing incorrect

1   Air cleaner restricted. Clean or replace element (Chapter 1).
2   Spark plug fouled, defective or worn out. See Chapter 1 for spark plug maintenance.
3   Spark plug cap or secondary wiring defective. See Chapters 1 and 4 for details of the ignition system.

4   Spark plug cap not in good contact. See Chapter 4.
5   Incorrect spark plug. Wrong type, heat range or cap configuration. Check and install correct plugs listed in Chapter 1. A cold plug or one with a recessed firing electrode will not operate at low speeds without fouling.
6   Breaker point models: Points worn, burned or gapped incorrectly (see Chapter 1).
7   CDI models: CDI unit defective. See Chapter 4.
8   Ignition coil defective. See Chapter 4.

15   Fuel/air mixture incorrect

1   Pilot screw out of adjustment. See Chapter 3 for adjustment procedures.
2   Main jet clogged. Dirt, water or other contaminants can clog the main jets. Clean the fuel tap strainer and in-tank strainer, the float bowl area, and the jets and carburetor orifices (Chapter 3).
3   Main jet wrong size. The standard jetting is for sea level atmospheric pressure and oxygen content. See Chapter 3 for high altitude adjustments.
4   Throttle shaft-to-carburetor body clearance excessive. Refer to Chapter 3 for inspection and part replacement procedures.
5   Air bleed holes clogged. Remove and overhaul carburetor (Chapter 3).
6   Air cleaner clogged, poorly sealed, or missing.
7   Air cleaner-to-carburetor boot poorly sealed. Look for cracks, holes or loose clamps, and replace or repair defective parts.
8   Float level too high or too low. Check float level and replace the float if necessary (Chapter 3).
9   Fuel tank air vent obstructed. Make sure the air vent passage in the filler cap is open.
10   Carburetor intake manifold loose. Check for cracks, breaks, tears or loose clamps or bolts. Repair or replace the rubber boots (Chapter 3).
11   Fuel tap clogged. Remove the tap and clean it (Chapter 1).
12   Fuel line clogged. Pull the fuel line loose and carefully blow through it.

16   Compression low

1   Spark plug loose. Remove the plug and inspect the threads. Reinstall and tighten to the specified torque (Chapter 1).
2   Cylinder head not sufficiently tightened down. If the cylinder head is suspected of being loose, then there's a chance that the gasket and head are damaged if the problem has persisted for any length of time. The head nuts and bolts should be tightened to the proper torque in the correct sequence (Chapter 2).
3   Improper valve clearance. This means that the valve is not closing completely and compression pressure is leaking past the valve. Check and adjust the valve clearances (Chapter 1).
4   Cylinder and/or piston worn. Excessive wear will cause compression pressure to leak past the rings. This is usually accompanied by worn rings as well. A top end overhaul is necessary (Chapter 2).
5   Piston rings worn, weak, broken, or sticking. Broken or sticking piston rings usually indicate a lubrication or carburetion problem that causes excess carbon deposits or seizures to form on the pistons and rings. Top end overhaul is necessary (Chapter 2).
6   Piston ring-to-groove clearance excessive. This is caused by excessive wear of the piston ring lands. Piston replacement is necessary (Chapter 2).
7   Cylinder head gasket damaged. If a head is allowed to become loose, or if excessive carbon build-up on the piston crown and combustion chamber causes extremely high compression, the head gasket may leak. Retorquing the head is not always sufficient to restore the seal, so gasket replacement is necessary (Chapter 2).
8   Cylinder head warped. This is caused by overheating or improp-

erly tightened head nuts and bolts. Machine shop resurfacing or head replacement is necessary (Chapter 2).
9   Valve spring broken or weak. Caused by component failure or wear; the spring(s) must be replaced (Chapter 2).
10   Valve not seating properly. This is caused by a bent valve (from over-revving or improper valve adjustment), burned valve or seat (improper carburetion) or an accumulation of carbon deposits on the seat (from carburetion or lubrication problems). The valves must be cleaned and/or replaced and the seats serviced if possible (Chapter 2).

17   Knocking or pinging

1   Carbon build-up in combustion chamber. Use of a fuel additive that will dissolve the adhesive bonding the carbon particles to the crown and chamber is the easiest way to remove the build-up. Otherwise, the cylinder head will have to be removed and decarbonized (Chapter 2).
2   Incorrect or poor quality fuel. Old or improper grades of fuel can cause detonation. This causes the piston to rattle, thus the knocking or pinging sound. Drain old fuel and always use the recommended fuel grade.
3   Spark plug heat range incorrect. Uncontrolled detonation indicates the plug heat range is too hot. The plug in effect becomes a glow plug, raising cylinder temperatures. Install the proper heat range plug (Chapter 1).
4   Improper air/fuel mixture. This will cause the cylinder to run hot, which leads to detonation. Clogged jets or an air leak can cause this imbalance. See Chapter 3.

18   Miscellaneous causes

1   Throttle valve doesn't open fully. Adjust the cable slack (Chapter 1).
2   Clutch slipping. May be caused by improper adjustment or loose or worn clutch components. Refer to Chapter 1 for adjustment or Chapter 2 for cable replacement and clutch overhaul procedures.
3   Timing not advancing.
4   Engine oil viscosity too high. Using a heavier oil than the one recommended in Chapter 1 can cause drag on the engine.
5   Brakes dragging. Usually caused by a dry brake cable (front), debris which has entered the brake cam, or from a warped disc or bent axle. Repair as necessary.

Overheating

19   Engine overheats

1   Engine oil level low. Check and add oil (Chapter 1).
2   Wrong type of oil. If you're not sure what type of oil is in the engine, drain it and fill with the correct type (Chapter 1).
3   Air leak at carburetor intake manifold. Check and tighten or replace as necessary (Chapter 3).
4   Fuel level low. Check and adjust if necessary (Chapter 3).
5   Clogged oil passages. Clean passages as necessary.
6   Clogged external oil line. Remove and check for foreign material (see Chapter 2).
7   Carbon build-up in the combustion chamber. Use of a fuel additive that will dissolve the adhesive bonding the carbon particles to the piston crown and chamber is the easiest way to remove the build-up. Otherwise, the cylinder head will have to be removed and decarbonized (Chapter 2).
8   Operation in high ambient temperatures.

20 Firing incorrect

1 Spark plug fouled, defective or worn out. See Chapter 1 for spark plug maintenance.
2 Incorrect spark plug (see Chapter 1).
3 Faulty ignition coil (Chapter 4).

21 Fuel/air mixture incorrect

1 Pilot screw out of adjustment (Chapter 3).
2 Main jet clogged. Dirt, water and other contaminants can clog the main jets. Clean the fuel tap strainer, the float bowl area and the jets and carburetor orifices (Chapter 3).
3 Main jet wrong size. The standard jetting is for sea level atmospheric pressure and oxygen content. See Chapter 3 for high altitude settings.
4 Air cleaner poorly sealed or missing.
5 Air cleaner-to-carburetor boot poorly sealed. Look for cracks, holes or loose clamps and replace or repair.
6 Fuel level too low. Check float level and replace the float if necessary (Chapter 3).
7 Fuel tank air vent obstructed. Make sure that the air vent passage in the filler cap is open.
8 Carburetor intake manifold loose. Check for cracks or loose clamps or bolts. Inspect the gasket and O-ring (Chapter 3).

22 Compression too high

1 Carbon build-up in combustion chamber. Use of a fuel additive that will dissolve the adhesive bonding the carbon particles to the piston crown and chamber is the easiest way to remove the build-up. Otherwise, the cylinder head will have to be removed and decarbonized (Chapter 2).
2 Improperly machined head surface or installation of incorrect gasket during engine assembly.

23 Engine load excessive

1 Clutch slipping. Can be caused by damaged, loose or worn clutch components. Refer to Chapter 2 for overhaul procedures.
2 Engine oil level too high. The addition of too much oil will cause pressurization of the crankcase and inefficient engine operation. Check the Specifications and drain to proper level (Chapter 1).
3 Engine oil viscosity too high. Using a heavier oil than the one recommended in Chapter 1 can cause drag on the engine.
4 Brakes dragging. Usually caused by a sticking brake cam or from a warped drum or bent axle. Repair as necessary (Chapter 6).

24 Lubrication inadequate

1 Engine oil level too low. Friction caused by intermittent lack of lubrication or from oil that is overworked can cause overheating. The oil provides a definite cooling function in the engine. Check the oil level (Chapter 1).
2 Poor quality engine oil or incorrect viscosity or type. Oil is rated not only according to viscosity but also according to type. Some oils are not rated high enough for use in this engine. Check the Specifications section and change to the correct oil (Chapter 1).
3 Camshaft or journals worn. Excessive wear causing drop in oil pressure. Replace cam or cylinder head. Abnormal wear could be caused by oil starvation at high rpm from low oil level or improper viscosity or type of oil (Chapter 1).

4 Crankshaft and/or bearings worn. Same problems as paragraph 3. Check and replace crankshaft assembly if necessary (Chapter 2).

25 Miscellaneous causes

Modification to exhaust system. Most aftermarket exhaust systems cause the engine to run leaner, which makes it run hotter. When installing an accessory exhaust system, always rejet the carburetor.

Clutch problems

26 Clutch slipping

1 Friction plates worn or warped. Overhaul the clutch (Chapter 2).
2 Steel plates worn or warped (Chapter 2).
3 Clutch spring(s) broken or weak. Old or heat-damaged spring(s) (from slipping clutch) should be replaced with new ones (Chapter 2).
4 Clutch release mechanism defective. Replace any defective parts (Chapter 2).
5 Clutch center or housing unevenly worn. This causes improper engagement of the plates. Replace the damaged or worn parts (Chapter 2).

27 Clutch not disengaging completely

1 Clutch improperly adjusted (see Chapter 1).
2 Clutch plates warped or damaged. This will cause clutch drag, which in turn will cause the machine to creep. Overhaul the clutch assembly (Chapter 2).
3 Sagged or broken clutch spring(s). Check and replace the spring(s) (Chapter 2).
4 Engine oil deteriorated. Old, thin, worn out oil will not provide proper lubrication for the discs, causing the clutch to drag. Replace the oil and filter (Chapter 1).
5 Engine oil viscosity too high. Using a thicker oil than recommended in Chapter 1 can cause the clutch plates to stick together, putting a drag on the engine. Change to the correct viscosity oil (Chapter 1).
6 Clutch housing seized on shaft. Lack of lubrication, severe wear or damage can cause the housing to seize on the shaft. Overhaul of the clutch, and perhaps transmission, may be necessary to repair the damage (Chapter 2).
7 Clutch release mechanism defective. Worn or damaged release mechanism parts can stick and fail to apply force to the pressure plate. Overhaul the release mechanism (Chapter 2).
8 Loose clutch center snap-ring. Causes housing and center misalignment putting a drag on the engine. Engagement adjustment continually varies. Overhaul the clutch assembly (Chapter 2).

Gear shifting problems

28 Doesn't go into gear or lever doesn't return

1 Clutch not disengaging. See Section 27.
2 Shift fork(s) bent or seized. May be caused by lack of lubrication. Overhaul the transmission (Chapter 2).
3 Gear(s) stuck on shaft. Most often caused by a lack of lubrication or excessive wear in transmission bearings and bushings. Overhaul the transmission (Chapter 2).
4 Shift drum binding. Caused by lubrication failure or excessive

wear. Replace the drum and bearing (Chapter 2).
5   Shift lever return spring weak or broken (Chapter 2).
6   Shift lever broken. Splines stripped out of lever or shaft, caused by allowing the lever to get loose. Replace necessary parts (Chapter 2).
7   Shift mechanism pawl broken or worn. Full engagement and rotary movement of shift drum results. Replace shaft assembly (Chapter 2).
8   Pawl spring broken. Allows pawl to float, causing sporadic shift operation. Replace spring (Chapter 2).

29   Jumps out of gear

1   Shift fork(s) worn. Overhaul the transmission (Chapter 2).
2   Gear groove(s) worn. Overhaul the transmission (Chapter 2).
3   Gear dogs or dog slots worn or damaged. The gears should be inspected and replaced. No attempt should be made to service the worn parts.

30   Overshifts

1   Pawl spring weak or broken (Chapter 2).
2   Shift drum stopper lever not functioning (Chapter 2).

Abnormal engine noise

31   Knocking or pinging

1   Carbon build-up in combustion chamber. Use of a fuel additive that will dissolve the adhesive bonding the carbon particles to the piston crown and chamber is the easiest way to remove the build-up. Otherwise, the cylinder head will have to be removed and decarbonized (Chapter 2).
2   Incorrect or poor quality fuel. Old or improper fuel can cause detonation. This causes the piston to rattle, thus the knocking or pinging sound. Drain the old fuel (Chapter 3) and always use the recommended grade fuel (Chapter 1).
3   Spark plug heat range incorrect. Uncontrolled detonation indicates that the plug heat range is too hot. The plug in effect becomes a glow plug, raising cylinder temperatures. Install the proper heat range plug (Chapter 1).
4   Improper air/fuel mixture. This will cause the cylinder to run hot and lead to detonation. Clogged jets or an air leak can cause this imbalance. See Chapter 3.

32   Piston slap or rattling

1   Cylinder-to-piston clearance excessive. Caused by improper assembly. Inspect and overhaul top end parts (Chapter 2).
2   Connecting rod bent. Caused by over-revving, trying to start a badly flooded engine or from ingesting a foreign object into the combustion chamber. Replace the damaged parts (Chapter 2).
3   Piston pin or piston pin bore worn or seized from wear or lack of lubrication. Replace damaged parts (Chapter 2).
4   Piston ring(s) worn, broken or sticking. Overhaul the top end (Chapter 2).
5   Piston seizure damage. Usually from lack of lubrication or overheating. Replace the pistons and bore the cylinder, as necessary (Chapter 2).
6   Connecting rod upper or lower end clearance excessive. Caused by excessive wear or lack of lubrication. Replace worn parts.

33   Valve noise

1   Incorrect valve clearances. Adjust the clearances by referring to Chapter 1.
2   Valve spring broken or weak. Check and replace weak valve springs (Chapter 2).
3   Camshaft or cylinder head worn or damaged. Lack of lubrication at high rpm is usually the cause of damage. Insufficient oil or failure to change the oil at the recommended intervals are the chief causes.

34   Other noise

1   Cylinder head gasket leaking.
2   Exhaust pipe leaking at cylinder head connection. Caused by improper fit of pipe, damaged gasket or loose exhaust flange. All exhaust fasteners should be tightened evenly and carefully. Failure to do this will lead to a leak.
3   Crankshaft runout excessive. Caused by a bent crankshaft (from over-revving) or damage from an upper cylinder component failure.
4   Engine mounting bolts or nuts loose. Tighten all engine mounting bolts and nuts to the specified torque (Chapter 2).
5   Crankshaft bearings worn (Chapter 2).
6   Camshaft chain tensioner defective. Replace according to the procedure in Chapter 2.
7   Camshaft chain, sprockets or guides worn (Chapter 2).

Abnormal driveline noise

35   Clutch noise

1   Clutch housing/friction plate clearance excessive (Chapter 2).
2   Loose or damaged pressure plate and/or bolts (Chapter 2).
3   Broken clutch springs (Chapter 2).

36   Transmission noise

1   Bearings worn. Also includes the possibility that the shafts are worn. Overhaul the transmission (Chapter 2).
2   Gears worn or chipped (Chapter 2).
3   Metal chips jammed in gear teeth. Probably pieces from a broken clutch, gear or shift mechanism that were picked up by the gears. This will cause early bearing failure (Chapter 2).
4   Engine oil level too low. Causes a howl from transmission. Also affects engine power and clutch operation (Chapter 1).

37   Final drive noise

1   Dry or dirty chain. Inspect, clean and lubricate (see Chapter 1).
2   Chain out of adjustment. Adjust chain slack (see Chapter 1).
3   Chain and sprockets damaged or worn. Inspect the chain and sprockets and replace them as necessary (see Chapter 4).

Abnormal chassis noise

38   Suspension noise

1   Spring weak or broken. Makes a clicking or scraping sound.
2   Steering head bearings worn or damaged. Clicks when braking. Check and replace as necessary (Chapter 5).
3   Front fork oil level incorrect. Check and correct oil level (see Chapter 5).

4 Front fork(s) assembled incorrectly. Disassemble the fork(s) and check for correct assembly (see Chapter 5).
5 Rear shock absorber fluid level incorrect. Indicates a leak caused by defective seal. Shock will be covered with oil. Replace shock (Chapter 5).
6 Defective shock absorber with internal damage. This is in the body of the shock and can't be remedied. The shock must be replaced with a new one (Chapter 5).
7 Bent or damaged shock body. Replace the shock with a new one (Chapter 5).

39 Brake noise

1 Brake linings worn or contaminated. Can cause scraping or squealing. Replace the shoes (Chapter 6).
2 Brake linings warped or worn unevenly. Can cause chattering. Replace the linings (Chapter 6).
3 Brake drum out of round. Can cause chattering. Replace brake drum (Chapter 6).
4 Loose or worn wheel bearings. Check and replace as needed (Chapter 5).

Excessive exhaust smoke

40 White smoke

1 Piston oil ring worn. The ring may be broken or damaged, causing oil from the crankcase to be pulled past the piston into the combustion chamber. Replace the rings with new ones (Chapter 2).
2 Cylinder worn, cracked, or scored. Caused by overheating or oil starvation. If worn or scored, the cylinder will have to be rebored and a new piston installed. If cracked, the cylinder will have to be replaced (see Chapter 2).
3 Valve oil seal damaged or worn. Replace oil seals with new ones (Chapter 2).
4 Valve guide worn. Perform a complete valve job (Chapter 2).
5 Engine oil level too high, which causes the oil to be forced past the rings. Drain oil to the proper level (Chapter 1).
6 Head gasket broken between oil return and cylinder. Causes oil to be pulled into the combustion chamber. Replace the head gasket and check the head for warpage (Chapter 2).
7 Abnormal crankcase pressurization, which forces oil past the rings. Clogged breather or hoses usually the cause (Chapter 2).

41 Black smoke

1 Air cleaner clogged. Clean or replace the element (Chapter 1).
2 Main jet too large or loose. Compare the jet size to the Specifications (Chapter 3).
3 Choke stuck open (Chapter 3).
4 Fuel level too high. Check the float level and replace the float if necessary (Chapter 3).
5 Inlet needle held off needle seat. Clean the float chamber and fuel line and replace the needle and seat if necessary (Chapter 3).

42 Brown smoke

1 Main jet too small or clogged. Lean condition caused by wrong size main jet or by a restricted orifice. Clean float chamber and jets and compare jet size to Specifications (Chapter 3).
2 Fuel flow insufficient. Fuel inlet needle valve stuck closed due to chemical reaction with old fuel. Float level incorrect; check and replace float if necessary. Restricted fuel line. Clean line and float chamber.
3 Carburetor intake tube loose (Chapter 3).
4 Air cleaner poorly sealed or not installed (Chapter 1).

Poor handling or stability

43 Handlebar hard to turn

1 Steering stem adjusting nut too tight (Chapter 5).
2 Steering stem bearings damaged. Roughness can be felt as the bars are turned from side-to-side. Replace bearings and races (Chapter 5).
3 Races dented or worn. Denting results from wear in only one position (e.g., straight ahead), striking an immovable object or hole or from dropping the machine. Replace races and bearings (Chapter 5).
4 Steering stem bearing lubrication inadequate. Causes are grease getting hard from age or being washed out by high pressure car washes. Remove steering stem, clean and lubricate bearings (Chapter 5).
5 Steering stem bent. Caused by a collision, hitting a pothole or by dropping the machine. Replace damaged part. Don't try to straighten the steering stem (Chapter 5).
6 Front tire air pressure too low (Chapter 1).

44 Handlebar shakes or vibrates excessively

1 Tires worn or out of balance (Chapter 1 or 6).
2 Swingarm bearings worn. Replace worn bearings (Chapter 5).
3 Wheel rim(s) warped or damaged. Inspect wheels (Chapter 6).
4 Wheel bearings worn. Worn front or rear wheel bearings can cause poor tracking. Worn front bearings will cause wobble (Chapter 6).
5 Handlebar clamp bolts loose (Chapter 5).
6 Steering stem or triple clamps loose. Tighten them to the specified torque (Chapters 1 and 5).
7 Motor mount bolts loose. Will cause excessive vibration with increased engine rpm (Chapter 2).

45 Handlebar pulls to one side

1 Frame bent. Definitely suspect this if the machine has been crashed. May or may not be accompanied by cracking near the bend. Replace the frame (Chapter 5).
2 Front and rear wheels out of alignment. Caused by uneven adjustment of the drive chain adjusters (see Chapter 1). May also be caused by improper location of the axle spacers or from bent steering stem or frame (see Chapter 5).
3 Swingarm bent or twisted. Caused by age (metal fatigue) or impact damage. Replace the swingarm (Chapter 5).
4 Steering stem bent. Caused by impact damage or by dropping the motorcycle. Replace the steering stem (Chapter 5).

46 Poor shock absorbing qualities

1 Too hard:
a) *Fork oil level excessive (see Chapter 5).*
b) *Fork oil viscosity too high. Use a lighter oil (see the Specifications in Chapter 5).*
c) *Fork tube bent. Causes a harsh, sticking feeling (see Chapter 5).*
d) *Fork internal damage (see Chapter 5).*
e) *Shock internal damage.*
f) *Tire pressures too high (Chapter 1).*
2 Too soft:
a) *Fork or shock oil insufficient and/or leaking (Chapter 5).*
b) *Fork oil level too low (see Chapter 5).*
c) *Fork springs weak or broken (Chapter 5).*

Braking problems

47   Brakes are weak, don't hold

1   Linings worn (Chapters 1 and 6).
2   Contaminated linings. Caused by contamination with oil, grease, etc. Clean or replace linings. Clean drum thoroughly with brake cleaner (Chapter 6).
3   Drum warped. Replace drum (Chapter 6).
4   Cable out of adjustment or stretched. Adjust or replace the cable (see Chapters 1 and 6).

48   Brake lever or pedal pulsates

1   Axle bent. Replace axle (Chapter 5).
2   Wheel warped or otherwise damaged (Chapter 6).

3   Wheel bearings damaged or worn (Chapter 6).
4   Brake drum out of round. Replace brake drum (Chapter 6).

49   Brakes drag

1   Cable sticking. Lubricate or replace cable (see Chapters 1 and 6).
2   Lever balky or stuck. Check pivot and lubricate (see Chapter 1).
3   Brake shoes damaged. Lining material separated from shoes. Usually caused by faulty manufacturing process or contact with chemicals. Replace shoes (see Chapter 6).
4   Shoes improperly installed (Chapter 6).
5   Brake pedal or lever freeplay insufficient (Chapter 1).
6   Brake springs weak. Replace brake springs (Chapter 6).

Chapter 1
Tune-up and routine maintenance

Contents

Specifications

Engine

Spark plugs
  80 and 100 models
    Type
      Standard .... NGK CR7HSA or ND U22FSR-U
      Extended high-speed riding .... NGK CR8HSA or ND U24FSR-U
      Cold climates (below 5-degrees C/41-degrees F) .... NGK CR6HSA or ND U20FSR-U
    Gap .... 0.6 to 0.7 mm (0.024 to 0.028 inch)
  50 and 70 models
    Type
      Standard .... NGK CR6HSA or ND U20FSR-U
      Extended high-speed riding .... NGK CR7HSA or ND U22FSR-U
      Cold climates (below 5-degrees C/41-degrees F) .... NGK CR5HSA or ND U16FSR-U
    Gap .... 0.6 to 0.7 mm (0.024 to 0.028 inch)
Points gap (breaker point models) .... 0.3 to 0.4 mm (0.012 to 0.016 inch)
Ignition timing speed (breaker point models)
  Advance starts at
    XR80R .... 1800 +/- 150 rpm
    XR100R .... 2050 +/- 150 rpm
  Full advance at
    XR80R .... 3400 +/- 200 rpm
    XR100R .... 3650 +/- 200 rpm
Engine idle speed
  XR80R .... 1500 +/- 100 rpm
  XR100R, CRF80F, CR100F .... 1400 +/- 100 rpm
  XR50R, XR70R, CRF50F, CRF70F .... 1700 +/- 100 rpm
Valve clearance (COLD engine, intake and exhaust) .... 0.05 mm (0.002 inch)

Miscellaneous

Brake shoe lining thickness	
New	4 mm (5/32-inch)
Wear limit	2 mm (3/32-inch)
Front brake lever freeplay	
XR70R, XR80R, XR100R, CRF80F, CRF100F	20 to 30 mm (3/4 to 1-1/4 inch)
XR50R, CRF50F, CRF70F	10 to 20 mm (3/8 to 13/16 inch)
Rear brake pedal freeplay	
XR70R, XR80R, XR100R, CRF80F, CRF100F	20 to 30 mm (3/4 to 1-1/4 inch)
XR50R, CRF50F, CRF70F	10 to 20 mm (3/8 to 13/16 inch)
Clutch lever freeplay	10 to 20 mm (3/8 to 3/4 inch)
Throttle grip freeplay	
All except XR50R and CRF50F	2 to 6 mm (3/32 to 1/4 inch)
XR50R and CRF50F	2 to 4 mm (3/32 to 3/16 inch)
Choke freeplay	Not adjustable
Minimum tire tread depth	
1985 through 1997	Not specified
1998 and later	
XR50R, CRF50F, XR80R, XR100R, CRF80F, CRF70F	3 mm (1/8-inch)
XR70R	
Front	1.5 m (1/16 inch)
Rear	2.0 mm (3/32 inch)
CRF70F	Not specified
Tire pressures (cold) (1)	
XR50R, XR80R, XR100R, CRF50F	
Front	15 psi
Rear	18 psi
CRF80F, CRF100F (front and rear)	14 psi
XR70R, CRF70F (front and rear)	15 psi
Tire sizes	
XR80R	
Front	2.50-16-4PR
Rear	3.60-14-4PR
XR100R	
Front	2.50-19-4PR
Rear	3.00-16-4PR
CRF80F	
Front	70/100-16 M/C 39M
Rear	80/100-14 M/C 43M
CRF100F	
Front	70/100-19 M/C 42M
Rear	90/100-16 M/C 51M
XR50R and CRF50F (front and rear)	2.50-10 33J
XR70R, CRF70F	
Front	2.50-14 4PR
Rear	3.00-12 4PR
Drive chain slack	
XR80R, XR100R, CRF80F, CRF100F	25 to 35 mm (1 to 3/8 inch)
XR70R, CRF80F	10 to 20 mm (3/8 to 3/4 inch)
CRF50F	15 to 25 mm (9/16 to 1inch)

Torque specifications

Oil drain plug	24 Nm (18 ft-lbs)
Spark plug	
XR80R, XR100R, CRF80F, CRF100F	14 Nm (120 inch-lbs)
XR50R, XR70R, CRF70F	12 Nm (108 inch-lbs)
CRF50F	
2004 through 2005	12 Nm (108 inch-lbs)
2006 and later	16 Nm (144 inch-lbs)
Wheel spokes	
All except CRF50F	3 Nm (24 inch-lbs)
XR50R, CRF50F	2 Nm (17 inch-lbs)
Rim lock locknut	12 Nm (108 inch-lbs)
Steering stem adjusting nut	
XR80R, XR100R	
Initial torque	29 Nm (22 ft-lbs)
Final torque	2 Nm (12 inch-lbs)
CRF80F, CRF100F	
Initial torque	25 Nm (18 ft-lbs)
Final torque	2.5 Nm (22 inch-lbs)

Torque specifications (continued)
Steering stem adjusting nut (continued)
    XR50R, XR70R, CRF50F, CRF70F
        Initial torque .... 25 Nm (18 ft-lbs)
        Final torque.. 2.9 Nm (26 inch-lbs)

Recommended lubricants and fluids
Engine/transmission oil
    Type .... API grade SG or higher*

*Oil must meet Japan Automobile Standards Organization (JASO) T 903 standard MA to prevent clutch slippage. Do not use oils with molybdenum additives.

Viscosity .... 10W-30 or 10W-40
Capacity
    Oil change
        XR80R .... 0.7 liters (0.74 US qt, 1.24 Imp pt)
        XR100R, CRF80F, CRF100F .... 0.9 liters (0.95 US qt, 1.58 Imp pt)
        XR50R, XR70R, CRF50F, CRF70F.......................... 0.6 liters (0.6 US qt, 1.0 Imp pt)
    After engine overhaul
        XR80R .... 0.9 liters (0.95 US qt, 1.58 Imp pt)
        XR100R .... 1.0 liters (1.06 US qt, 1.76 Imp pt)
        CRF80F, CRF100F .... 1.1 liters (1.2 US qt, 2.0 Imp pt)
        XR50R, XR70R, CRF50F, CRF70F.......................... 0.8 liters (0.8 US qt, 1.4 Imp pt)
Air filter oil.. Pro Honda foam filter oil or equivalent

Miscellaneous
Wheel bearings... Medium weight, lithium-based multi-purpose grease (NLGI no. 3)
Swingarm pivot bushings.. Molybdenum disulfide paste grease containing 40-percent or more molybdenum disulfide
Cables and lever pivots .... Medium weight, lithium-based multi-purpose grease (NLGI no. 3)
Brake pedal/shift lever/throttle lever pivots............................. Medium weight, lithium-based multi-purpose grease (NLGI no. 3)

Honda XR and CRF50/70/80/100 Routine maintenance intervals

Note: *The pre-ride inspection outlined in the owner's manual covers checks and maintenance that should be carried out on a daily basis. It's condensed and included here to remind you of its importance. Always perform the pre-ride inspection at every maintenance interval (in addition to the procedures listed). The intervals listed below are the shortest intervals recommended by the manufacturer for each particular operation during the model years covered in this manual. Your owner's manual may have different intervals for your model.*

Daily or before riding

    Check the engine oil level
    Check the fuel level and inspect for leaks
    Check the operation of both brakes - check the front brake lever
        and rear brake pedal for correct freeplay
    Check the tires for damage, the presence of foreign objects and
        correct air pressure
    Check the throttle for smooth operation and correct freeplay
    Make sure the steering operates smoothly
    Make sure the engine kill switch works properly
    Check the air cleaner drain tube and clean it if necessary
    Check all fasteners, including axle nuts, for tightness
    Check for mud or debris that could start a fire or interfere with
        motorcycle operation

Every 300 miles

    Clean, inspect and lubricate the drive chain*
*More often in dusty, sandy or wet conditions.

Every 600 miles

Perform all of the daily checks plus:
    Check the brake shoes and cables for wear
    Inspect breaker points and check the gap (except CDI models)
    Adjust cam chain tension
    Check and adjust the valve clearances
    Clean the air filter element*
    Clean the air cleaner housing drain tube
    Check/adjust the throttle lever freeplay
    Check choke operation
    Check/adjust the idle speed
    Change the engine oil and clean the strainer screen
    Check the tightness of all fasteners
    Inspect the suspension
    Clean and gap the spark plug
    Adjust the clutch
    Check the exhaust system for leaks and check fastener
        tightness; clean the spark arrester
    Inspect the wheels and tires
    Check the cleanliness of the fuel system and the condition of
        the fuel line
    Clean the fuel tap strainer screen
    Inspect the steering system and steering head bearings
    Check the sidestand operation

2.1a Decals on the motorcycle include maintenance information such as drive chain adjustment . . .

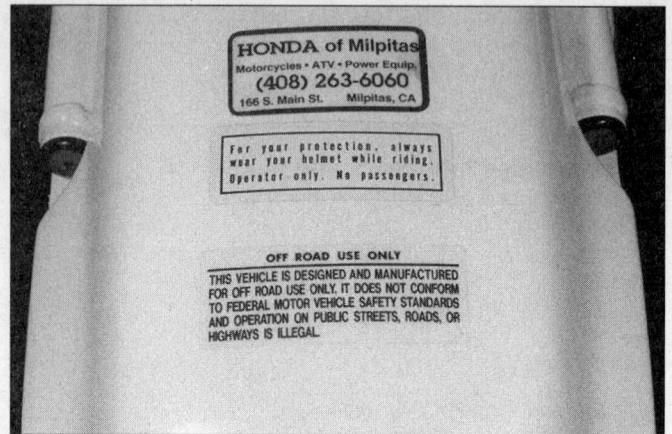

2.1b . . . as well as safety information

2   Introduction to tune-up and routine maintenance

Refer to illustrations 2.1a and 2.1b

This Chapter covers in detail the checks and procedures necessary for the tune-up and routine maintenance of your motorcycle. Section 1 includes the routine maintenance schedule, which is designed to keep the machine in proper running condition and prevent possible problems. The remaining Sections contain detailed procedures for carrying out the items listed on the maintenance schedule, as well as additional maintenance information designed to increase reliability. Maintenance information is also printed on decals, which are mounted in various locations on the motorcycle **(see illustrations)**. Where information on the decals differs from that presented in this Chapter, use the decal information.

Since routine maintenance plays such an important role in the safe and efficient operation of your motorcycle, it is presented here as a comprehensive check list. For the rider who does all his own maintenance, these lists outline the procedures and checks that should be done on a routine basis.

Deciding where to start or plug into the routine maintenance schedule depends on several factors. If you have a motorcycle whose warranty has recently expired, and if it has been maintained according to the warranty standards, you may want to pick up routine maintenance as it coincides with the next mileage or calendar interval. If you have owned the machine for some time but have never performed any maintenance on it, then you may want to start at the nearest interval and include some additional procedures to ensure that nothing important is overlooked. If you have just had a major engine overhaul, then you may want to start the maintenance routine from the beginning. If you have

a used machine and have no knowledge of its history or maintenance record, you may desire to combine all the checks into one large service initially and then settle into the maintenance schedule prescribed.

The Sections which actually outline the inspection and maintenance procedures are written as step-by-step comprehensive guides to the actual performance of the work. They explain in detail each of the routine inspections and maintenance procedures on the check list. References to additional information in applicable Chapters is also included and should not be overlooked.

Before beginning any actual maintenance or repair, the machine should be cleaned thoroughly, especially around the oil filter housing, spark plug, valve cover, side covers, carburetor, etc. Cleaning will help ensure that dirt does not contaminate the engine and will allow you to detect wear and damage that could otherwise easily go unnoticed.

3   Engine oil level - check

Refer to illustration 3.3a and 3.3b

1   Support the motorcycle in a level position, then start the engine and allow it to reach normal operating temperature. **Warning:** *Do not run the engine in an enclosed space such as a garage or shop.*

2   Stop the engine and allow the machine to sit undisturbed in a level position for about five minutes.

3   With the engine off, unscrew the dipstick from the right side of the crankcase. Pull it out, wipe it off with a clean rag, and reinsert it (let the dipstick rest on the threads; don't screw it back in). Pull the dipstick out and check the oil level on the dipstick scale. The oil level should be between the Maximum and Minimum level marks on the scale **(see illustration)**.

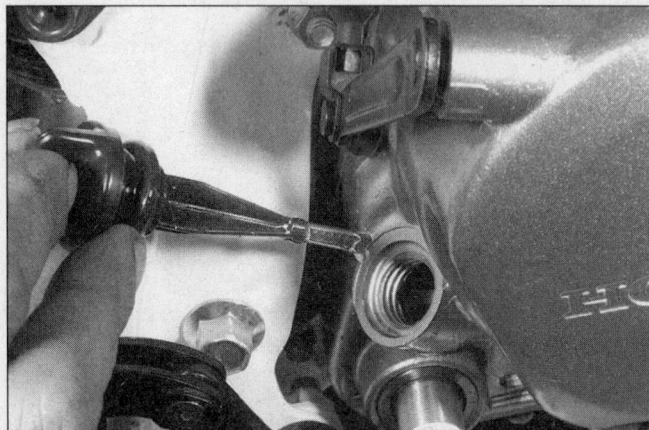

3.3a The engine oil level must be between the upper and lower marks on the dipstick (here's the 80/100 dipstick) . . .

3.3b . . . here's the 50/70 dipstick

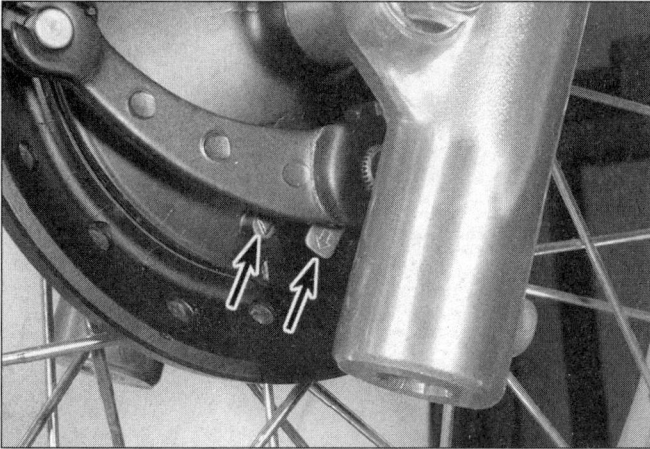

4.5 If the pointer (right arrow) aligns with the mark (left arrow) when the brake is applied, it's time to replace the brake shoes (front brake shown; rear brake similar)

5.3 Loosen the lockwheel (left arrow) and turn the adjuster (right arrow) to adjust freeplay

4   If the level is below the Minimum mark, add oil through the dipstick hole. Add enough oil of the recommended grade and type to bring the level up to the Maximum mark. Do not overfill.

4   Brake system - general check

Refer to illustration 4.5

1   A routine general check of the brakes will ensure that any problems are discovered and remedied before the rider's safety is jeopardized.
2   Check the brake lever and pedal for loose connections, excessive play, bends, and other damage. Replace any damaged parts with new ones (see Chapter 6).
3   Make sure all brake fasteners are tight. Check the brakes for wear as described below.
4   Operate the rear brake lever and pedal. If operation is rough or sticky, refer to Section 10 and lubricate the cables.
5   With the rear brake lever and pedal freeplay properly adjusted (see Section 5), check the wear indicator on the brake panel **(see illustration)**. If the pointer lines up with the indicator when the lever is pulled or the pedal is pressed, refer to Chapter 6 and replace the brake shoes.

5   Brake lever and pedal freeplay - check and adjustment

Front brake lever

Refer to illustrations 5.3 and 5.4

1   Squeeze the front brake lever and note how far the lever travels (measure at the tip of the lever). If it exceeds the limit listed in this Chapter's Specifications, adjust the front brake as described below.
2   If lever travel needs to be adjusted, there are two methods. Minor adjustments can be made at the adjuster on the brake lever. Major adjustments can be made at the adjuster on the brake panel.
3   Pull back the rubber cover from the handlebar adjuster **(see illustration)**. Loosen the lockwheel, turn the adjuster as needed to set freeplay, then tighten the lockwheel.
4   If freeplay can't be brought within specifications at the lockwheel adjuster, loosen the locknut at the brake panel adjuster **(see illustration)**. Turn the adjusting nut to bring freeplay within the specified range, then tighten the locknut.

Rear brake

Refer to illustrations 5.5 and 5.6

5   To adjust brake pedal height, loosen the locknut and turn the adjusting bolt **(see illustration)**. Honda doesn't specify pedal height.

5.4 Major adjustments to the front brake are made at the lower end of the cable

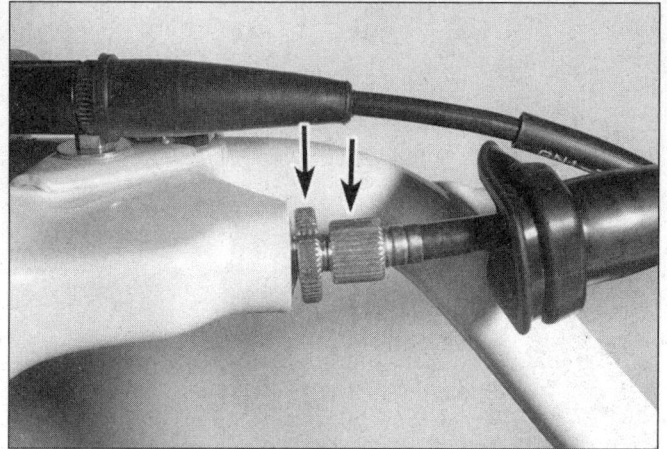

5.5 Loosen the locknut (arrow) and turn the adjusting bolt to change pedal height

5.6 The wear indicator on rear brakes is at the rear of the panel (lower arrow); adjustments are made with the wingnut (upper arrow)

6   Check the play of the brake pedal **(see illustration)**. If it exceeds the limit listed in this Chapter's Specifications, adjust it with the wingnut at the rear end of the brake rod.

6   Tires/wheels - general check

Refer to illustrations 6.4, 6.5 and 6.7

1   Routine tire and wheel checks should be made with the realization that your safety depends to a great extent on their condition.
2   Check the tires carefully for cuts, tears, embedded nails or other sharp objects and excessive wear. Operation of the motorcycle with excessively worn tires is extremely hazardous, as traction and handling are directly affected. Check the tread depth at the center of the tire. Honda doesn't specify a minimum tread depth for these models, but as a general rule, tires should be replaced with new ones when the tread knobs are worn to 3 mm (1/8 inch) or less.
3   Repair or replace punctured tires as soon as damage is noted. Do not try to patch a torn tire, as wheel balance and tire reliability may be impaired.
4   Check the tire pressures when the tires are cold and keep them properly inflated **(see illustration)**. Proper air pressure will increase tire life and provide maximum stability and ride comfort. Keep in mind that low tire pressures may cause the tire to slip on the rim or come off,

6.4 Check tire pressure with a gauge

while high tire pressures will cause abnormal tread wear and unsafe handling.
5   The wheels should be kept clean and checked periodically for cracks, bending, loose spokes and rust. Never attempt to repair damaged wheels; they must be replaced with new ones. Loose spokes can be tightened with a spoke wrench **(see illustration)**, but be careful not to overtighten and distort the wheel rim.
6   Check the valve stem locknuts to make sure they're tight. Also, make sure the valve stem cap is in place and tight. If it is missing, install a new one made of metal or hard plastic.
7   Check the tightness of the locknut on the rim lock **(see illustration)**. Tighten it if necessary to the torque listed in this Chapter's Specifications.

7   Clutch - check and freeplay adjustment

Refer to illustrations 7.2, 7.4 and 7.5

80 and 100 models

1   Operate the clutch lever and measure freeplay at the tip of the lever. If it's not within the range listed in this Chapter's Specifications, adjust it as follows.
2   Pull back the rubber cover from the adjuster at the handlebar **(see illustration)**. Loosen the lockwheel and turn the adjuster to change freeplay.

6.5 Check the tension of the spokes periodically, but don't over-tighten them

6.7 Tighten the nut on the rim lock to the specified torque

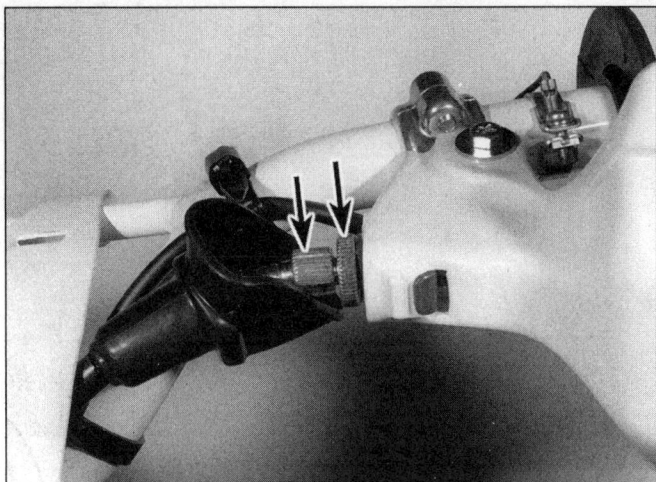

7.2 Loosen the lockwheel (right arrow) and turn the adjuster wheel (left arrow) to make fine adjustments in clutch lever freeplay

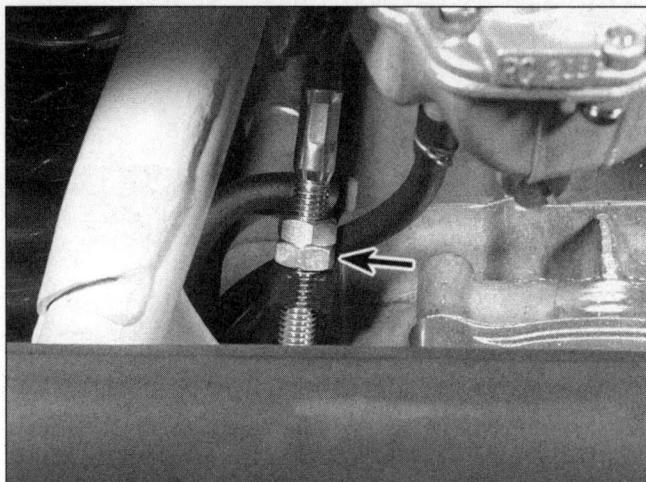

7.4 The in-line adjuster is located near the lower end of the clutch cable

3   If freeplay can't be brought within specifications by using the handlebar adjuster, turn the handlebar adjuster in all the way, then unscrew it two turns.

4   Loosen the locknuts on the lower cable adjuster and turn it in all the way **(see illustration)**.

5   Loosen the adjusting screw locknut in the right engine cover **(see illustration)**. Turn the adjusting screw counterclockwise just until you feel resistance, then turn it back in 1/8 to 1/4-turn. Hold the screw in this position and tighten the locknut.

6   Turn the lower cable adjuster back out until freeplay at the tip of the clutch lever is 25 mm (one inch), then tighten the nuts.

7   Repeat Step 2 to bring clutch lever freeplay within the range listed in this Chapter's Specifications.

8   If freeplay still can't be adjusted to within the specified range, the cable is probably stretched and should be replaced with a new one.

50 and 70 models

Refer to illustration 7.10

9   The clutch disengages automatically when the gearshift pedal is moved from one gear position to another.

10   Loosen the adjuster locknut **(see illustration)**. Carefully turn the adjusting screw one full turn clockwise (but don't force it).

11   Turn the screw back (counterclockwise) just until you feel resistance. Then turn it clockwise 1/8 turn. Hold the screw in this position

with the screwdriver and tighten the locknut.

12   Ride the bike and check clutch operation. You should be able to shift gears without grinding, and the clutch should not slip.

8   Throttle and choke operation/grip freeplay - check and adjustment

Throttle check

1   Make sure the throttle twistgrip moves easily from fully closed to fully open with the front wheel turned at various angles. The grip should return automatically from fully open to fully closed when released. If the throttle sticks, check the throttle cable for cracks or kinks in the housings. Also, make sure the inner cable is clean and well-lubricated.

2   Check for a small amount of freeplay at the twistgrip and compare the freeplay to the value listed in this Chapter's Specifications.

Throttle adjustment

Refer to illustration 8.4

3   Freeplay adjustments can be made at the throttle lever end of the accelerator cable. On 1985 models only, freeplay can also be adjusted at the carburetor end of the cable.

4   Pull back the rubber cover from the adjuster and loosen the lock-

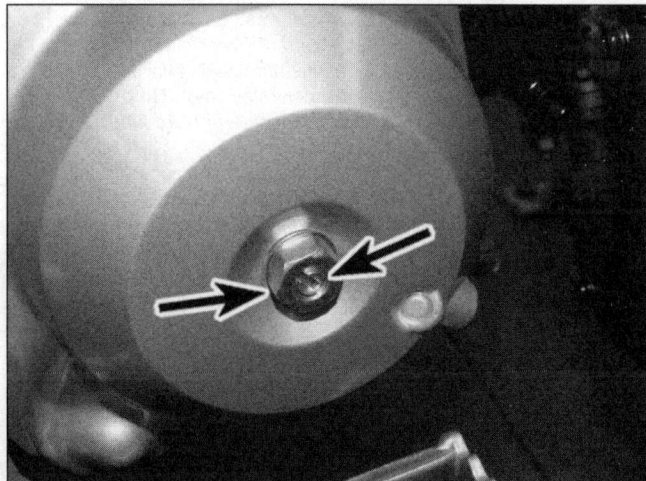

7.5 The 80/100 clutch adjusting screw and locknut are located in the bottom of the right engine cover (arrow)

7.10 The 50/70 clutch adjusting screw and locknut (arrows) are located in the center of the right engine cover

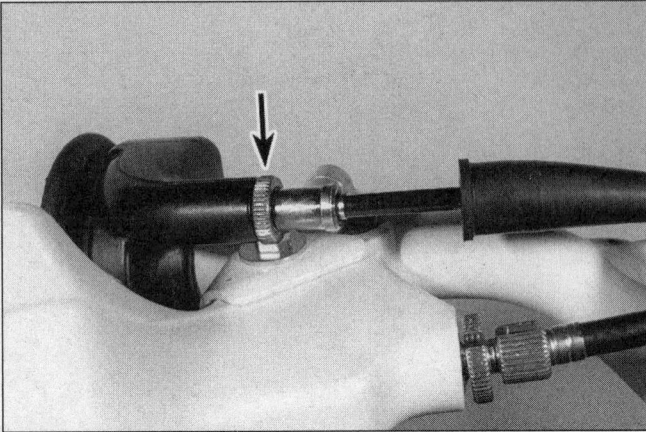

8.4 Make throttle freeplay adjustments at the handlebar; on 1985 models only, adjustments can also be made at the carburetor

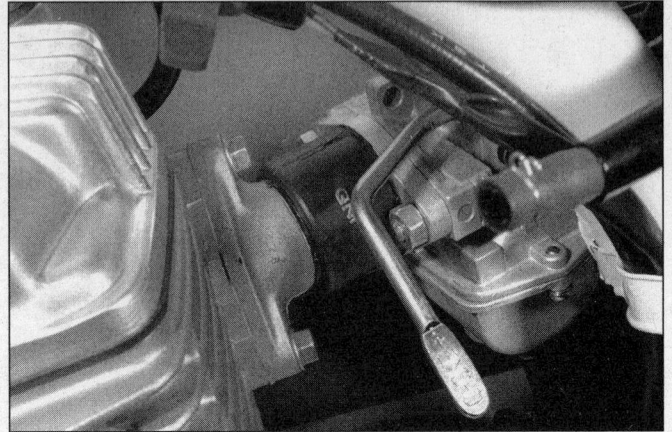

9.1 Move the choke lever back and forth and check for smooth operation

wheel on the cable **(see illustration)**. Turn the adjuster until the desired freeplay is obtained, then tighten the lockwheel.

5   If the freeplay can't be adjusted at the grip end on 1985 models, adjust the cable at the carburetor end. To do this, first remove the fuel tank (see Chapter 3). Loosen the locknut on the throttle cable. Turn the adjusting nut to set freeplay, then tighten the locknut securely.

9   Choke - operation check

Refer to illustration 9.1
1   Operate the choke lever on the carburetor while you feel for smooth operation **(see illustration)**.
2   If the lever doesn't move smoothly, refer to Chapter 3 and check the choke mechanism for worn or damaged parts.

10   Lubrication - general

Refer to illustration 10.3
1   Since the controls, cables and various other components of a motorcycle are exposed to the elements, they should be lubricated periodically to ensure safe and trouble-free operation.
2   The throttle twistgrip, brake lever, brake pedal, kickstarter pivot and sidestand pivot should be lubricated frequently. In order for the lubricant to be applied where it will do the most good, the component should be disassembled. However, if chain and cable lubricant is being used, it can be applied to the pivot joint gaps and will usually work its way into the areas where friction occurs. If motor oil or light grease is being used, apply it sparingly as it may attract dirt (which could cause the controls to bind or wear at an accelerated rate). **Note:** *One of the best lubricants for the control lever pivots is a dry-film lubricant (available from many sources by different names).*
3   The throttle and brake cables should be removed and treated with a commercially available cable lubricant which is specially formulated for use on motorcycle control cables. Small adapters for pressure lubricating the cables with spray can lubricants are available and ensure that the cable is lubricated along its entire length **(see illustration)**. When attaching the cable to the lever, be sure to lubricate the barrel-shaped fitting at the end with multi-purpose grease.
4   To lubricate the cables, disconnect them at the lower end, then lubricate the cable with a pressure lube adapter **(see illustration 10.3)**. See Chapter 3 (throttle cable) or Chapter 6 (brake cables).
5   Refer to Chapter 5 for the following lubrication procedures:
   a) *Swingarm bearing and dust seals*
   b) *Rear suspension linkage and dust seals*
   c) *Steering head bearings*
6   Refer to Chapter 6 for the following lubrication procedures:

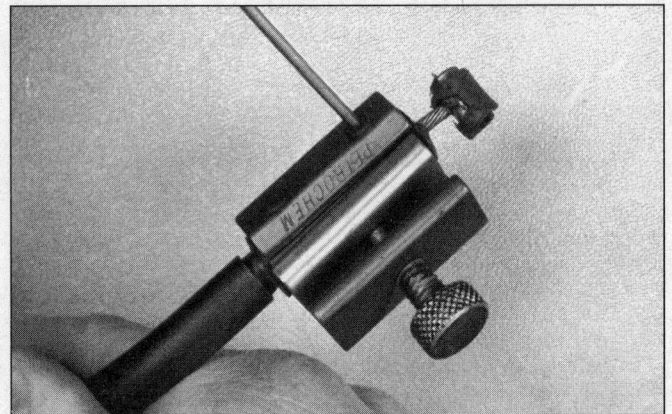

10.3 Lubricating a cable with a pressure lube adapter (make sure the tool seats around the inner cable)

   a) *Front and rear wheel bearings*
   b) *Brake pedal pivot*

11   Engine oil change and filter screen cleaning

Refer to illustrations 11.5a, 11.5b, 11.7a, 11.7b, 11.10a and 11.10b
1   Consistent routine oil changes and filter screen cleaning are the single most important maintenance procedure you can perform on these models. The oil not only lubricates the internal parts of the engine, transmission and clutch, but it also acts as a coolant, a cleaner, a sealant, and a protectant. Because of these demands, the oil takes a terrific amount of abuse and should be replaced often with new oil of the recommended grade and type. Saving a little money on the difference in cost between a good oil and a cheap oil won't pay off if the engine is damaged. Honda recommends against using the following:
   a) *Oils with graphite or molybdenum additives*
   b) *Non-detergent oils*
   c) *Castor or vegetable based oils*
   d) *Oil additives*
2   Before changing the oil and cleaning the filter screen, warm up the engine so the oil will drain easily. Be careful when draining the oil, as the exhaust pipe, the engine and the oil itself can cause severe burns.
3   Park the motorcycle over a clean drain pan.
4   Remove the dipstick/oil filler cap to vent the crankcase and act as a reminder that there is no oil in the engine.
5   Next, remove the drain plug from the engine **(see illustrations)** and allow the oil to drain into the pan. Do not lose the sealing washer on the drain plug.

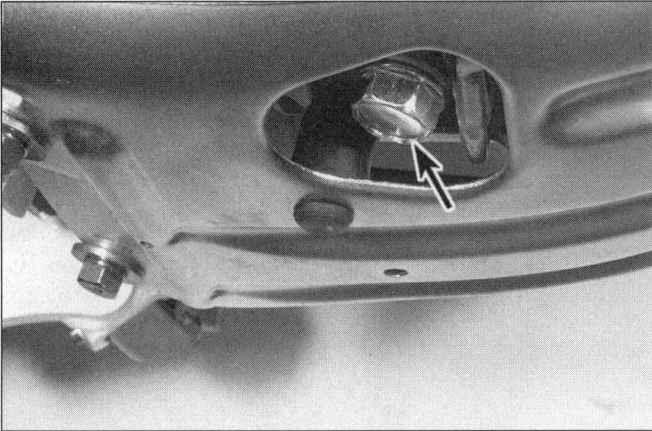

11.5a The engine oil drain plug is accessible through a hole in the skid plate (80/100 models)

11.5b Here's the 50/70 engine oil drain plug (arrow) - the plug on the far side of the engine is for the cam chain tensioner

11.7a The right-side engine cover must be removed for access to the oil strainer screen (this is an 80/100 strainer screen)

11.7b . . . and this is the 50/70 design

6   As the oil is draining, remove the kickstarter pedal (see Chapter 2). Remove the brake pedal (80 and100 models) or remove the pedal spring and lower the pedal (50 and 70 models) (see Chapter 6). Refer to the clutch section of Chapter 2 and remove the right-side engine cover. If additional maintenance is planned for this time period, check or service another component while the oil is allowed to drain completely.

7   Pull the filter screen out of its slot in the crankcase (see illustrations). Clean it thoroughly with a high flash point solvent, then dry it completely (blow it dry with compressed air, if available).

8   Check the condition of the drain plug threads. Replace the plug if the threads are damaged.

9   Install the filter screen in its slot.

10   If you're working on a 50 or 70 model, clean the centrifugal oil filter. To do this, remove the clutch lifter lever and cam plate (see Chapter 2). Clean all oil and deposits from the clutch housing center groove and from the inside of the outer cover (see illustration). Remove all traces of old gasket from the clutch housing and outer cover, then rein-

11.10a Remove the cover screws (arrows) . . .

11.10b . . . remove the cover and clean the area inside the clutch housing (arrow) - use a new gasket

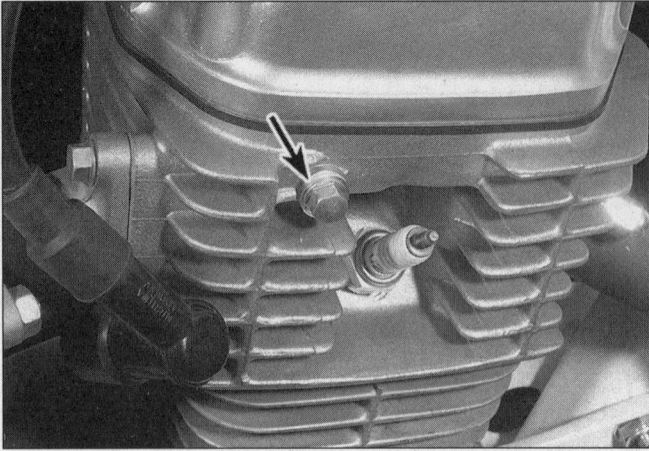

11.13 With the engine idling, loosen (but don't remove) the oil check bolt (arrow); oil should seep from around the bolt

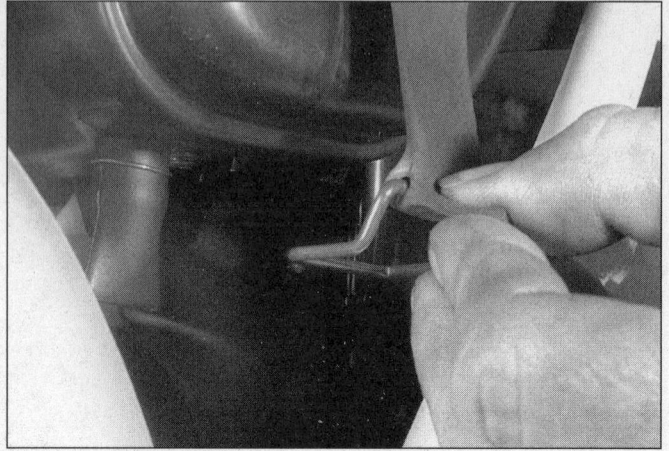

12.2 Unhook the retaining band and take off the filter cover

stall the outer cover, using a new gasket.

11   On all models, refer to Chapter 2 and install the right engine cover.

12   Slip a new sealing washer over the drain plug, then install and tighten the plug to the torque listed in this Chapter's Specifications. Avoid overtightening, as damage to the engine case will result.

13   Before refilling the engine, check the old oil carefully. If the oil was drained into a clean pan, small pieces of metal or other material can be easily detected. If the oil is very metallic colored, then the engine is experiencing wear from break-in (new engine) or from insufficient lubrication. If there are flakes or chips of metal in the oil, then something is drastically wrong internally and the engine will have to be disassembled for inspection and repair.

14   If there are pieces of fiber-like material in the oil, the clutch is experiencing excessive wear and should be checked.

15   If the inspection of the oil turns up nothing unusual, refill the crankcase to the proper level with the recommended oil and install the dipstick/filler cap. Start the engine, let it run and check for leaks.

16   If you're working on an 80 or 100 model, loosen (but don't remove) the oil check bolt with the engine running **(see illustration)**. Oil should seep from around the bolt. If it doesn't, shut it off and find the problem before running it further. **Warning:** *Don't remove the check bolt with the engine running.*

17   If oil does seep from around the check bolt, shut the engine off, wait a few minutes, then check the oil level. If necessary, add more oil to bring the level up to the upper level mark on the dipstick. Check around the drain plug and right engine cover for leaks.

18   The old oil drained from the engine cannot be reused in its present

state and should be disposed of. Check with your local refuse disposal company, disposal facility or environmental agency to see if they will accept the oil for recycling. Don't pour used oil into drains or onto the ground. After the oil has cooled, it can be drained into a suitable container (capped plastic jugs, topped bottles, milk cartons, etc.) for transport to one of these disposal sites.

12   Air cleaner - filter element and drain tube cleaning

Element cleaning
80 and 100 models
Refer to illustrations 12.2, 12.3, 12.4 and 12.8

1   Remove the left side cover (see Chapter 7).

2   Unclip the cover retaining band, then lift it off and remove the cover **(see illustration)**.

3   Unclip the retaining band that secures the filter element and pull the element out **(see illustration)**.

4   Separate the foam element from the metal core **(see illustration)**.

5   Clean the element and core in a high flash point solvent, squeeze the solvent out of the foam and let the core and element dry completely.

6   Soak the foam element in the type of oil listed in this Chapter's Specifications, then squeeze it firmly to remove the excess oil.

7   Place the element on the core.

8   The remainder of installation is the reverse of the removal steps. Be sure the retaining bands are hooked securely **(see illustration)**.

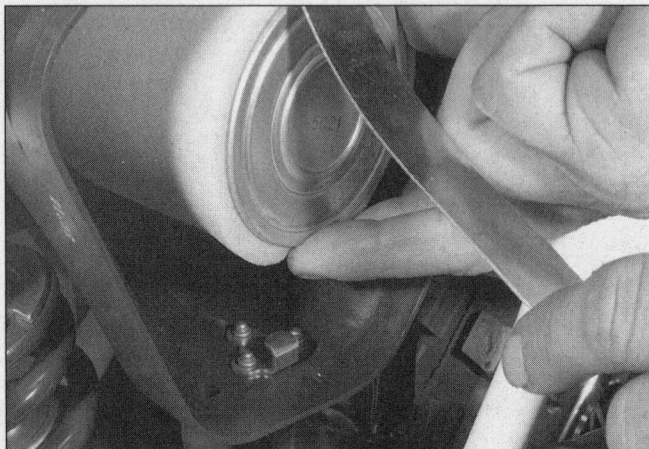

12.3 Unclip the filter retaining band and pull the filter out of the case

12.4 Separate the foam element from the core for cleaning and re-oiling

12.8 Make sure the retaining bands for the element and cover are securely installed

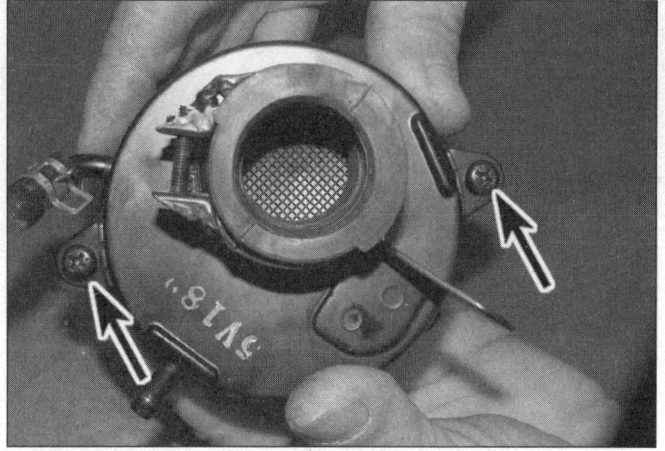

12.9a Remove the cover screws (arrows) (filter housing removed for clarity)

12.9b The cover slot aligns with the housing tab (arrows)

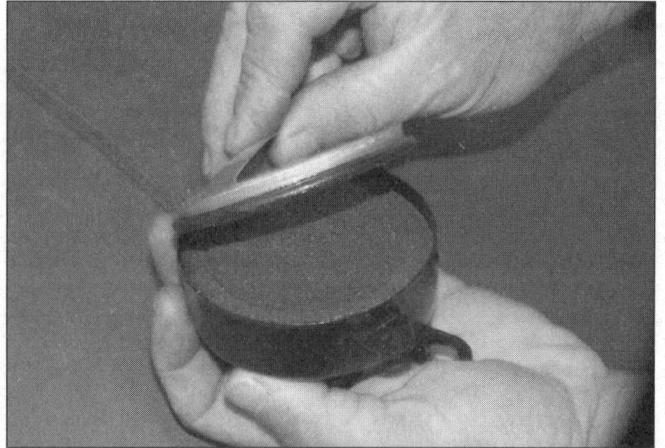

12.10a Remove the element holder . . .

50 and 70 models

Refer to illustrations 12.9a, 12.9b, 12.10a, 12.10b and 12.13

9   Remove the screws and take the cover off the air cleaner **(see illustrations)**. **Note:** *On 50 models, you may find it easier to remove the air cleaner housing from the engine (see Chapter 3).*

10   Pull the element holder and element out of the housing **(see illustrations)**.

11   Clean the element and soak it in oil as described in Steps 5 and 6 above.

12   Reinstall the element in the housing, then install the holder. Align the holder slot with the tab on the cover.

13   Pack the rim groove of the housing with multi-purpose grease **(see illustration)**. Install the cover, aligning its slot with the tab on the housing, and secure it with the screws.

12.10b . . . and the element

12.13 Pack the housing groove with multipurpose grease

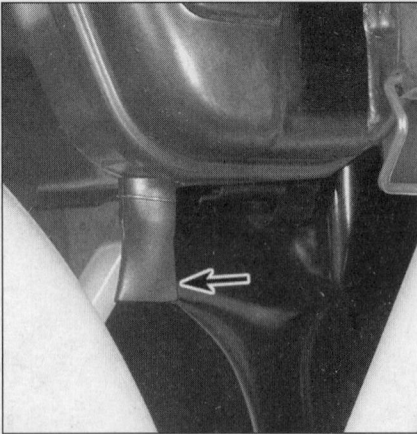

12.14 Open the drain tube (arrow) to release accumulated oil and water; if it's clogged, remove it for cleaning

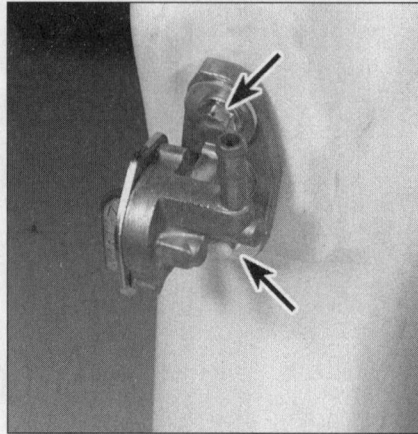

13.5 Remove the bolts (arrows) and take the fuel tap off the tank

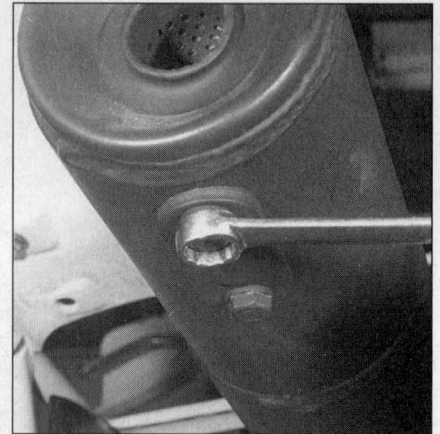

14.3a Unbolt the plate . . .

Drain tube and crankcase breather

Refer to illustration 12.14

14   Squeeze the drain tube to let accumulated water and oil run out **(see illustration)**. If the tube is clogged, squeeze its clamp, remove it from the air cleaner housing and clean it out. Install the drain tube on the housing and secure it with the clamp.

15   On models so equipped, remove the plug from the end of the crankcase breather tube. On 80 and 100 models, it's located below and behind the kickstart lever. On 50 and 70 models, it's next to the shift pedal. Drain accumulated deposits from the tube, then reinstall the plug.

13   Fuel system - check and filter cleaning

Refer to illustration 13.5

Warning: *Gasoline is extremely flammable, so take extra precautions when you work on any part of the fuel system. Don't smoke or allow open flames or bare light bulbs near the work area, and don't work in a garage where a natural gas-type appliance (such as a water heater or clothes dryer) is present. Since gasoline is carcinogenic, wear latex gloves when there's a possibility of being exposed to fuel, and, if you spill any fuel on your skin, rinse it off immediately with soap and water. Mop up any spills immediately and do not store fuel-soaked rags where they could ignite. When you perform any kind of work on the fuel system, wear safety glasses and have an extinguisher suitable for a class B type fire (flammable liquids) on hand.*

1   Check the carburetor, fuel tank, the fuel tap and the line for leaks and evidence of damage.

2   If carburetor gaskets are leaking, the carburetor should be disassembled and rebuilt (refer to Chapter 3).

3   If the fuel tap is leaking at the gasket, tightening the screws may help. If leakage persists, the tap should be removed and a new gasket installed. The tap can't be disassembled, so if it's leaking around the handle, it should be replaced with a new one.

4   If the fuel line is cracked or otherwise deteriorated, replace it with a new one.

5   Place the fuel tap lever in the Off position. Disconnect and plug the fuel line, remove the bolts and take the tap out of the fuel tank **(see illustration)**.

6   Clean the strainer. If it's too heavily clogged to clean, replace the fuel tap.

7   Installation is the reverse of the removal steps. Tighten the fuel tap screws securely, but don't overtighten them and strip out the threads.

8   After installation, run the engine and check for fuel leaks.

9   If the motorcycle will be stored for a month or more, remove and drain the fuel tank. Also loosen the float chamber drain screw and drain the fuel from the carburetor (see Chapter 3).

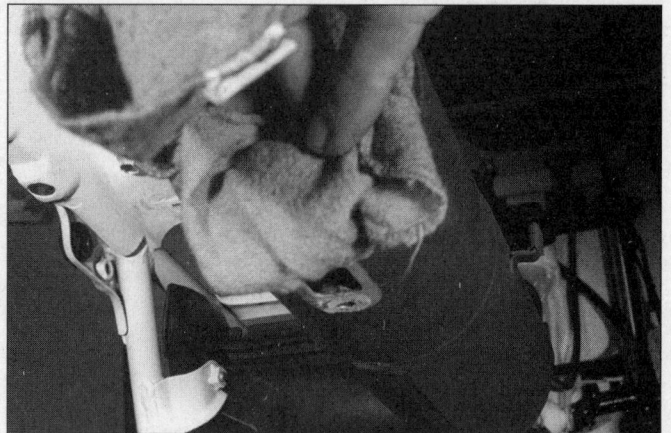

14.3b . . . then hold a rag against the muffler opening and rev the engine a few times to blow carbon out of the spark arreste

14   Exhaust system - inspection and spark arrester cleaning

Refer to illustrations 14.3a and 14.3b

1   Periodically check the exhaust system for leaks and loose fasteners. If tightening the holder nuts at the cylinder head fails to stop any leaks, replace the gasket with a new one (a procedure which requires removal of the system).

2   The exhaust pipe flange nuts at the cylinder head are especially prone to loosening, which could cause damage to the head. Check them frequently and keep them tight.

80 and 100 models

3   **Warning:** *Make sure the exhaust system is cool before doing this procedure.* At the specified interval, remove the plate or plug from under the rear end of the muffler **(see illustration)**. Hold a rag firmly over the hole at the rear end of the muffler **(see illustration)**. Have an assistant start the engine and rev it a few times to blow out carbon, then shut the engine off.

4   After the exhaust system has cooled, install the plate and gasket. Tighten the bolts securely.

50 and 70 models

Refer to illustration 14.5

5   Remove the three bolts that secure the spark arrester to the muffler **(see illustration)**. Pull the spark arrester out and remove the gasket.

14.5 On 50/70 models, remove the bolts (arrows) and pull the spark arrester out of the muffler housing

15.2a Unscrew the plug with a spark plug socket (here's the 80/100 plug location)

15.2b . . . and here's the 50/70 plug location

15.6a Spark plug manufacturers recommend using a wire type gauge when checking the gap - if the wire doesn't slide between the electrodes with a slight drag, adjustment is required

15.6b To change the gap, bend the side electrode only, as indicated by the arrows, and be very careful not to crack or chip the ceramic insulator surrounding the center electrode

6   Clean the spark arrester screen with a wire brush, using solvent if necessary. Check it for breaks, tears or other damage and replace it if problems are found.

7   Installation is the reverse of the removal steps. Use a new gasket. Tighten the bolts evenly and securely, but don't overtighten them and strip the threads.

15 Spark plug - replacement

Refer to illustrations, 15.2a, 15.2b, 15.6a and 15.6b

1   Twist the spark plug cap to break it free from the plug, then pull it off.

2   If available, use compressed air to blow any accumulated debris from around the spark plug. Remove the plug **(see illustrations)**.

3   Inspect the electrodes for wear. Both the center and side electrodes should have square edges and the side electrode should be of uniform thickness. Look for excessive deposits and evidence of a cracked or chipped insulator around the center electrode. Compare your spark plugs to the color spark plug chart on the inside of the back cover. Check the threads, the washer and the ceramic insulator body for cracks and other damage.

4   If the electrodes are not excessively worn, and if the deposits can be easily removed with a wire brush, the plug can be regapped and

reused (if no cracks or chips are visible in the insulator). If in doubt concerning the condition of the plug, replace it with a new one, as the expense is minimal.

5   Cleaning the spark plug by sandblasting is permitted, provided you clean the plug with a high flash-point solvent afterwards.

6   Before installing a new plug, make sure it is the correct type and heat range. Check the gap between the electrodes, as it is not pre-set. For best results, use a wire-type gauge rather than a flat gauge to check the gap **(see illustration)**. If the gap must be adjusted, bend the side electrode only and be very careful not to chip or crack the insulator nose **(see illustration)**. Make sure the washer is in place before installing the plug.

7   Since the cylinder head is made of aluminum, which is soft and easily damaged, thread the plug into the head by hand. Slip a short length of hose over the end of the plug to use as a tool to thread it into place. The hose will grip the plug well enough to turn it, but will start to slip if the plug begins to cross-thread in the hole - this will prevent damaged threads and the accompanying repair costs.

8   Once the plug is finger tight, the job can be finished with a socket. If a torque wrench is available, tighten the spark plug to the torque listed in this Chapter's Specifications. If you do not have a torque wrench, tighten the plug finger tight (until the washer bottoms on the cylinder head) then use a wrench to tighten it an additional 1/4-turn. Regardless of the method used, do not over-tighten it.

9   Reconnect the spark plug cap.

16.1 Loosen the retaining plate bolt and turn the eccentric adjuster with a screwdriver to quiet the cam chain; if the chain is still noisy with the punch mark all the way to the right (arrow), you'll need to make adjustments at the lower adjuster

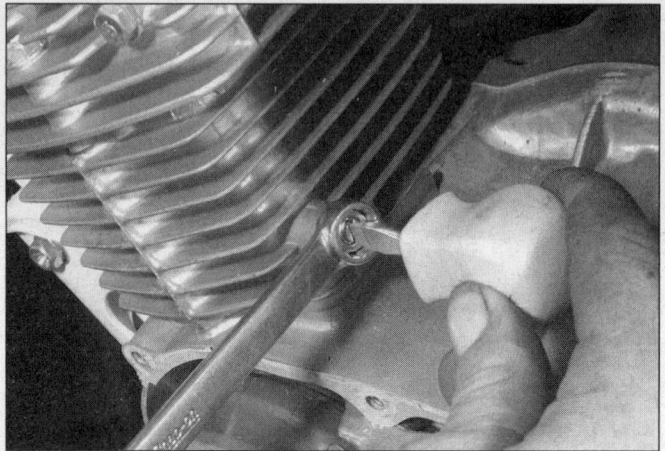

16.2 Loosen the locknut and turn the adjusting screw in to take up slack in the cam chain

16   Cam chain tensioner (80/100 models) - adjustment

Refer to illustrations 16.1 and 16.2

1   With the engine idling, loosen the retaining plate bolt on the eccentric adjuster **(see illustration)**. Turn the eccentric adjuster back and forth with a screwdriver until the cam chain noise is reduced as much as possible, then tighten the retaining plate bolt.
2   If the cam chain is still noisy with the adjuster punch mark in the position shown in illustration 17.1, shut off the engine. Loosen the locknut on the tensioner's lower adjusting screw **(see illustration)**. Tighten the adjusting screw to take up slack in the cam chain, then tighten the locknut.
3   Loosen the retaining plate bolt again, and turn the eccentric adjuster so its punch mark is straight down.
4   Restart the engine. At idle speed, readjust the eccentric adjuster as described in Step 1 until the cam chain is at its quietest.

17   Valve clearances - check and adjustment

Refer to illustrations 17.3a, 17.3b, 17.5, 17.7a, 17.7b and 17.7c

1   The engine must be completely cool for this maintenance procedure (below 35-degrees C/95-degrees F), so if possible let the machine

sit overnight before beginning.
2   Refer to Section 15 and remove the spark plug.
3   If you're working on an 80 or 100 model, remove the valve cover (see Chapter 2). If you're working on a 50 or 70, remove the valve adjusting hole covers **(see illustrations)**.
4   Refer to Chapter 4 and remove the left engine cover.
5   Position the piston at Top Dead Center (TDC) on the compression stroke. Do this by turning the crankshaft while feeling for compression at the spark plug hole with your finger. When you begin to feel compression, continue turning the crankshaft until the T mark on the rotor is aligned with the timing pointer on the crankcase **(see illustration)**. You should now be able to wiggle the rocker arms with your fingers. If you can't, the piston is on the exhaust stroke; rotate the crankshaft one full turn to bring the T mark into position. On 80 and 100 models, confirm the piston position by checking to make sure the cam sprocket timing mark is straight up (you can also do this on 50 and 70 models, but you'll need to remove the right and left cylinder head covers as described in Chapter 2B). If it isn't straight up, the piston is on the exhaust stroke; rotate the crankshaft one full turn to bring the T mark into position.
6   With the engine in this position, both of the valves can be checked.
7   To check, insert a feeler gauge of the thickness listed in this Chapter's Specifications between the valve stem and rocker arm **(see illustrations)**. Pull the feeler gauge out slowly - you should feel a slight

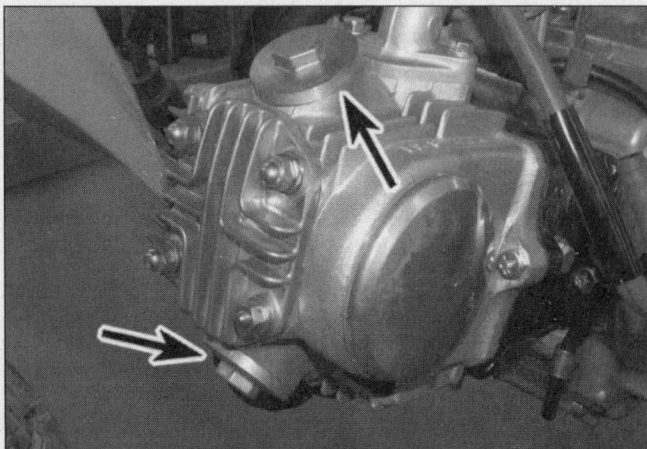

17.3a On 50/70 models, unscrew the valve adjusting hole covers (arrows) . . .

17.3b . . . and inspect the O-rings

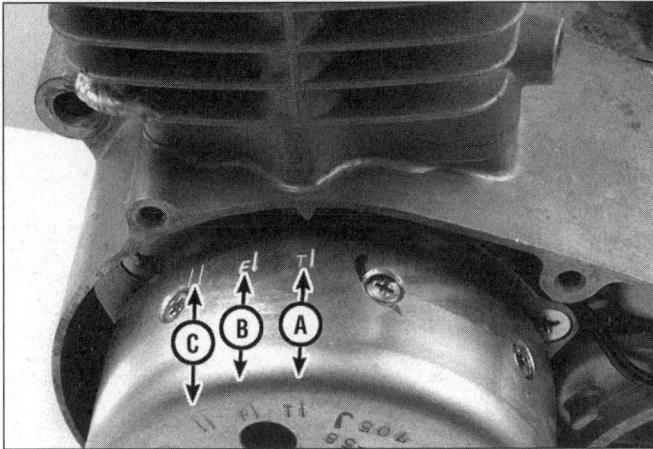

17.5a You'll need to remove the left engine cover to see the timing marks; for valve adjustment, the pointer should align with the T mark

a) Top dead center mark
b) Timing mark (engine at idle speed)
c) Advance timing mark (some models)

17.5b The camshaft sprocket mark (arrow) should be straight up

drag. If there's no drag, the clearance is too loose. If there's a heavy drag, the clearance is too tight.

8   If the clearance is incorrect, loosen the adjuster locknut with a box wrench. Turn the adjusting screw until the correct clearance is achieved, then tighten the locknut. The adjusting screws on some models have square heads. They can be turned with a special tool (Honda part no. 07708-0030100 or equivalent), or with an open-end wrench if you don't have the special tool.

9   After adjusting, recheck the clearance with the feeler gauge to make sure it wasn't changed when the locknut was tightened.

10   Now measure the other valve, following the same procedure you used for the first valve. Make sure to use a feeler gauge of the specified thickness.

11   With both of the clearances within the Specifications, install the left engine cover and the valve cover.

17.7a Measure valve clearance with a feeler gauge; to adjust it, loosen the locknut and turn the adjusting screw (this is the 80/100 design) . . .

18 Breaker points - inspection and adjustment

Refer to illustrations 18.3 and 18.5

1   Ignition timing on models equipped with breaker points can be

changed by varying the points gap. On CDI models, ignition timing is fixed and can't be adjusted.

2   Remove the left engine cover (see Chapter 4).

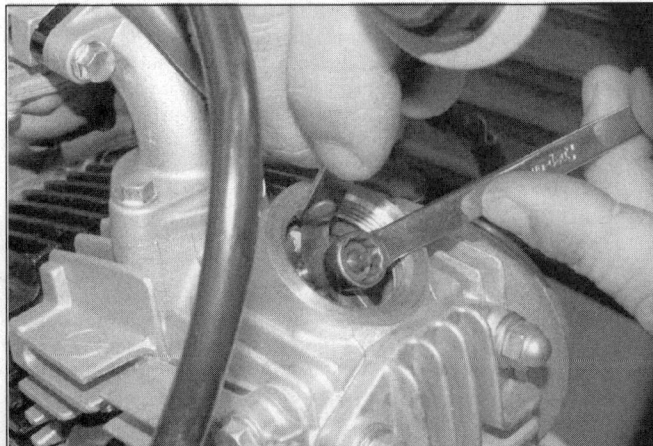

17.7b . . . and this is the 50/70 design

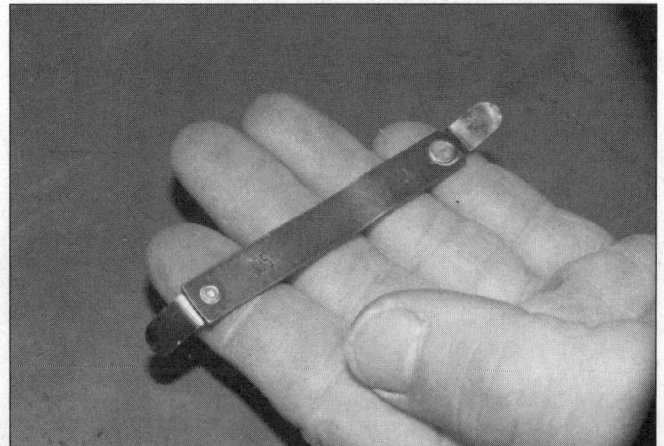

17.7c A bent feeler gauge like this one, available inexpensively at motorcycle dealers, will make valve adjustment easier on 50/70 models

18.3 Breaker point details (alternator rotor removed for clarity)

a) *Contacts*
b) *Wire retaining nut*
c) *Points screw*
d) *Adjusting slot*

18.5 Insert a feeler gauge between the contacts to measure points gap

3   Pry apart the points and inspect the contact surfaces (see illustration). If they're lightly pitted or have a gray color, file them clean with a points file, then spray them with electrical contact cleaner to remove any contamination. If the points are heavily pitted, if significant amounts of metal have been transferred from one points surface to the other or if the surfaces are worn at angle, replace the points with a new set.
4   To replace the points, remove the nut that secures the points wire (see illustration 18.3). Disconnect the wire, remove the attaching screw and lift the points off. Install the new points and connect the wire, then adjust points gap as described below.
5   To adjust the gap, turn the alternator rotor counterclockwise until the breaker cam opens the points to the maximum. You can do this by rolling the bike with the transmission in gear, or by turning the crankshaft with a wrench placed on the alternator rotor nut. Insert a feeler gauge between the points to measure the gap (see illustration). If it's not within the range listed in this Chapter's Specifications, loosen the points screw slightly, insert the tip of a screwdriver in the adjusting slot and rotate the screwdriver to set the gap (see illustration 18.3).
6   When the gap is correct, tighten the points screw, then recheck the gap to make sure it hasn't changed.

19   Ignition timing (breaker point models) - check and adjustment

1   With the points gap set correctly, ignition timing can be checked. There are two methods, static timing and dynamic timing. The first uses a 12-volt battery and test light. The second uses a timing light and tachometer and will provide more accurate results. In addition, the timing light method allows advance timing to be checked.
2   If you haven't already done so, remove the left engine cover.

Static timing

3   Follow the wiring harness from the alternator to the connectors and unplug the connectors. Connect a 12-volt test light between the black/white wire and the positive terminal of a fully charged 12-volt battery. Connect a jumper wire between the battery negative terminal and bare metal on the engine. **Note:** *Since the motorcycle doesn't have a battery, you'll need one from another source. A battery from a car or another motorcycle will work.*
4   The test light should come on at this point. Slowly turn the alternator rotor counterclockwise until the F mark aligns with the timing pointer (see illustration 18.5a). The light should dim.

5   If the light doesn't dim at the proper time, readjust the points gap to change timing. Increasing the gap advances timing (the light will dim sooner). Decreasing the gap retards timing (the light will dim later).
6   If the points gap can't be adjusted to obtain correct ignition timing, replace the points with a new set.

Dynamic timing

7   Connect a timing light and tune-up tachometer to the engine, following manufacturer's instructions.
8   Start the engine. Let it idle and compare idle speed with this Chapter's Specifications. If necessary, adjust idle speed (see Section 20).
9   At idle, the timing light should flash when the F mark on the alternator rotor is aligned with the timing pointer on the crankcase (see illustration 17.5a).
10   Operate the throttle to slowly increase engine speed. At the engine speed listed in this Chapter's Specifications, the timing should start to advance. The timing light should flash at a point between the F mark and the double line on the alternator rotor.
11   Keep increasing engine speed to the full advance speed listed in this Chapter's Specifications. At that point, the timing light should flash when the timing pointer on the crankcase is between the full advance marks (parallel lines) on the alternator rotor (see illustration 17.5a).
12   If the light doesn't flash at the proper time, readjust the points gap to change timing. Increasing the gap advances timing (the light will flash sooner). Decreasing the gap retards timing (the light will flash later).
13   If the points gap can't be adjusted to obtain correct ignition timing at idle, replace the points with a new set.
14   If timing is correct at idle but not at advanced timing speeds, refer to Chapter 4 and inspect the spark advancer.

20   Idle speed - check and adjustment

Refer to illustrations 20.3a, 20.3b and 20.3c
1   Before adjusting the idle speed, make sure the valve clearances, spark plug gap and breaker point gap (models so equipped) are correct. Also, turn the handlebars back-and-forth and see if the idle speed changes as this is done. If it does, the throttle cable may not be adjusted correctly, or it may be worn out. Be sure to correct this problem before proceeding.
2   The engine should be at normal operating temperature, which is usually reached after 10 to 15 minutes of stop and go riding. Make sure the transmission is in Neutral.

20.3a Turn the throttle stop screw (arrow) to set idle speed (this is an 80 model) . . .

a)   Throttle stop screw
b)   Air screw

3   Turn the throttle stop screw **(see illustrations)** until the idle speed listed in this Chapter's Specifications is obtained.
4   Snap the throttle open and shut a few times, then recheck the idle speed. If necessary, repeat the adjustment procedure.
5   If a smooth, steady idle can't be achieved, the fuel/air mixture may be incorrect. Refer to Chapter 3 for additional carburetor information.

21 Fasteners - check

1   Since vibration of the machine tends to loosen fasteners, all nuts, bolts, screws, etc. should be periodically checked for proper tightness. Also make sure all cotter pins or other safety fasteners are correctly installed.
2   Pay particular attention to the following:

Spark plug
Engine oil drain plug
Gearshift lever
Brake pedal
Kickstarter pedal
Footpegs
Engine mount bolts
Steering stem locknut
Front axle nut
Rear axle nut
Skid plate bolts

3   If a torque wrench is available, use it along with the torque specifications at the beginning of this or other Chapters.

22 Suspension - check

1   The suspension components must be maintained in top operating condition to ensure rider safety. Loose, worn or damaged suspension parts decrease the motorcycle's stability and control.
2   Lock the front brake and push on the handlebars to compress the front forks several times. See if they move up-and-down smoothly without binding. If binding is felt, the forks should be disassembled and inspected as described in Chapter 6.
3   Check the tightness of all front suspension nuts and bolts to be sure none have worked loose.
4   Inspect the rear shock absorber for fluid leakage and tightness of the mounting nuts and bolts. If leakage is found, the shock should be replaced.

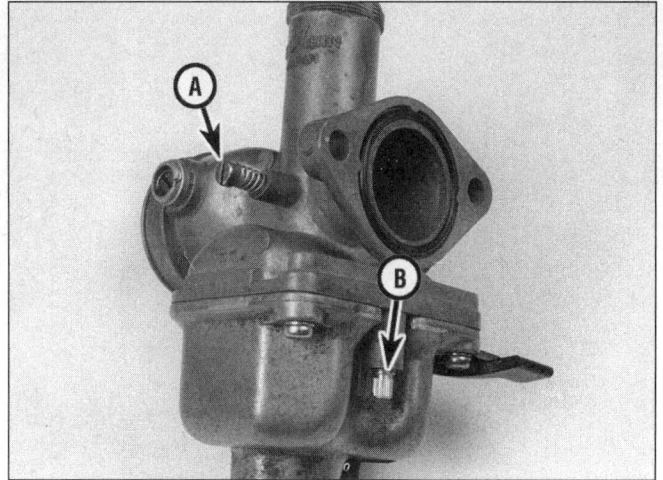

20.3b . . . this is a 100 model . . .

a)   Throttle stop screw
b)   Pilot screw

5   Support the motorcycle securely upright with its rear wheel off the ground. Grab the swingarm on each side, just ahead of the axle. Rock the swingarm from side to side - there should be no discernible movement at the rear. If there's a little movement or a slight clicking can be heard, make sure the swingarm pivot shaft is tight. If the pivot shaft is tight but movement is still noticeable, the swingarm will have to be removed and the bearings replaced as described in Chapter 5.
6   Inspect the tightness of the rear suspension nuts and bolts.

23 Steering head bearings - check and adjustment

Inspection

1   This motorcycle is equipped with ball-and-cone type steering head bearings, which can become dented, rough or loose during normal use of the machine. In extreme cases, worn or loose steering head bearings can cause steering wobble that is potentially dangerous.
2   To check the bearings, Lift up the front end of the motorcycle and place a secure support beneath the engine so the front wheel is off the ground.

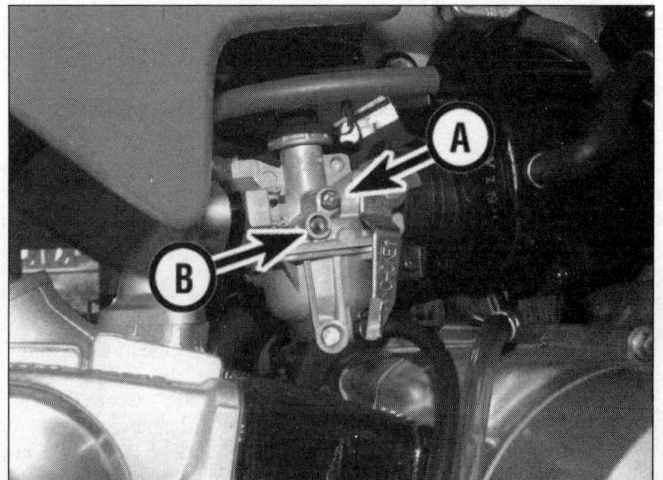

20.3c . . . and this is a 50 (70 similar)

a)   Throttle stop screw
b)   Pilot screw

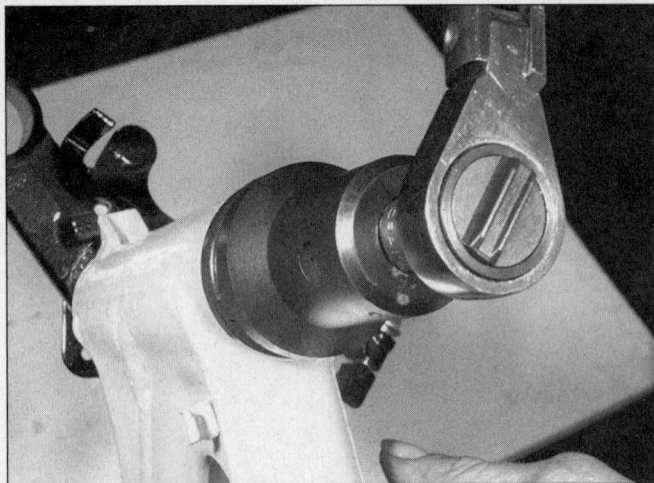

23.6 The best way to adjust the steering stem bearings is with a torque wrench and a special socket . . .

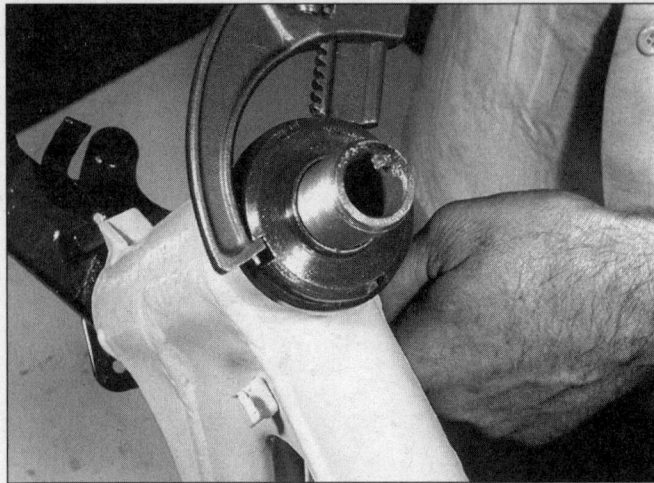

23.9 . . . but an adjustable spanner can also be used; be very sure there's no binding or looseness in the bearings

3   Point the wheel straight ahead and slowly move the handlebars from side-to-side. Dents or roughness in the bearing will be felt and the bars will not move smoothly. **Note:** *Make sure any hesitation in movement is not being caused by the cables and wiring harnesses that run to the handlebars.*

4   Next, grasp the fork legs and try to move the wheel forward and backward. Any looseness in the steering head bearings will be felt. If play is felt in the bearings, adjust the steering head as follows.

Adjustment

Refer to illustrations 23.6 and 23.9

5   Remove the handlebars and upper triple clamp (see Chapter 5).

6   Loosen the bearing adjusting nut, then tighten it to the torque listed in this Chapter's Specifications **(see illustration)**.

7   Turn the lower triple clamp from lock-to-lock (all the way to the left and all the way back to the right) four or five times to seat the bearings.

8   Loosen the adjusting nut all the way, then tighten it to the final torque listed in this Chapter's Specifications.

9   An adjustable spanner wrench can be used to adjust the bearings if you don't have the special socket **(see illustration)**. Since this tool can't be used with a torque wrench, it will be necessary to estimate the tightness of the nut. Be sure the final result is that the steering stem turns from side-to-side freely, but there is no side-to-side or vertical play of the steering stem in the bearings.

24   Drive chain and sprockets - check, adjustment and lubrication

Refer to illustrations 24.3 and 24.6

1   A neglected drive chain won't last long and can quickly damage the sprockets. Routine chain adjustment isn't difficult and will ensure maximum chain and sprocket life.

2   To check the chain, support the bike securely with the rear wheel off the ground. Place the transmission in neutral.

3   Push up on the bottom run of the chain and measure the slack midway between the two sprockets **(see illustration)**, then compare the measurements to the value listed in this Chapter's Specifications. As wear occurs, the chain will actually stretch, which means adjustment by removing some slack from the chain. In some cases where lubrication has been neglected, corrosion and galling may cause the links to bind and kink, which effectively shortens the chain's length. If the chain is tight between the sprockets, rusty or kinked, it's time to replace it with a new one. **Note:** *Repeat the chain slack measurement along the length of the chain - ideally, every inch or so. If you find a tight area,*

mark it with felt pen or paint and repeat the measurement after the bike has been ridden. If the chain's still tight in the same areas, it may be damaged or worn. Because a tight or kinked chain can damage the transmission countershaft bearing, it's a good idea to replace it.

4   Check the entire length of the chain for damaged rollers, loose links and loose pins.

5   Look through the slots in the left engine cover and inspect the engine sprocket. Check the teeth on the engine sprocket and the rear sprocket for wear. Refer to Chapter 5 for the sprocket replacement procedure if the sprockets appear to be worn excessively.

6   On 80 and 100 models, check the chain slider on the swingarm near the front **(see illustration)**. If it's worn, measure its thickness. If it's less than the value listed in the Chapter 5 Specifications, replace it (see Chapter 5).

Adjustment

Refer to illustration 24.8

7   Rotate the rear wheel until the chain is positioned with the least amount of slack present.

8   Loosen the rear axle nut **(see illustration)**. Turn the adjusting nut on each side of the swingarm evenly until the proper chain tension is obtained (get the adjuster on the chain side close, then set the adjuster on the opposite side). Be sure to turn the adjusting nuts evenly to keep the wheel in alignment. If the adjusting nuts pull the adjusters to the end of their travel, the chain is excessively worn and should be replaced

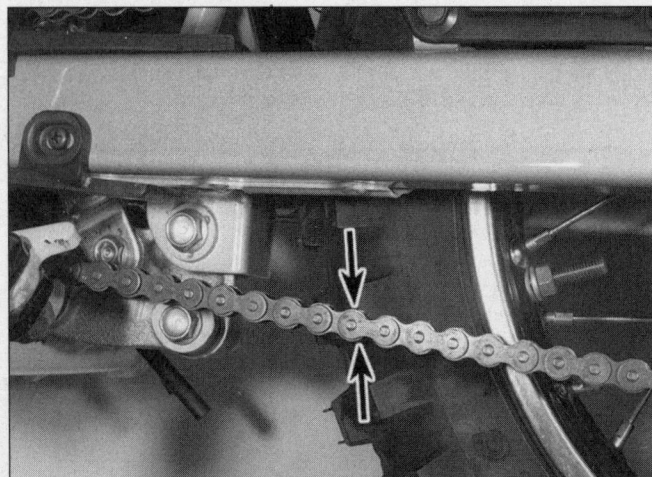

24.3 Check drive chain freeplay midway along the lower chain run

24.6 Inspect the slider at the front of the swingarm and replace it if it's worn

24.8 Chain adjuster details

a)	Axle nut	c)	Alignment marks
b)	Chain adjuster nut		

with a new one (see Chapter 5).

9   When the chain has the correct amount of slack, make sure the marks on the adjusters correspond to the same relative marks on each side of the swingarm **(see illustration 24.8)**. Tighten the axle nut to the torque listed in the Chapter 5 Specifications.

Lubrication

Note: *If the chain is dirty, it should be removed and cleaned before it's lubricated (see Chapter 5).*

10   The best time to lubricate the chain is after the motorcycle has been ridden. When the chain is warm, the lubricant will penetrate the joints between the side plates, pins, bushings and rollers to provide lubrication of the internal bearing areas. Use a good quality chain lubricant and apply it to the area where the side plates overlap - not the middle of the rollers. Apply the lubricant along the top of the lower chain run, so that when the bike is ridden centrifugal force will move the lubricant into the chain, rather than throwing it off.

11   After applying the lubricant, let it soak in a few minutes before wiping off any excess.

25 Front fork oil change

1   Although fork oil changes are not a regularly scheduled maintenance procedure, the oil should be changed if it becomes contaminated. The following steps apply to models equipped with fork drain screws. If you're working on a bike that doesn't have a drain screw, you'll need to disassemble the forks part-way to drain the oil (see Chapter 5). The forks on XR50R and CRF50F models are packed with grease and do not use fork oil.

2   Support the motorcycle securely upright.

3   Remove the handlebars (see Chapter 5).

4   Remove the fork cap bolts **(see illustration 3.3 in Chapter 5)**.

5   Wrap a rag around the top of the fork to catch dripping oil, the lift out the fork spring from each fork.

6   Place a pan under the fork drain bolt and remove the drain bolt and gasket. **Warning:** *Do not allow the fork oil to drip onto the tire. If it does, wash it off with soap and water before riding the motorcycle.*

7   After most of the oil has drained, slowly compress and release the forks to pump out the rest of the oil. An assistant may be needed to do this.

8   Check the drain bolt gasket for damage and replace it if necessary. Clean the threads of the drain bolt with solvent and let it dry, then reinstall the bolt and gasket, tightening it securely.

9   Pour the type and amount of fork oil listed in the Chapter 5 Specifications into the fork tube through the opening at the top. Slowly pump the forks a few times to purge air from the upper and lower chambers.

10   Fully compress the front forks (you may need an assistant to do this). Insert a stiff tape measure into the fork tube and measure the distance from the oil to the top of the fork tube **(see illustration 4.14b in Chapter 5)**. Compare your measurement to the value listed in the Chapter 5 Specifications. Drain or add oil as necessary until the level is correct.

11   Check the O-ring on the fork cap bolt and replace it with a new one if it's deteriorated, broken or otherwise damaged. Install the fork spring. Install the cap bolt and tighten it to the torque listed in this Chapter's Specifications.

12   Repeat the procedure for the other fork. It is essential that the oil quantity and level are identical in each fork.

13   Install the handlebar, being sure to locate it correctly in the brackets, and tighten the handlebar bracket bolts to the torque listed in the Chapter 5 Specifications.

26 Sidestand - check

The sidestand should be checked to make sure it stays down when extended and up when retracted. Refer to Chapter 7 and check tightness of the sidestand mounting bolts. Check the spring for cracks or rust and replace it if any problems are found.

Notes

Chapter 2 Part A
Engine, clutch and transmission
(80 and 100 models)

Contents

Specifications

Note: *For wear tolerance and service limit specifications, refer to Chapter 2C.*

Torque specifications

Engine front mounting bolts	
1985 through 1997	30 to 40 Nm (22 to 29 ft-lbs)
1998 through 2000	
To frame	26 Nm (20 ft-lbs)
To engine	34 Nm (25 ft-lbs)
2001 and later	34 Nm (25 ft-lbs)
Engine rear mounting bolts	
1985 through 1997	40 to 50 Nm (29 to 36 ft-lbs)
1998 through 2000	34 Nm (25 ft-lbs)
2001 and later	44 Nm (33 ft-lbs)
Valve cover bolts	
1985 through 1997	Not specified
1998 and later	12 Nm (108 inch-lbs)
Cam sprocket bolts	12 Nm (108 inch-lbs)*
Rocker assembly (cylinder stud) nuts	20 Nm (14 ft-lbs)
Right engine cover bolts	Not specified
Clutch spring bolts	Not specified
Primary drive gear locknut	39 Nm (29 ft-lbs)

The bolt with the dowel goes on the intake side (toward the rear of the engine).

1   General information

The engine/transmission unit is of the air-cooled, single-cylinder four-stroke design. The two valves are operated by an overhead cam-shaft which is chain driven off the crankshaft. The engine/transmission assembly is constructed from aluminum alloy. The crankcase is divided vertically.

The crankcase incorporates a wet sump, pressure-fed lubrication system which uses a gear-driven rotor-type oil pump, an oil filter and separate strainer screen.

Power from the crankshaft is routed to the transmission via a wet, multi-plate type clutch. The transmission has five forward gears.

2   Operations possible with the engine in the frame

The components and assemblies listed below can be removed without having to remove the engine from the frame. If, however, a number of areas require attention at the same time, removal of the engine is recommended.

External shift mechanism external components
Clutch
Camshaft
Rocker arm assembly
Oil pump

3   Operations requiring engine removal

It is necessary to remove the engine/transmission assembly from the frame and separate the crankcase halves to gain access to the fol-lowing components:

Cylinder head
Cylinder and piston
Crankshaft and connecting rod
Transmission shafts
Shift drum and forks

4   Major engine repair - general note

1   It is not always easy to determine when or if an engine should be completely overhauled, as a number of factors must be considered.
2   High mileage is not necessarily an indication that an overhaul is needed, while low mileage, on the other hand, does not preclude the need for an overhaul. Frequency of servicing is probably the single most important consideration. An engine that has regular and frequent oil and filter changes, as well as other required maintenance, will most likely give many miles of reliable service. Conversely, a neglected engine, or one which has not been broken in properly, may require an overhaul very early in its life.
3   Exhaust smoke and excessive oil consumption are both indications that piston rings and/or valve guides are in need of attention. Make sure oil leaks are not responsible before deciding that the rings and guides are bad. Refer to Chapter 1 and perform a cylinder compression check to determine for certain the nature and extent of the work required.
4   If the engine is making obvious knocking or rumbling noises, the connecting rod and/or main bearings are probably at fault.
5   Loss of power, rough running, excessive valve train noise and high fuel consumption rates may also point to the need for an overhaul, espe-cially if they are all present at the same time. If a complete tune-up does not remedy the situation, major mechanical work is the only solution.
6   An engine overhaul generally involves restoring the internal parts to the specifications of a new engine. During an overhaul the piston rings are replaced and the cylinder walls are bored and/or honed. If a rebore is done, then a new piston is also required. The crankshaft and connecting rod are permanently assembled, so if one of these compo-nents needs to be replaced both must be. Generally the valves are ser-viced as well, since they are usually in less than perfect condition at this

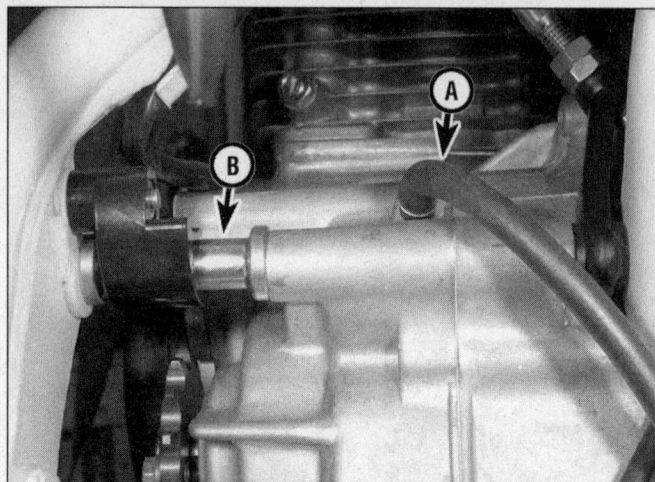

5.9 Disconnect the breather hose

a)   *Breather hose*
b)   *Upper rear engine mounting bolt spacer*

point. While the engine is being overhauled, other components such as the carburetor can be rebuilt also. The end result should be a like-new engine that will give as many trouble-free miles as the original.
7   Before beginning the engine overhaul, read through all of the related procedures to familiarize yourself with the scope and requirements of the job. Overhauling an engine is not all that difficult, but it is time con-suming. Plan on the motorcycle being tied up for a minimum of two (2) weeks. Check on the availability of parts and make sure that any neces-sary special tools, equipment and supplies are obtained in advance.
8   Most work can be done with typical shop hand tools, although a number of precision measuring tools are required for inspecting parts to determine if they must be replaced. Often a dealer service department or repair shop will handle the inspection of parts and offer advice con-cerning reconditioning and replacement. As a general rule, time is the primary cost of an overhaul so it doesn't pay to install worn or substan-dard parts.
9   As a final note, to ensure maximum life and minimum trouble from a rebuilt engine, everything must be assembled with care in a spotlessly clean environment.

5   Engine - removal and installation

Note: *Engine removal and installation should be done with the aid of an assistant to avoid damage or injury that could occur if the engine is dropped.*

Removal

Refer to illustrations 5.9, 5.12a and 5.12b

1   Drain the engine oil (see Chapter 1).
2   Remove the seat (see Chapter 7).
3   Remove the fuel tank, exhaust system and carburetor (see Chap-ter 3). The throttle cable can be left connected to the carburetor.
4   Disconnect the spark plug wire (see Chapter 1).
5   Label and disconnect the wires above the engine (refer to Chap-ter 4 for component location if necessary). Detach the wires from their clips on the frame.
6   Remove the drive chain (see Chapter 5).
7   Remove the skid plate from beneath the engine **(see illustrations 8.2 and 8.3 in Chapter 7)**.
8   Disconnect the clutch cable (see Section 16).
9   Disconnect the crankcase breather tube from the top of the engine **(see illustration)**.
10   Support the bike securely upright so it can't fall over during the remainder of this procedure.

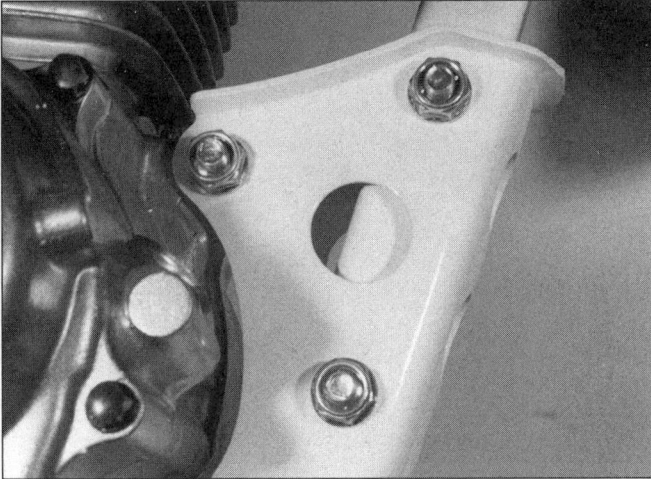

5.12a Remove the lower front engine mounting bolts and bracket

5.12b Remove the lower rear engine mount through-bolt

11   Temporarily remove the left footpeg bracket and sidestand to provide access to the engine lower mount bolt (see Chapter 7).
12   Remove the engine mounting bolts, nuts and brackets at the upper front, upper rear lower rear **(see illustration 5.9 and the accompanying illustrations)**.
13   Reinstall the footpeg/sidestand bracket.
14   Have an assistant help you lift the engine out of the frame.
15   Set the engine to a suitable work surface.

Installation

16   Have an assistant help lift the engine to align the mounting bolt holes, then install the brackets, bolts and nuts. Tighten them to the torques listed in this Chapter's Specifications.
17   The remainder of installation is the reverse of the removal steps, with the following additions:

a) *Use new gaskets at the exhaust pipe connection.*
b) *Adjust the throttle cable and clutch cable following the procedures in Chapter 1.*
c) *Fill the engine with oil, also following the procedures in Chapter 1.*
d) *Run the engine and check for oil or exhaust leaks.*

6   Valve cover - removal, inspection and installation

Refer to illustrations 6.2 and 6.3
Note: *The valve cover can be removed with the engine in the frame. If*

the engine has been removed, ignore the steps which don't apply.
1   Remove the fuel tank (see Chapter 3).
2   Remove the valve cover bolts and lift the cover off the engine **(see illustration)**. If it's stuck, don't attempt to pry it off - tap around the sides of it with a plastic hammer to dislodge it.
3   Remove the gasket from the valve cover groove **(see illustration)**. Check it for brittleness, cracks or deterioration and replace it if any problems are found.
4   Check the seals on the valve cover bolts. Check them for brittleness, crushing or deterioration and replace them if any problems are found.
5   Installation is the reverse of the removal steps, with the following additions:

a) *Make sure the gasket is securely seated in its groove.*
b) *Tighten the cover bolts securely, but don't overtighen them and force the gasket out of its groove.*

7   Rocker arms and camshaft - removal and installation

Removal

Refer to illustrations 7.4a, 7.4b and 7.7
1   Refer to Section 6 and remove the valve cover.
2   Refer to Valve clearance - check and adjustment in Chapter 1 and place the piston at top dead center on the compression stroke.

6.2 Loosen the cover bolts evenly in two or three stages

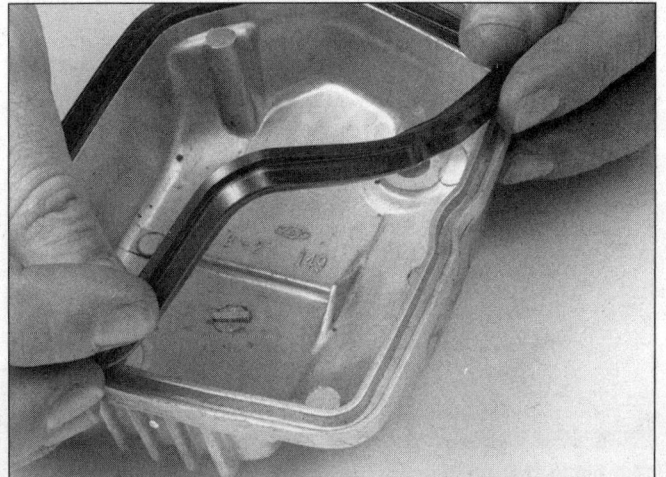

6.3 Lift off the cover and remove the gasket from the groove

7.4a Rotate the camshaft sprocket so one bolt is accessible, then remove the bolt . . .

7.4b . . . rotate the sprocket to remove the other bolt, then turn it back so the bolt holes are even with the cylinder head surface and the sprocket timing mark is straight up

3   Loosen the cam chain tensioner locknut and back off the adjuster (see Chapter 1). Pry the chain guide away from the chain to release the tension, then tighten the locknut.

4   Turn the cam sprocket so one of the bolts is accessible and remove it **(see illustration)**. Turn the engine so the other bolt is accessible, remove it and turn the engine back to TDC compression **(see illustration)**.

5   Remove the rocker assembly nuts **(see illustration 7.4b)** and washers. Lift the assembly off the studs.

6   Disengage the sprocket from the cam chain. Support the cam chain so it won't drop into the engine, then remove the sprocket.

7   Lift the camshaft out of the cylinder head **(see illustration)**.

8   Refer to Chapter 2C for inspection procedures.

Installation

Refer to illustration 7.9

9   Coat the rocker shafts and rocker arm bores with moly-based grease. Install the rocker shafts and rocker arms in the rocker assembly. The intake rocker arm has a notch that aligns with one of the stud holes in the rocker assembly **(see illustration)**. The exhaust rocker shaft has threads in one end; be sure the threaded end faces out. Be sure to install the intake and exhaust rocker arms and shafts in the correct side of the assembly.

10   Make sure the bearing surfaces in the cylinder head and rocker assembly are clean.

11   Lubricate the cam bearing journals with molybdenum disulfide grease. Lay the camshaft in the cylinder head with the lobes pointing down **(see illustration 7.7)**.

12   Engage the sprocket with the chain so its timing mark will be straight up **(see illustration 7.4b)**. Place the sprocket on the camshaft so its bolt holes align with the camshaft bolt holes. Rotate the sprocket as needed for access, install the bolts and tighten them to the torque listed in this Chapter's Specifications. The bolt with the dowel goes toward the intake (rear) side of the engine.

13   Turn the sprocket so its timing mark is straight up and the bolts are aligned with the cylinder head gasket surface.

14   Recheck the crankshaft timing mark to make sure it's still at the TDC position (see *Valve clearance - check and adjustment* in Chapter 1). If it's out of position and the camshaft sprocket is aligned as described in Step 19, you'll need to remove the chain from the sprocket and reposition it. Don't run the engine with the marks out of alignment or severe engine damage could occur.

15   Install the cam chain guides if they were removed.

16   Coat the cam lobes with moly-based grease or assembly lube. Fill the oil pocket in the top of the cylinder head with engine oil.

17   Install the rocker assembly and washers. Install the nuts and

7.7 Lift the camshaft out of the head (note how the cam chain is supported by a screwdriver)

7.9 Align the notch in the intake rocker shaft (arrow) with the bolt hole in the rocker assembly

8.3 Remove the bolt that secures the head to the cylinder

8.5 Remove the gasket, dowels and O-ring (they may have stuck to the bottom of the cylinder head)

tighten them evenly, in a criss-cross pattern, to the torque listed in this Chapter's Specifications.

18   Adjust the cam chain tension and the valve clearances (see Chapter 1).

19   The remainder of installation is the reverse of removal.

8   Cylinder head - removal and installation

Caution: *The engine must be completely cool before beginning this procedure, or the cylinder head may become warped.*

Removal

Refer to illustrations 8.3, 8.5 and 8.6

1   Remove the engine from the frame (see Section 5).

2   Remove the valve cover, rocker assembly and camshaft (Sections 6 and 7).

3   Remove the remaining bolt that secures the cylinder head to the cylinder **(see illustration)**.

4   Lift the cylinder head off the cylinder. If the head is stuck, tap around the side of the head with a rubber mallet to jar it loose, or use two wooden dowels inserted into the intake or exhaust ports to lever the head off. Don't attempt to pry the head off by inserting a screwdriver

between the head and the cylinder block - you'll damage the sealing surfaces.

5   Support the cam chain so it won't drop into the cam chain tunnel, and stuff a clean rag into the tunnel to prevent the entry of debris. Once this is done, remove the gasket, O-ring and two dowel pins from the cylinder **(see illustration)**.

6   If the front (exhaust) side chain guide is worn, lift it out of its notches **(see illustration)**.

7   Check the cylinder head gasket and the mating surfaces on the cylinder head and cylinder for leakage, which could indicate warpage. Refer to Chapter 2C and check the flatness of the cylinder head.

8   Clean all traces of old gasket material from the cylinder head and cylinder. Be careful not to let any of the gasket material fall into the crankcase, the cylinder bore or the bolt holes.

Installation

Refer to illustration 8.9

9   Install the two dowel pins, then lay the new gasket in place on the cylinder block and install the O-ring **(see illustration)**. Never reuse the old gasket and don't use any type of gasket sealant.

10   Make sure the cam chain front guide fits in its notches **(see illustration 8.6)**.

11   Carefully lower the cylinder head over the studs and dowels. It is helpful to have an assistant support the camshaft chain with a piece of

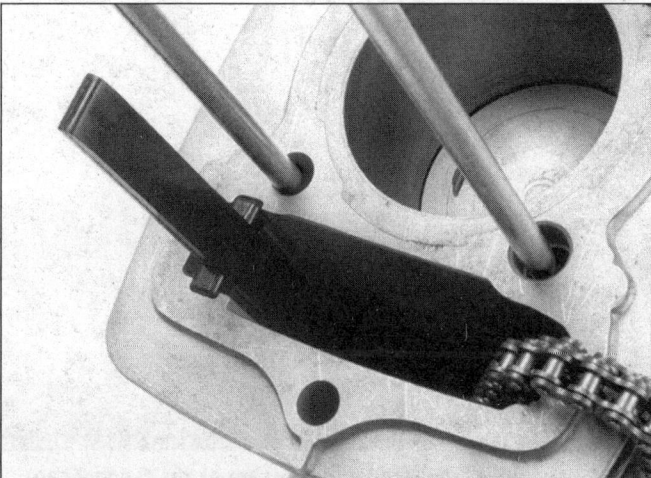

8.6 Lift the exhaust side cam chain guide out of its notches

8.9 Fit the O-ring after installing the dowels and gasket

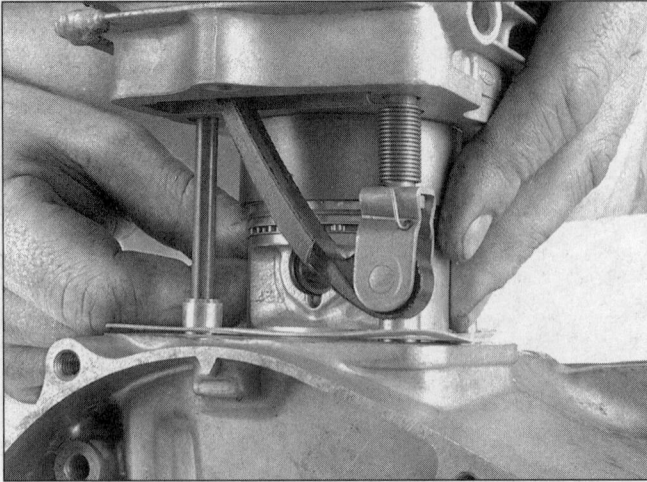

9.3 Lift the cylinder off together with the cam chain tensioner

9.4a Locate the dowels and remove the base gasket

wire so it doesn't fall and become kinked or detached from the crank-shaft. When the head is resting on the cylinder, wire the cam chain to another component to keep tension on it.

12   The remainder of installation is the reverse of the removal steps.

13   Change the engine oil (see Chapter 1).

9   Cylinder - removal and installation

Removal

Refer to illustrations 9.3, 9.4a and 9.4b

1   Following the procedure given in Section 8, remove the cylinder head. Make sure the crankshaft is positioned at Top Dead Center (TDC).

2   Lift out the cam chain front guide (see illustration 8.6).

3   Lift the cylinder straight up to remove it (see illustration). If it's stuck, tap around its perimeter with a soft-faced hammer (but don't tap on the cooling fins or they may break). Don't attempt to pry between the cylinder and the crankcase, as you'll ruin the sealing surfaces.

4   Locate the dowel pins (they may have come off with the cylinder or still be in the crankcase) (see illustration). Be careful not to let these drop into the engine. Stuff rags around the piston and remove the gas-ket and all traces of old gasket material from the surfaces of the cylinder

and the crankcase (see illustration).

5   Refer to Chapter 2C for inspection procedures.

Installation

Refer to illustration 9.9

6   Lubricate the cylinder bore with plenty of clean engine oil. Apply a thin film of moly-based grease to the piston skirt.

7   Install the dowel pins, then lower a new cylinder base gasket over them (see illustration 9.4a).

8   Attach a piston ring compressor to the piston and compress the piston rings. A large hose clamp can be used instead - just make sure it doesn't scratch the piston, and don't tighten it too much.

9   Install the cylinder over the studs and carefully lower it down until the piston crown fits into the cylinder liner (see illustration). While doing this, pull the camshaft chain up, using a hooked tool or a piece of stiff wire. Push down on the cylinder, making sure the piston doesn't get cocked sideways, until the bottom of the cylinder liner slides down past the piston rings. A wood or plastic hammer handle can be used to gently tap the cylinder down, but don't use too much force or the piston will be damaged.

10   Remove the piston ring compressor or hose clamp, being careful not to scratch the piston.

11   The remainder of installation is the reverse of the removal steps.

9.4b Pack clean rags into the crankcase opening
to keep out debris

9.9 If you're experienced and very careful, the cylinder can
be installed over the rings without a ring compressor, but a
compressor is recommended

10.4a Unhook the tensioner spring from the ridge in the cylinder casting (arrow) . . .

10.4b . . . then pull the tensioner out of its bore

10 Cam chain tensioner - removal, inspection and installation

Removal

Refer to illustrations 10.4a and 10.4b

1   Refer to Section 8 and remove the cylinder head, then lift the exhaust side cam chain guide out of its notches **(see illustration 8.6)**.
2   Refer to Section 9 and remove the cylinder.
3   Loosen the adjuster screw locknut and back the adjuster screw and O-ring all the way out of the cylinder (see Chapter 1).
4   Unhook the tensioner spring from the ridge inside the cam chain tunnel, then pull the tensioner out of its bore **(see illustrations)**.

Inspection

Refer to illustration 10.5

5   Check the intake side chain guide for wear or damage **(see illustration)**. Check for looseness where the chain guide pivots on the tensioner rod and replace the tensioner if problems are found.
6   Check the tensioner spring for breakage and replace it if necessary.
7   Replace the O-rings on the adjusters if they're brittle, cracked or deteriorated.

Installation

Refer to illustration 10.8

8   Install the tensioner rod in its bore in the cam chain tunnel, then hook the spring over the cast ridge **(see illustrations 10.4a and 10.4b and the accompanying illustration)**.
9   The remainder of installation is the reverse of the removal steps.
10   Adjust the cam chain tension (see Chapter 1).

11 Clutch - removal, inspection and installation

Cable

Removal

1   Loosen the cable adjuster at the handlebar grip all the way (see Chapter 1). Rotate the cable so the inner cable aligns with the slot in the lever, then slip the cable end fitting out of the lever.
2   Loosen the locknut and adjusting nut at the midline adjuster (see Chapter 1). Slip the cable out of the bracket, then disengage it from the lifter lever in the right engine cover.

Inspection

3   Slide the inner cable back and forth in the housing and make sure it moves freely. If it doesn't, try lubricating it as described in Chapter 1. If that doesn't help, replace the cable.

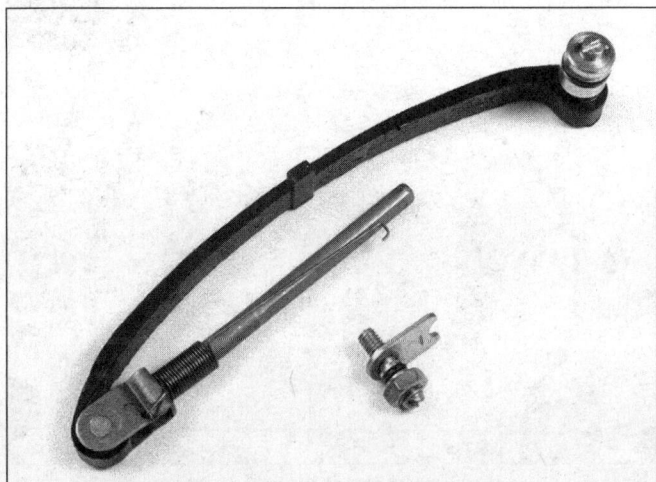

10.5 Cam chain tensioner details

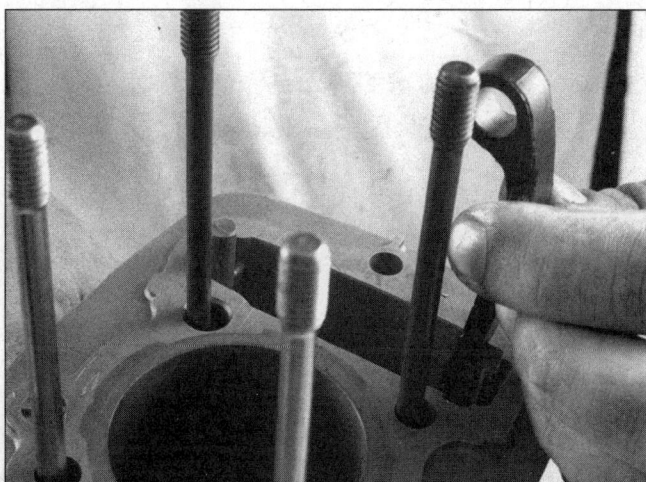

10.8 The intake side chain guide is installed like this

11.7 Remove the cover bolts and take off the right-side engine cover to expose the clutch

a)   Cover bolts (without dowels)
b)   Cover bolts (with dowels)
c)   Clutch adjuster locknut and bolt
d)   Kickstarter pedal pinch bolt

Installation

4   Installation is the reverse of the removal steps. Refer to Chapter 1 and adjust clutch freeplay.

Release mechanism

Removal

Refer to illustrations 11.7 and 11.9

5   Disconnect the clutch cable from the lifter lever as described above.
6   Remove the kickstarter pedal (Section 16) and the brake pedal (Chapter 6).
7   Remove the right-side engine cover bolts and take the cover off the engine **(see illustration)**.
8   Unscrew the locknut from the clutch adjuster bolt **(see illustration 11.7)**. Unscrew the adjuster bolt from the cover.
9   Inside the cover, unhook the lifter arm spring and remove the lifter arm **(see illustration)**. Remove the cotter pin from the lifter arm shaft, then pull out the lifter arm and remove the lifter cam.

11.9 Release mechanism details

a)   Lifter arm   c)   Cotter pin
b)   Lifter arm spring   d)   Lifter cam

Inspection

10   Check for visible wear or damage at the contact points of the lifter shaft and cam and the friction points of the lifter arm and adjusting bolt **(see illustration 11.9)**. Check the spring for bending or distortion. Replace any parts that show problems. Replace the lifter shaft O-ring in the engine cover whenever it's removed.

Installation

11   Installation is the reverse of the removal steps, with the following additions:

a)   Use a new engine cover gasket and be sure the cover dowels are in position **(see illustration 11.7)**.
b)   Refill the engine oil and adjust the clutch (see Chapter 1).

Clutch

Removal

Refer to illustrations 11.13a through 11.13j

12   Remove the right engine cover as described above.
13   Refer to the accompanying illustrations to remove the clutch components **(see illustrations)**.
14   Refer to Chapter 2C for inspection procedures.

11.13a Remove the spring bolts . . .

11.13b . . . and take off the lifter plate, together with the pushrod and release bearing

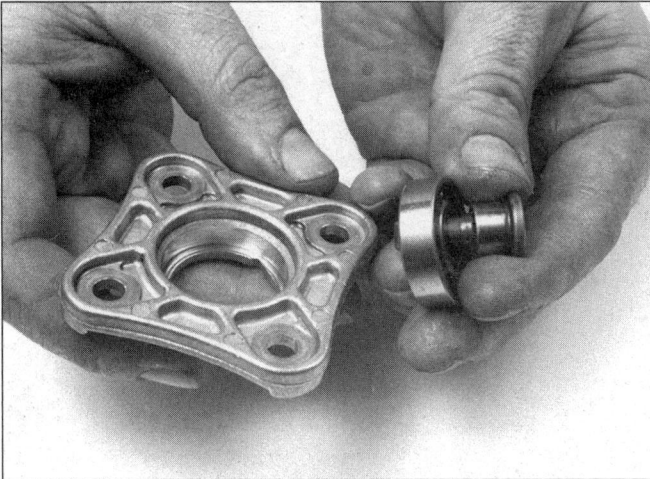

11.13c Separate the pushrod and release bearing from the lifter plate

11.13d Take the springs off the posts

11.13e Remove the snap-ring

11.13f On some models, there's a washer behind the snap-ring; if so, lift it off

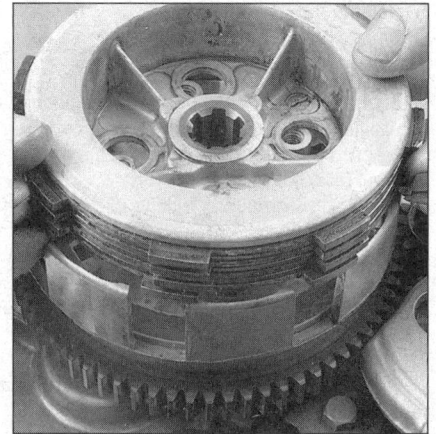

11.13g Lift out the clutch center, friction plates and metal plates as a set

11.13h On some models, there's a thrust washer behind the clutch center; if so remove it from the countershaft - this design has a raised steel boss (arrow)

11.13i Lift the pressure plate (arrow) out of the clutch housing

11.13j Take the thrust washer (if equipped) and clutch housing off the countershaft

a) Thrust washer location
b) Clutch housing

11.15 Install the clutch housing, thrust washer (if equipped), pressure plate, and a friction plate . . .

11.16a . . . then install a metal plate; alternate the remaining friction and metal plates

Installation

Refer to illustrations 11.15, 11.16a, 11.16b and 11.17

15   Install the clutch housing and the pressure plate on the mainshaft, then coat a friction plate with engine oil and install it on the pressure plate **(see illustration)**. If the bike has a separate thrust washer between the clutch housing and clutch center, install it in the clutch housing **(see illustration 11.13h)**.

16   Coat the remaining friction plates with engine oil. Install a metal plate on the friction plate, then alternate the remaining friction and metal plates until they're all installed (there are three friction plates and two metal plates). Friction plates go on first and last, so the friction material contacts the metal surfaces of the clutch center and the pressure plate **(see illustrations)**.

17   Install the clutch center over the posts **(see illustration)**.

18   Install the washer (if equipped) on the mainshaft **(see illustration 11.13f)**.

19   Install the snap-ring and make sure it's securely seated in its groove.

20   Install the clutch springs, the lifter plate, push piece and release bearing **(see illustrations 11.13a through 11.13d)**. Tighten the bolts evenly in a criss-cross pattern until they are tight, but don't overtighten them and strip out the threads.

21   The remainder of installation is the reverse of the removal steps.

12 Oil pump - removal, disassembly, reassembly and installation

Note: *The oil pump can be removed with the engine in the frame.*

Removal

Refer to illustrations 12.2a and 12.2b

1   Refer to Section 16 and remove the right-side engine cover.

2   Remove the mounting screws, then pull the pump out of the engine and remove the O-rings **(see illustrations)**.

Disassembly

Refer to illustrations 12.3, 12.4a, 12.4b, 12.5a, 12.5b and 12.5c

3   Remove the screws and lift off the pump cover **(see illustration)**.

4   Remove the rotors **(see illustrations)**.

5   Turn the pump over and remove the gear cover, gear and shaft **(see illustrations)**.

6   Refer to Chapter 2C for inspection procedures.

Assembly and installation

7   Assembly and installation are the reverse of removal, with the following additions:

a) *Install new O-rings* **(see illustration 12.2b)**.

b) *Tighten the oil pump mounting screws securely, but don't overtighten them.*

11.16b A friction plate goes on last

11.17 Install the clutch center

12.2a Remove the oil pump mounting screws (arrows) . . .

12.2b . . . then pull the pump off the crankcase and remove the O-rings

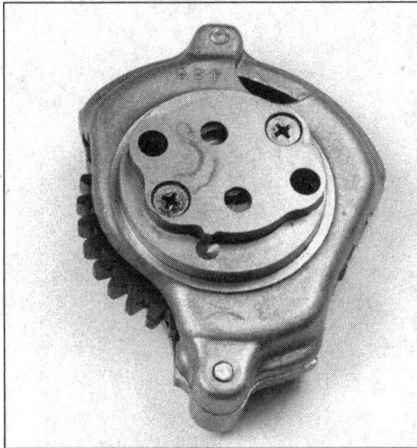

12.3 Remove the pump cover screws

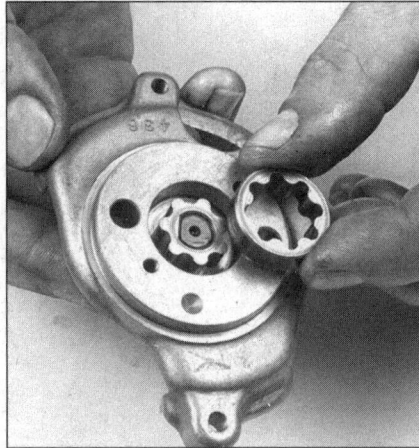

12.4a Lift out the outer rotor . . .

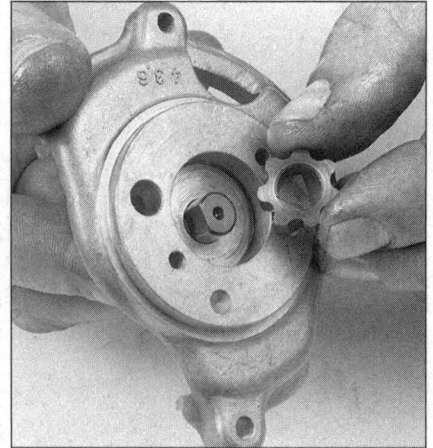

12.4b . . . and the inner rotor

12.5a Remove the gear cover bolts . . .

12.5b . . . lift off the gear cover . . .

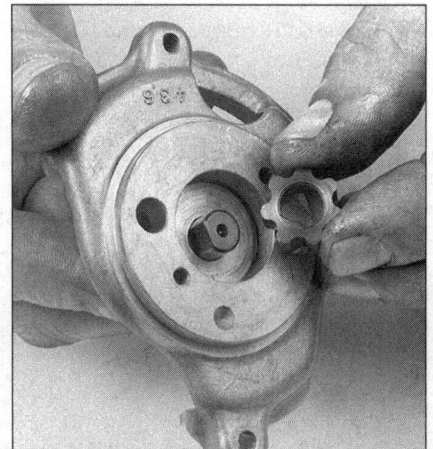

12.5c . . . then pull out the shaft and remove the gear

13.1 Wedge a rag between the primary drive and driven gears (arrow) and loosen the locknut

13.2 Pull the oil orifice (arrow) out of the crankshaft

13.3a Unscrew the locknut

13.3b Remove the drive pin and lockwasher

13 Primary drive gear - removal, inspection and installation

Removal

Refer to illustrations 13.1, 13.2, 13.3a, 13.3b and 13.4

1   Wedge a rag between the teeth of the primary drive gear and the primary driven gear on the clutch housing **(see illustration)**.
2   Pull the oil orifice out of end of the crankshaft **(see illustration)**.
3   Unscrew the drive gear locknut and remove the oil orifice drive pin and lockwasher from the end of the crankshaft **(see illustrations)**.
4   Slide the primary drive gear off the crankshaft and remove the spacer **(see illustration)**.

Inspection

5   Check the drive gear for obvious damage such as chipped or broken teeth. Replace it if any of these problems are found.
6   Check the lockwasher for flattening. Its ends should be apart from each other; if they've been flattened together, replace the lockwasher.
7   Check the oil orifice drive pin for bending or wear and replace it if its condition is in any doubt.

13.4 Slide the primary drive gear off the crankshaft and remove the spacer (arrow)

13.8 Don't forget to reinstall the oil orifice drive pin

14.1 If you don't see a punch mark on the end of the spindle, make your own to align with the slit in the pedal (arrow)

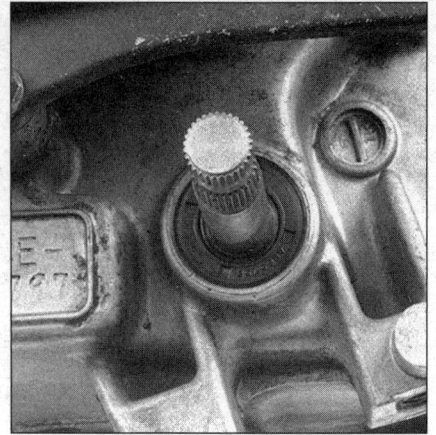

14.4 If the shift shaft seal has been leaking, replace it

Installation

Refer to illustration 13.8

8   Installation is the reverse of the removal steps, with the following additions:

a) *Be sure the oil orifice drive pin is in position before installing the locknut* **(see illustration)**.

b) *Tighten the locknut to the torque listed in this Chapter's Specifications.*

14 External shift mechanism - removal, inspection and installation

Shift pedal
Removal

Refer to illustration 14.1

1   Look for alignment marks on the end of the shift pedal and shift shaft **(see illustration)**. If they aren't visible, make your own marks with a sharp punch.
2   Remove the shift pedal pinch bolt and slide the pedal off the shaft.

Inspection

Refer to illustration 14.4

3   Check the shift pedal for wear or damage such as bending. Check the splines on the shift pedal and shaft for stripping or step wear. Replace the pedal or shaft if these problems are found.
4   Check the shift shaft seal for signs of oil leakage **(see illustration)**. If it has been leaking, refer to Chapter 4 and remove the left-side engine cover. Pry the seal out of the cover and install a new one. You may be able to push the seal in with your thumbs; if not, tap it in with a hammer and block of wood or a socket the same diameter as the seal.

Installation

5   Line up the punch marks, install the shift pedal and tighten the pinch bolt.

External shift linkage
Removal

Refer to illustrations 14.8a, 14.8b, 14.9a, 14.9b, 14.10 and 14.11

6   Remove the shift pedal as described above.
7   Remove the right engine cover (see Section 16) and the left engine cover (see Chapter 4).
8   Pull down the stopper arm and disengage the shift shaft pawls from the shift drum **(see illustration)**. Pull the shift shaft out of the crankcase **(see illustration)**.

14.8a Pull down the stopper arm (arrow), disengage the shift shaft pawls from the shift drum center . . .

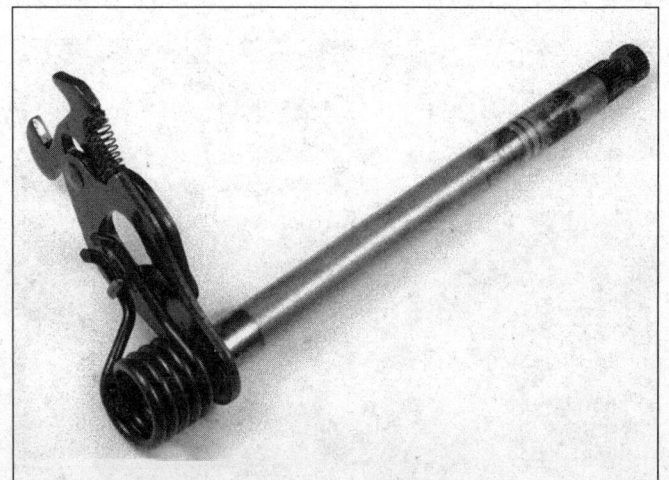

14.8b . . . and pull the shift shaft out of the crankcase

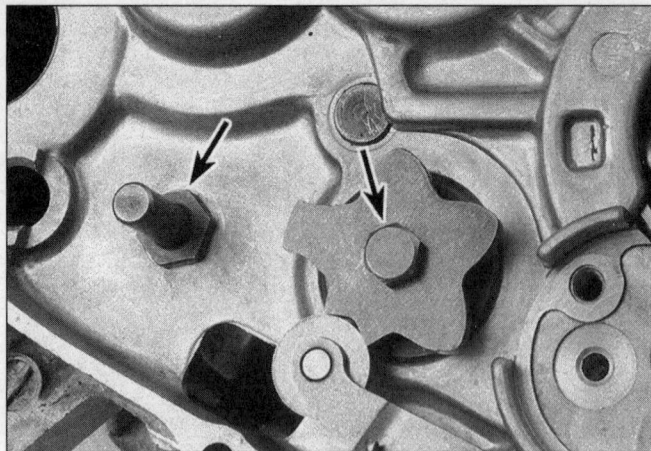

14.9a Remove the bolt (right arrow) from the drum center; the return spring post (left arrow) should be checked for looseness

14.9b Pull down the stopper arm and remove the drum center

9   Remove the bolt from the shift drum center and take the drum center off the drum **(see illustrations)**.

10   Remove the dowel pins from the shift drum **(see illustration)**.

11   Unbolt the stopper arm, then remove the arm and its spring **(see illustration)**.

Inspection

12   Check the shift shaft for bends and damage to the splines **(see illustration 14.8b)**. If the shaft is bent, you can attempt to straighten it, but if the splines are damaged it will have to be replaced. Pry the return spring apart, then slide it and the shift arm down the shaft. Check the condition of the shift arm and the pawl spring. Replace them if they're worn, cracked or distorted. If the arm, spring and shaft are good, reassemble them.

13   Make sure the return spring pin isn't loose **(see illustration 14.9a)**. If it is, unscrew it, apply a non-hardening locking compound to the threads, then reinstall it and tighten it securely.

Installation

14   Position the spring on the stopper arm, then install the stopper arm on the engine and tighten its bolt securely **(see illustration 14.11)**.

15   Install the dowel pins in the shift drum **(see illustration 14.10)**.

16   Pull down the stopper arm and install the drum center on the shift drum, making sure its dowel pins engage the holes in the drum center. Apply non-permanent thread locking agent to the threads of the drum center bolt, then install it and tighten securely. Make sure the stopper arm spring is correctly installed and that the roller end of the stopper

arm engages a notch in the drum center **(see illustration 14.9a)**.

17   Slide the shift shaft into the engine, taking care not to damage the seal as the splines pass through it. Pull down the stopper arm, slide the shaft all the way in and make sure the pawls engage the shift drum dowel pins **(see illustration 14.8a)**.

18   The remainder of installation is the reverse of the removal steps.

19   Check the engine oil level and add some, if necessary (see Chapter 1).

---

15   Crankcase - disassembly and reassembly

---

1   To examine and repair or replace the cam chain, crankshaft, connecting rod, bearings, kickstarter and transmission components, the crankcase must be split into two parts.

Disassembly

Refer to illustrations 15.11, 15.12 and 15.13

2   Remove the engine from the vehicle (see Section 5).

3   Remove the carburetor (see Chapter 3).

4   Remove the alternator rotor (see Chapter 4).

5   Remove the clutch (see Section 11).

6   Remove the external shift mechanism (see Section 14).

7   Remove the oil pump (see Section 12).

8   Remove the valve cover, rocker assembly and camshaft, cylinder head, cylinder, cam chain tensioner and piston (see Sections 6, 7, 8, 9, 10 and Chapter 2C).

14.10 Remove the dowel pins from the shift drum

14.11 Unbolt the stopper arm and remove it together with its spring

15.11 Remove the crankcase bolts (arrows)

15.12 Lift the right crankcase half off the left half; the crankshaft will stay in the left half

9 Remove the kickstarter spring and spacer from the kickstarter shaft (see Section 16).
10 Check carefully to make sure there aren't any remaining components that attach the upper and lower halves of the crankcase together.
11 Loosen the two crankcase bolts evenly in two or three stages **(see illustration)**.
12 Carefully pry the crankcase apart and lift the right half off the left half **(see illustration)**. Don't pry against the mating surfaces or they'll develop leaks.
13 Locate the two crankcase dowels **(see illustration)**.
14 Refer to Sections 17 and 18 and Chapter 2C for information on the internal components of the crankcase.

Reassembly

15 Remove all traces of old gasket and sealant from the crankcase mating surfaces with a sharpening stone or similar tool. Be careful not to let any fall into the case as this is done and be careful not to damage the mating surfaces.
16 Check to make sure the two dowel pins are in place in their holes in the mating surface of the left crankcase half **(see illustration 15.13)**.
17 Pour some engine oil over the transmission and kickstarter gears, the right crankshaft bearing and the shift drum. Don't get any oil on the crankcase mating surface.
18 Install a new gasket on the crankcase mating surface.
19 Carefully place the right crankcase half onto the left crankcase half. While doing this, make sure the transmission shafts, shift drum, crankshaft and kickstarter fit into their bearings in the right crankcase half.

20 Install the crankcase bolts and tighten them so they are just snug. Then tighten them evenly in two or three stages until they are secure, but don't overtighten them and strip out the threads.
21 Turn the transmission mainshaft to make sure it turns freely. Also make sure the crankshaft turns freely.
22 The remainder of assembly is the reverse of disassembly.

16 Kickstarter - removal, inspection and installation

Removal
Pedal
1 The kickstarter pedal is accessible from outside the engine. The spindle spring and spacer can be reached by removing the right engine cover. The engine must be removed and the crankcase disassembled to remove the kickstarter mechanism.
2 Look for a punch mark on the end of the kickstarter spindle **(see illustration 11.7)**. If you can't see one, make your own to align with the slit in the pedal. Loosen the pinch bolt and slide the pedal off the spindle.

Spring and collar
Refer to illustration 16.4
3 Remove the right engine cover (see Section 16).
4 Unhook the spring from its lug on the crankcase casting and slide the spring and collar off the spindle **(see illustration)**.

15.13 Locate the dowels (A), remove the gasket (B) and make sure the thrust washer (C) is on the kickstarter spindle

16.4 Unhook the kickstarter spring from the crankcase (arrow)

16.6   Check the ratchet guide bolts for looseness

16.8   The punch marks on the spindle and ratchet should be aligned when the kickstarter is assembled

Ratchet mechanism

Refer to illustrations 16.6, 16.8, 16.9a and 16.9b

5   Refer to Section 15 and separate the crankcase halves.

6   Check the ratchet guide bolts for looseness (**see illustration**). The guide need not be removed to remove the kickstarter, but if the bolts are loose, unscrew them, apply non-hardening thread locking agent to the threads, then reinstall the guide and bolts. Tighten the bolts securely, but don't overtighten them and strip out the threads in the crankcase.

7   Remove the thrust washer from the kickstarter spindle and lift the spindle out of the crankcase (**see illustration 15.13**).

8   Look for punch marks on the spindle and the ratchet (**see illustration**). If you don't see them, make your own marks so the ratchet can be reinstalled in the correct relationship to the spindle.

9   Remove the snap-ring and take the spring and ratchet off the spindle (**see illustration**). Remove the thrust washer behind the ratchet and if necessary remove the remaining snap-ring (**see illustration**).

Inspection

10   Check all parts for wear or damage, paying special attention to the teeth on the ratchet and the matching teeth on the pinion gear. Replace worn or damaged parts.

11   Measure the inside diameter of the pinion gear and the outside diameter of the spindle where the pinion rides. If either is worn beyond the limit listed in this Chapter's Specifications, replace the worn part.

Installation

Ratchet mechanism

12   Apply moly-based grease to the splines on the spindle and ratchet. Install the snap-ring, thrust washer, ratchet, spring and remaining snap-ring on the spindle. Be sure the punch marks on the ratchet and spindle are aligned (**see illustrations 16.9a, 16.9b and 16.8**).

13   Install the spindle in the crankcase, then install the pinion gear and thrust washer.

14   Refer to Section 15 and reassemble the crankcase halves.

Spring and collar

15   Engage the spring with the slot in the collar and slip them onto the spindle (**see illustrations 16.9a and 16.4**).

Pedal

16   Slip the pedal onto the kickstarter spindle, aligning the marks. Install the pinch bolt and tighten it securely.

---

17   Shift drum and forks - removal, inspection and installation

Removal

Refer to illustrations 17.2a and 17.2b

1   Refer to Section 15 and disassemble the crankcase halves.

16.9a   Remove the snap-ring (left arrow) and spring from the end of the spindle - note how the end of the kickstarter spring fits into the slot in the collar (right arrow)

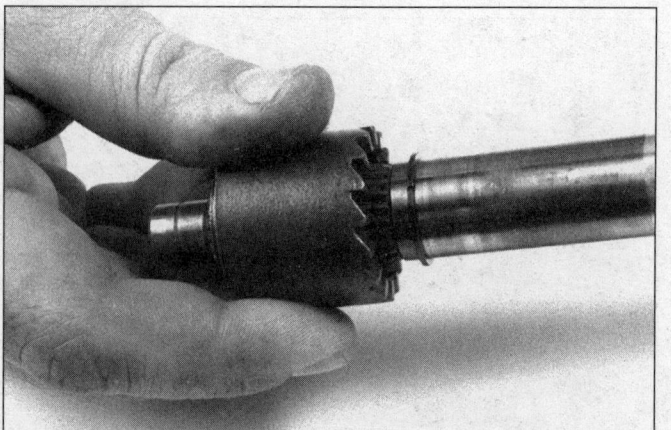

16.9b   Remove the ratchet, thrust washer and if necessary, the remaining snap-ring

17.2a Note the positions of the left and right forks . . .

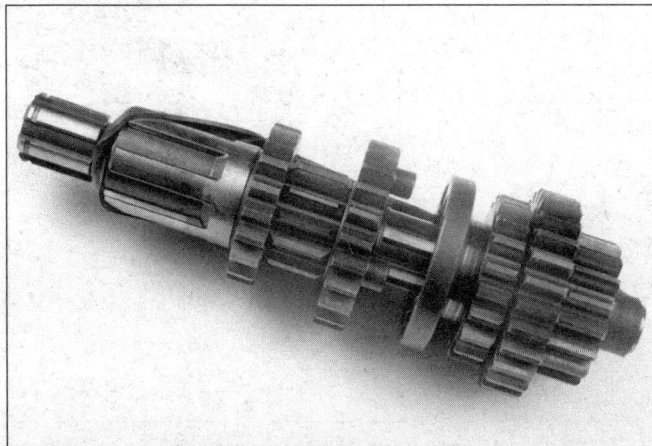

17.2b . . . and the center fork

2   Note how the forks fit in the gear grooves, then pull out the fork shaft **(see illustrations)**.
3   Disengage the forks from the gears and lift them out.

Installation

4   Installation is the reverse of the removal steps, with the following addition: Refer to the identifying letters on the forks and make sure they're installed in the correct position.

18 Transmission shafts - removal, disassembly, inspection, assembly and installation

Note: *When disassembling the transmission shafts, place the parts on a long rod or thread a wire through them to keep them in order and facing in the proper direction.*

Removal

Refer to illustrations 18.4a and 18.4b

1   Remove the engine, then separate the case halves (see Sections 5 and 15).
2   The transmission components and shift drum remain in the left case half when the case is separated.
3   Refer to Section 17 and remove the shift drum and forks.
4   Lift the transmission shafts out of the case together, then separate them. If you're not planning to disassemble them right away, place a large rubber band over both ends of each shaft so the gears won't slide off **(see illustrations)**.

18.4a Use large rubber bands to secure the gears to the countershaft . . .

Disassembly

Refer to illustrations 18.5a through 18.5o

5   Refer to accompanying illustrations to disassemble the transmission shafts **(see illustrations)**.

18.4b . . . and the mainshaft

18.5a Remove mainshaft second gear . . .

18.5b ... fifth gear, thrust washer and snap-ring ...

18.5c ... third gear ...

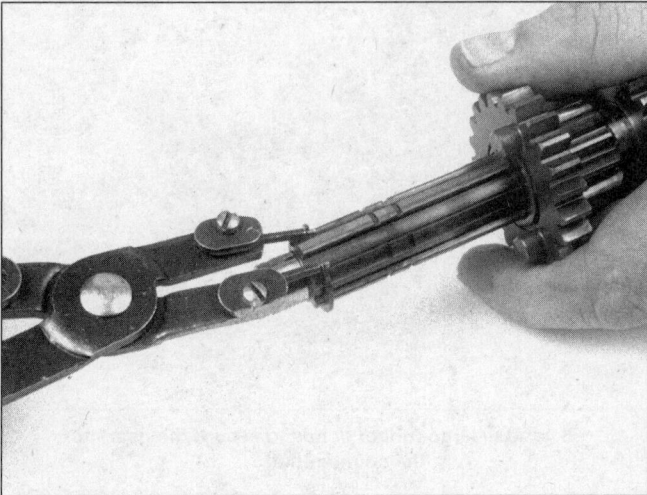

18.5d ... the snap-ring ...

18.5e ... spline washer and fourth gear ...

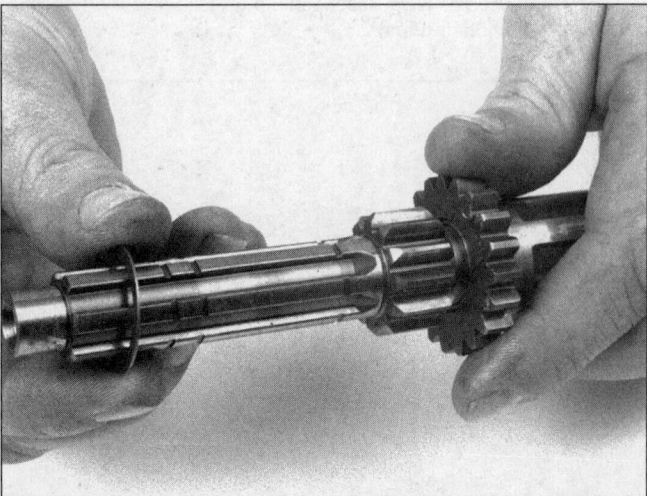

18.5f ... the thrust washer ...

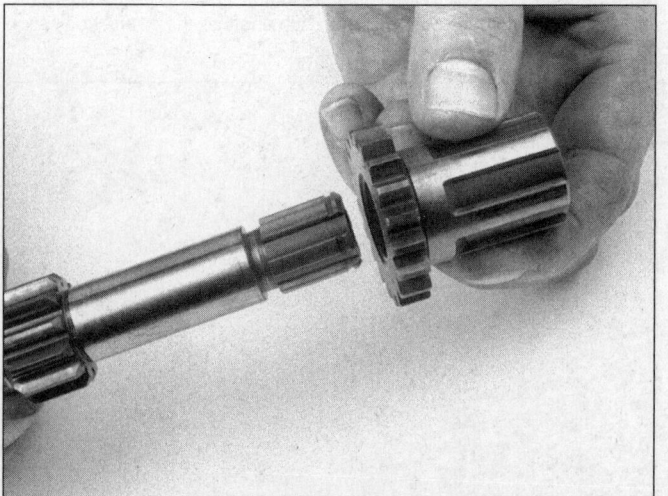

18.5g ... and primary starter gear

18.5h From the countershaft, remove the thrust washer and starter idler gear . . .

18.5i . . . first gear . . .

18.5j . . . the first gear collar (XR100R only) . . .

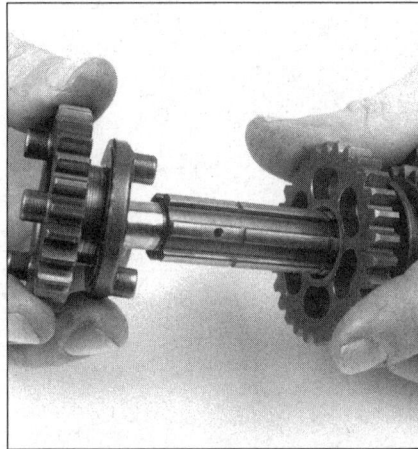

18.5k . . . a spline washer, snap-ring and fourth gear . . .

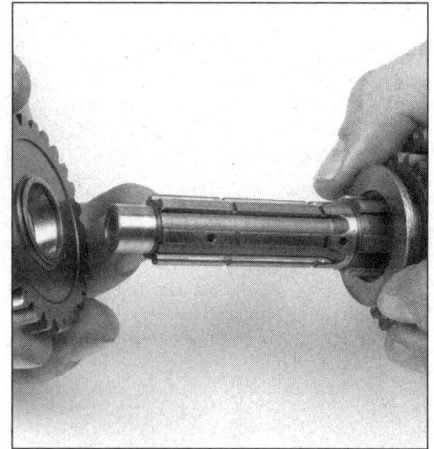

18.5l . . . a snap-ring, spline washer and third gear (and on XR100R models, another thrust washer) . . .

18.5m . . . and fifth gear

18.5n From the other end of the countershaft, remove the ball bearing (if it didn't stay in the crankcase), the thrust washer . . .

18.5o . . . second gear (all models) and thrust washer (XR100R)

Notes

Chapter 2 Part B
Engine, clutch and transmission
(50 and 70 models)

Contents

Specifications

Note: *For wear tolerance and service limit specifications, refer to Chapter 2C.*

Torque specifications

Engine mounting bolts and nuts	31 Nm (23 ft-lbs)
Cylinder head cover nuts	11 Nm (96 inch-lbs)
Cylinder head right side cover bolts	9.8 Nm (84 inch-lbs)
Cam sprocket bolts	8.8 Nm (78 inch-lbs)
Cam chain guide roller pin bolt	9.8 Nm (84 inch-lbs)
Cam tensioner bolt	24 Nm (204 inch-lbs)
Clutch outer cover screw	4.4 Nm (40 inch-lbs)
Clutch locknut	42 Nm (31 ft-lbs)
Clutch assembly screw	5.9 Nm (52 inch-lbs)
External lift linkage stopper arm bolt	
All except CRF70F	13 Nm (108 inch-lbs)
CRF70F	9.8 Nm (84 inch-lbs)
Return spring pin	
All except CRF70F	29 Nm (22 ft-lbs)
CRF70F	Not specified
Shifter cam plate bolts	17 Nm (144 inch-lbs)
Shift drum retaining bolt	12 Nm (108 inch-lbs)

1 General information

The engine/transmission unit is of the air-cooled, single-cylinder four-stroke design. The two valves are operated by an overhead camshaft which is chain driven off the crankshaft. The engine/transmission assembly is constructed from aluminum alloy. The crankcase is divided vertically.

The crankcase incorporates a wet sump, pressure-fed lubrication system which uses a gear-driven rotor-type oil pump, an oil filter and separate strainer screen.

Power from the crankshaft is routed to the transmission via a wet, multi-plate type clutch which engages and disengages automatically when the shift lever is operated. The transmission has three forward gears.

5.5a   Disconnect the electrical connectors on the left side of the frame . . .

5.5b   . . . and the ground wire under the frame (this bolt also secures the air cleaner housing)

2   Operations possible with the engine in the frame

The components and assemblies listed below can be removed without having to remove the engine from the frame. If, however, a number of areas require attention at the same time, removal of the engine is recommended.

External shift mechanism external components
Clutch
Camshaft
Rocker arm assembly
Cylinder head
Cylinder and piston
Oil pump

3   Operations requiring engine removal

It is necessary to remove the engine/transmission assembly from the frame and separate the crankcase halves to gain access to the following components:

Kickstarter
Crankshaft and connecting rod
Transmission shafts
Shift drum and forks

4   Major engine repair - general note

1   It is not always easy to determine when or if an engine should be completely overhauled, as a number of factors must be considered.

2   High mileage is not necessarily an indication that an overhaul is needed, while low mileage, on the other hand, does not preclude the need for an overhaul. Frequency of servicing is probably the single most important consideration. An engine that has regular and frequent oil and filter changes, as well as other required maintenance, will most likely give many miles of reliable service. Conversely, a neglected engine, or one which has not been broken in properly, may require an overhaul very early in its life.

3   Exhaust smoke and excessive oil consumption are both indications that piston rings and/or valve guides are in need of attention. Make sure oil leaks are not responsible before deciding that the rings and guides are bad. Refer to Chapter 1 and perform a cylinder compression check to determine for certain the nature and extent of the work required.

4   If the engine is making obvious knocking or rumbling noises, the connecting rod and/or main bearings are probably at fault.

5   Loss of power, rough running, excessive valve train noise and high

fuel consumption rates may also point to the need for an overhaul, especially if they are all present at the same time. If a complete tune-up does not remedy the situation, major mechanical work is the only solution.

6   An engine overhaul generally involves restoring the internal parts to the specifications of a new engine. During an overhaul the piston rings are replaced and the cylinder walls are bored and/or honed. If a rebore is done, then a new piston is also required. The crankshaft and connecting rod are permanently assembled, so if one of these components needs to be replaced both must be. Generally the valves are serviced as well, since they are usually in less than perfect condition at this point. While the engine is being overhauled, other components such as the carburetor can be rebuilt also. The end result should be a like-new engine that will give as many trouble-free miles as the original.

7   Before beginning the engine overhaul, read through all of the related procedures to familiarize yourself with the scope and requirements of the job. Overhauling an engine is not all that difficult, but it is time consuming. Plan on the motorcycle being tied up for a minimum of two (2) weeks. Check on the availability of parts and make sure that any necessary special tools, equipment and supplies are obtained in advance.

8   Most work can be done with typical shop hand tools, although a number of precision measuring tools are required for inspecting parts to determine if they must be replaced. Often a dealer service department or repair shop will handle the inspection of parts and offer advice concerning reconditioning and replacement. As a general rule, time is the primary cost of an overhaul so it doesn't pay to install worn or substandard parts.

9   As a final note, to ensure maximum life and minimum trouble from a rebuilt engine, everything must be assembled with care in a spotlessly clean environment.

5   Engine - removal and installation

Note: *Engine removal and installation should be done with the aid of an assistant to avoid damage or injury that could occur if the engine is dropped.*

Removal

Refer to illustrations 5.5a, 5.5b and 5.12

1   Drain the engine oil (see Chapter 1).

2   Remove the seat and right side cover (see Chapter 7).

3   Remove the fuel tank, exhaust system, carburetor and intake manifold (see Chapter 3). The throttle cable can be left connected to the carburetor.

4   Disconnect the spark plug wire (see Chapter 1).

5   Label and disconnect the wires on the left side of the engine **(see illustration)**. Detach the wires from their clips on the frame. Discon-

5.12 Remove the engine mount nuts (arrows) and through-bolts

6.1 Remove the top cover nuts (arrows) - nut A has a copper washer

nect the ground wire (its bolt also secures the air cleaner housing to the frame) **(see illustration)**.

6   Remove the drive chain (see Chapter 5).

7   Remove the shift pedal (see Section 13).

8   Remove the kickstarter pedal (see Section 15).

9   Disconnect the crankcase breather tube from the engine.

10   Support the bike securely upright so it can't fall over during the remainder of this procedure.

11   Disconnect the brake pedal return spring and unbolt the left foot-peg bracket (see Chapters 6 and 7).

12   Remove the engine mounting bolts and nuts at the top and rear of the engine **(see illustration)**.

13   Have an assistant help you lift the engine out of the frame.

14   Set the engine to a suitable work surface.

Installation

15   Have an assistant help lift the engine to align the mounting bolt holes, then install the brackets, bolts and nuts. Tighten them to the torques listed in this Chapter's Specifications.

16   The remainder of installation is the reverse of the removal steps, with the following additions:

a)   Use new gaskets at the exhaust pipe connection.

b)   Adjust the throttle cable and clutch cable following the procedures in Chapter 1.

c)   Fill the engine with oil, also following the procedures in Chapter 1.

d)   Run the engine and check for oil or exhaust leaks.

6   Cylinder head covers - removal, inspection and installation

Refer to illustrations 6.1, 6.2a, 6.2b, 6.5a and 6.5b

1   Remove the top cover nuts and lift the cover off the engine **(see illustration)**. If it's stuck, don't attempt to pry it off - tap around the sides of it with a plastic hammer to dislodge it.

2   Unbolt the right side cover **(see illustration)**. Tap on the head of the center bolt (the one with the sealing washer) to free the left side cover and take it off **(see illustration)**. Then remove the right side cover and gasket. If it's stuck, don't attempt to pry it off - tap around the sides of it with a plastic hammer to dislodge it.

3   Remove the gaskets from the covers. Check for brittleness, cracks or deterioration and replace it if any problems are found.

4   Check the sealing washer on the right side cover's center bolt. Replace it if it's condition is in doubt.

5   Installation is the reverse of the removal steps, with the following additions:

a)   Use new gaskets.

6.2a The right side cover is secured by three bolts (arrows) - the center bolt . . .

6.2b . . . goes all the way through the engine to secure the left side cover

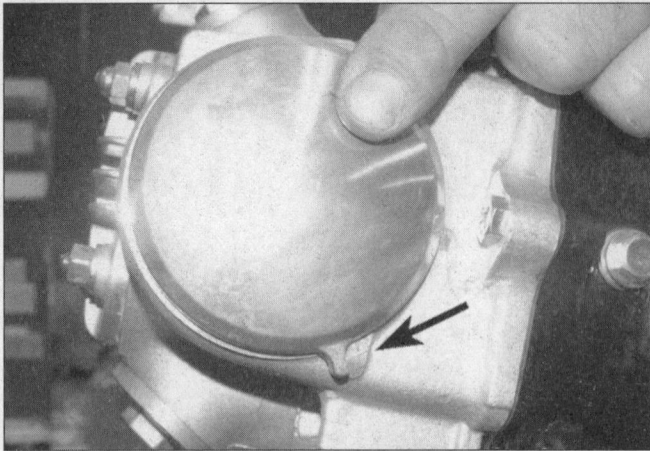

6.5a Position the left side cover's tab against the stop on the cylinder head

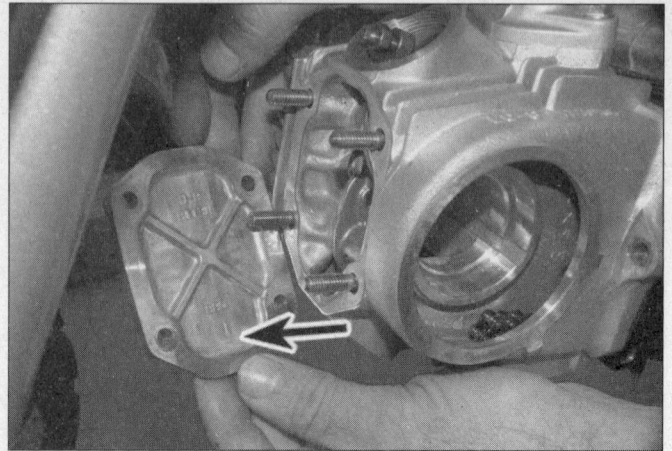

6.5b The arrow mark inside the top cover (arrow) points downward

7.1 Loosen the valve adjusting screws as far as they will go without falling out of the rocker arms

7.4 Align the TDC mark on the cam sprocket with the notch in the cylinder head (arrows)

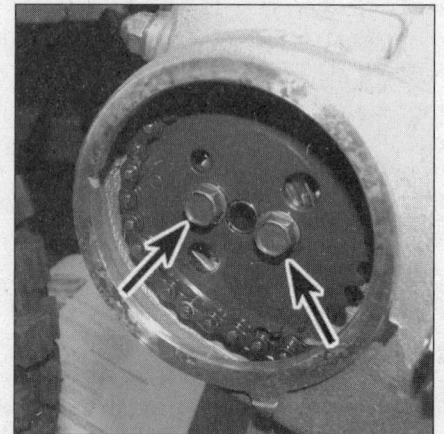

7.5a Remove the sprocket bolts (arrows) . . .

b) *Place the tab of the left-hand cover against the stop on the cylinder head* **(see illustration)**.
c) *The arrow mark inside the top cover faces down* **(see illustration)**.
d) *Use a new copper washer on the top cover's lower right stud* **(see illustration 6.1)**.
e) *Tighten the cover bolts and nuts securely, but don't overtighen them and strip the threads.*

7   Camshaft - removal and installation

Removal

Refer to illustrations 7.1, 7.4, 7.5a, 7.5b, 7.6, 7.7a and 7.7b

1   Referring to *Valve clearance - check and adjustment* in Chapter 1, unscrew the valve adjusting hole caps and place the piston at top dead center on the compression stroke. Loosen the valve adjusting screws all the way **(see illustration)**.
2   Refer to Section 6 and remove the left and right cylinder head covers.
3   Remove the cam chain tensioner plug, spring and piston (see Section 10). The lever and roller need not be removed.
4   Make sure the stamped circle on the camshaft sprocket aligns with the pointer cast in the cylinder head **(see illustration)**.
5   Unbolt the cam sprocket from the camshaft **(see illustration)**. Dis-

engage the sprocket from the chain and remove it from the camshaft **(see illustration)**.
6   Thread the cam sprocket bolts back into the camshaft to use as handles, then pull the camshaft out of the engine **(see illustration)**.

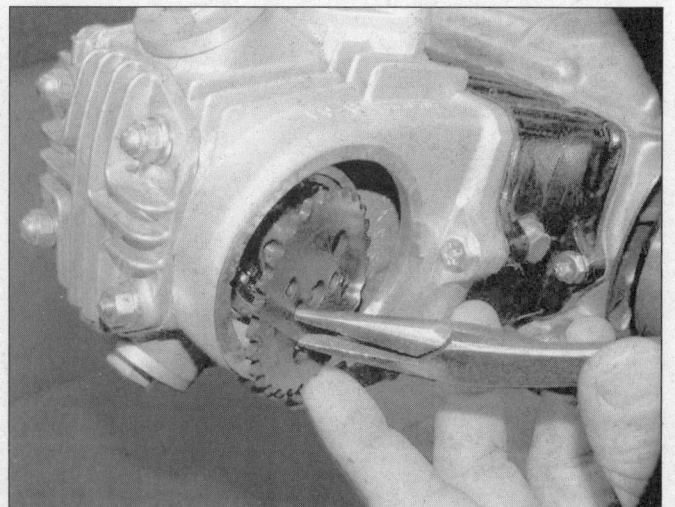

7.5b . . . disengage the sprocket from the chain and remove it

7.6 Pull the camshaft out with the lobes pointing in the directions shown

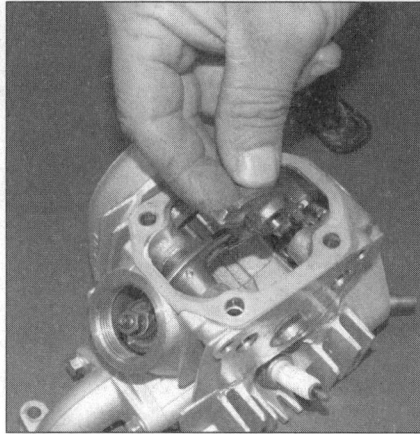

7.7a Note the directions of the rocker arms . . .

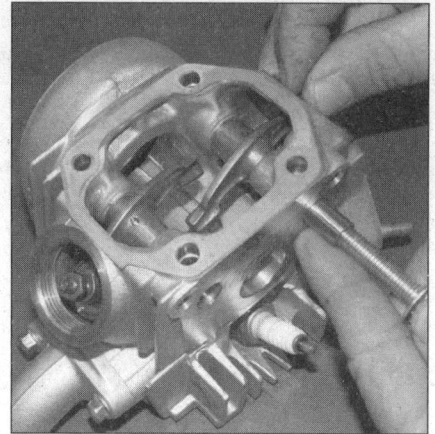

7.7b . . . then thread a bolt into each rocker shaft, pull it out and remove the rocker arms

7   To remove the rocker arms, thread an 8mm bolt into each of the rocker shafts and pull it out **(see illustration)**. Take the rocker arm out of the head **(see illustration)** and place it back on its shaft so they won't be mixed up. Label the intake and exhaust rocker arms and shafts so they can be returned to their original locations.

8   Refer to Chapter 2C for inspection procedures.

Installation

9   Lubricate the camshaft lobes and bearings with clean engine oil. Place the camshaft in the cylinder head with the lobes pointing toward the cylinder **(see illustration 7.6)**.

10   Engage the sprocket with the chain so its stamped circle mark will be align with the timing pointer **(see illustration 7.4)**. Place the sprocket on the camshaft so its bolt holes align with the camshaft bolt holes. Install the bolts and tighten them to the torque listed in this Chapter's Specifications.

11   Recheck the crankshaft timing mark to make sure it's still at the TDC position (see *Valve clearance - check and adjustment* in Chapter 1). If it's out of position and the camshaft sprocket is aligned as described in Step 19, you'll need to remove the chain from the sprocket and reposition it. Don't run the engine with the marks out of alignment or severe engine damage could occur.

12   Adjust the valve clearances (see Chapter 1).

13   The remainder of installation is the reverse of removal.

8 Cylinder head and rocker arms - removal and installation

Caution: *The engine must be completely cool before beginning this procedure, or the cylinder head may become warped.*

Removal

Refer to illustrations 8.2, 8.3, 8.4a and 8.4b

1   Remove the cylinder head covers and camshaft (Sections 6 and 7). Remove the front fender (see Chapter 7).

2   Remove the remaining hex-headed screw that secures the cylinder head to the cylinder **(see illustration)**. **Note:** *This screw is difficult to get at, since it's very close to the head. If it's tight (and it probably will be), use an impact driver with an extension. A box wrench won't fit. A Phillips screwdriver or open-end wrench might work, but they might strip out the screw slots or hex.*

3   Lift the cylinder head off the cylinder studs. If the head is stuck, tap around the side of the head with a rubber mallet to jar it loose, or use two wooden dowels inserted into the intake or exhaust ports to lever the head off. Don't attempt to pry the head off by inserting a screwdriver between the head and the cylinder - you'll damage the sealing surfaces. **Note:** *If the cylinder head contacts the front tire before coming off the studs, let the air out of the tire and compress it with your fingers* **(see illustration)**. *This should provide enough clearance to get the head all the way off.*

8.2 You'll need an impact driver with an extension and Phillips bit to remove the screw that holds the head to the cylinder

8.3 If there isn't enough room to get the head all the way off the studs, let the air out of the tire and compress the tire with your fingers

8.4a Take the head gasket off . . .

8.4b . . . then remove the O-ring and internal collar and locate the dowels (arrows)

9.2 Remove the screw that holds the cylinder to the crankcase (arrow) . . .

4   Support the cam chain so it won't drop into the cam chain tunnel, and stuff a clean rag into the tunnel to prevent the entry of debris. Once this is done, remove the gasket, O-ring with internal collar and two dowel pins from the cylinder **(see illustrations)**.

5   Check the cylinder head gasket and the mating surfaces on the cylinder head and cylinder for leakage, which could indicate warpage. Refer to Chapter 2C and check the flatness of the cylinder head.

6   Clean all traces of old gasket material from the cylinder head and cylinder. Be careful not to let any of the gasket material fall into the crankcase, the cylinder bore or the bolt holes.

Installation

7   Install the two dowel pins and the O-ring with internal collar, then lay the new gasket in place on the cylinder block **(see illustrations 8.4a and 8.4b)**. Never reuse the old gasket and don't use any type of gasket sealant.

8   Carefully lower the cylinder head over the studs and dowels. It is helpful to have an assistant support the camshaft chain with a piece of wire so it doesn't fall and become kinked or detached from the crankshaft. When the head is resting on the cylinder, wire the cam chain to another component to keep tension on it.

9   The remainder of installation is the reverse of the removal steps.

10   Change the engine oil (see Chapter 1).

---

9   Cylinder - removal and installation

Removal

Refer to illustrations 9.2, 9.3 and 9.4

1   Following the procedure given in Section 8, remove the cylinder head. Make sure the crankshaft is positioned at Top Dead Center (TDC).

2   Remove the hex head bolt that secures the cylinder and the pin bolt and sealing washer that secure the cam chain roller **(see illustration)**.

3   Lift the cylinder straight along the studs to remove it **(see illustration)**. If it's stuck, tap around its perimeter with a soft-faced hammer (but don't tap on the cooling fins or they may break). Don't attempt to pry between the cylinder and the crankcase, as you'll ruin the sealing surfaces. Once the cylinder is partway off, lift out the roller.

4   Locate the dowel pins and O-ring (they may have come off with the cylinder or still be in the crankcase) **(see illustration)**. Be careful not to let these drop into the engine. Stuff rags around the piston and remove the gasket and all traces of old gasket material from the surfaces of the cylinder and the crankcase **(see illustration 9.4b in Chapter 2A)**.

5   Refer to Chapter 2C for inspection procedures.

9.3 . . . pull the cylinder partway off and remove the timing chain roller . . .

9.4 . . . then remove the cylinder the rest of the way, remove the gasket and locate the dowels (arrows)

Installation

6   Lubricate the cylinder bore with plenty of clean engine oil. Apply a thin film of moly-based grease to the piston skirt.

7   Install the dowel pins and O-ring, then lower a new cylinder base gasket over them **(see illustration 9.4)**.

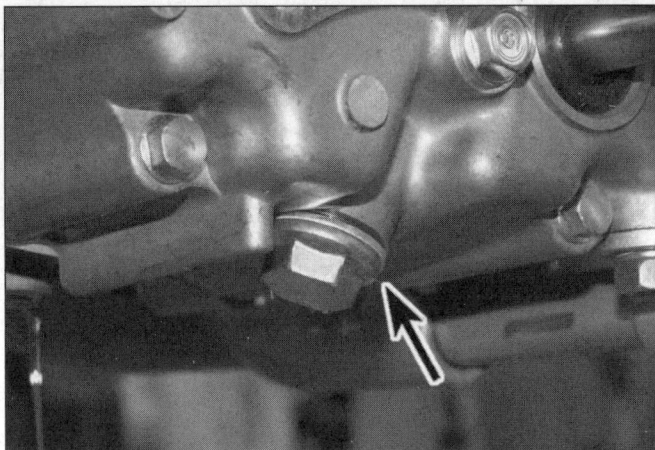

10.2a Remove the tensioner bolt (arrow) - oil will run out when you do this

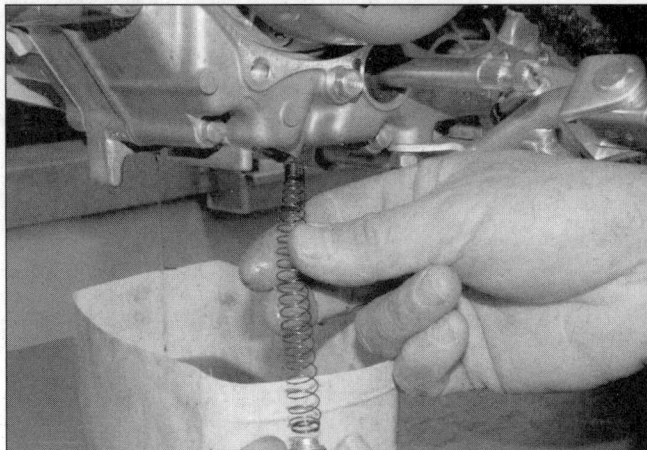

10.2b Pull out the tensioner spring (its narrow end goes upward on installation) . . .

8   Attach a piston ring compressor to the piston and compress the piston rings. A large hose clamp can be used instead - just make sure it doesn't scratch the piston, and don't tighten it too much.
9   Install the cylinder over the studs and carefully lower it down until the piston crown fits into the cylinder liner (see illustration 9.3). While doing this, pull the camshaft chain up, using a hooked tool or a piece of stiff wire. Push down on the cylinder, making sure the piston doesn't get cocked sideways, until the bottom of the cylinder liner slides down past the piston rings. A wood or plastic hammer handle can be used to gently tap the cylinder down, but don't use too much force or the piston will be damaged.
10   Remove the piston ring compressor or hose clamp, being careful not to scratch the piston.
11   The remainder of installation is the reverse of the removal steps.

10 Cam chain and tensioner - removal, inspection and installation

Removal

Refer to illustrations 10.2a, 10.2b, 10.2c, 10.3 and 10.4

1   Remove the alternator rotor, stator and stator base plate (see Chapter 4).
2   Place a drain pan beneath the tensioner bolt (oil will run out when it's removed, even if the oil has been drained). Unscrew the tensioner bolt and sealing washer from the bottom of the engine, then lower the tensioner spring and pushrod out of the bore (see illustrations). Note:

10.2c . . . then lower the piston out - its rubber-tipped end goes upward on installation

If you're removing the tensioner just to remove the camshaft, this is all that is necessary.
3   If you're planning to remove the cam chain, remove the cylinder head (see Section 8) and the roller inside the cylinder jacket (see Section 9). Disengage the chain from the crankshaft sprocket and take it out of the engine (see illustration)
4   Remove the tensioner arm pivot bolt, then remove the arm and rollers (see illustration).

10.3 Disengage the cam chain from the crankshaft sprocket and take it out

10.4 Remove the tensioner pivot bolt and rollers (arrows)

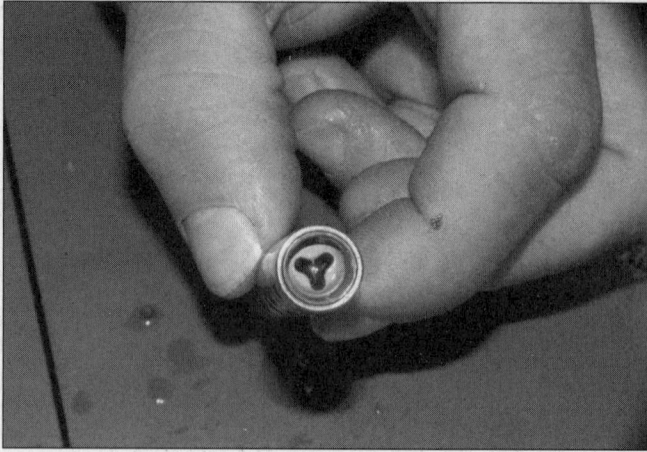

10.6 Check the one-way valve in the end of the pushrod for clogging or damage

11.4a Remove the crankcase cover bolts (arrows) . . .

Inspection

Refer to illustration 10.6

5   Check the tensioner pivot bolt and roller for wear or damage. Replace them if problems are found.
6   Check the tensioner pushrod for wear or damage along its length. Check the one-way valve in the end of the pushrod for damage or clogging **(see illustration)**. If the one-way valve is damaged, or if clogging can't be removed, replace the pushrod.
7   Check the tensioner spring for breakage and replace it if necessary. Measure its free length and compare it to the value listed in this Chapter's Specifications. If it's too short, replace it.

Installation

8   Installation is the reverse of the removal steps. Use a new sealing washer on the tensioner bolt. Tighten the pivot bolt and tensioner bolt to the torque listed in this Chapter's Specifications.

---

11 Clutch and primary drive gear - removal, inspection and installation

Release mechanism

Removal

Refer to illustrations 11.4a, 11.4b and 11.5

1   Drain the engine oil (see Chapter 1).
2   Remove the kickstarter pedal (Section 15).

11.4b . . . then take off the cover, remove the gasket and locate the dowels (arrows)

3   Unbolt the footpeg bracket (see Chapter 7). Unhook the brake pedal return spring. Loosen the brake pedal adjusting locknut and turn the adjusting nut to lower the pedal to provide removal clearance for the right crankcase cover (see Chapter 1).
4   Remove the right crankcase cover bolts and take the cover off the engine **(see illustration)**. **Note:** *Oil will run out when the cover is removed, even if the oil has been drained. It's a good idea to place a wide drain pan below the engine.* Locate the dowels **(see illustration)**. They may come off with the cover or stay in the engine.
5   Remove the ball retainer and spring **(see illustration)**. They may come off with the cover, as happened in this case, or stay on the lifter plate in the engine.
6   Unscrew the locknut from the clutch adjuster bolt **(see illustration 7.10 in Chapter 1)**. Unscrew the adjuster bolt from the cover and remove it together with the clutch lifter **(see illustration 11.5)**.

Inspection

7   Check for visible wear or damage at the contact points of the lifter and the three balls on the lifter cam and at the friction points of the lifter arm and adjusting bolt **(see illustration 11.5)**. Check the spring for bending or distortion. Replace any parts that show problems. Replace the lifter shaft O-ring in the crankcase cover whenever it's removed.

Installation

Refer to illustration 11.8

8   Installation is the reverse of the removal steps, with the following additions:

11.5 The ball retainer and spring may come off with the cover (shown here) or stay on the clutch

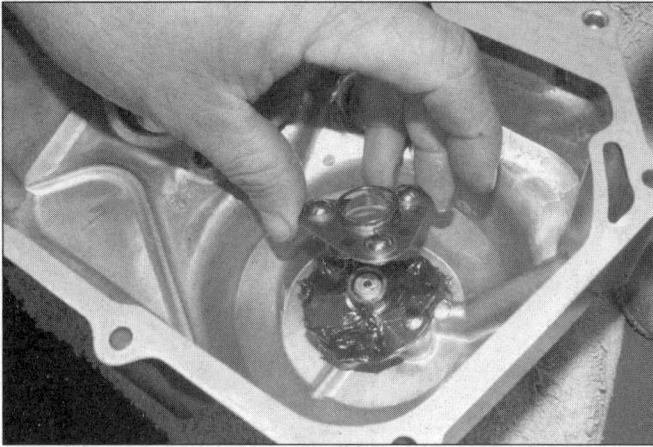

11.8 Stick the ball retainer to the lifter with dabs of grease for installation

11.10a Note how the lifter lever (lower arrow) and lifter cam plate (upper arrow) are installed . . .

11.10b . . . then slide the lifter lever off the gearshift spindle and remove the lifter cam plate

11.10c Remove the lifter cam plate (the bearing may come off with it or stay in the clutch outer cover)

a) Stick the ball retainer and spring to the lifter with dabs of grease (see illustration).
b) Use a new crankcase cover gasket and be sure the cover dowels are in position (see illustration 11.4b).
c) Refill the engine oil and adjust the clutch (see Chapter 1).

Clutch

Removal

Refer to illustrations 11.10a through 11.10i

9   Remove the right crankcase cover as described above.
10   Refer to the accompanying illustrations to remove the clutch components (see illustrations). **Note:** *Removal of the clutch locknut*

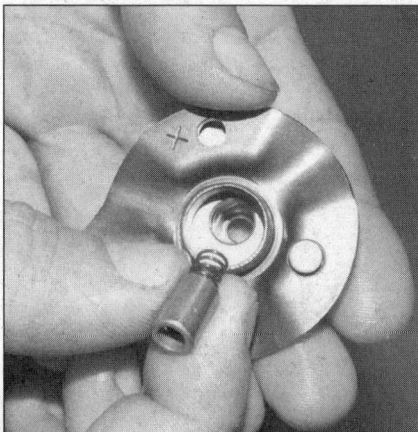

11.10d The oil passage and spring fit in the lifter cam plate like this

11.10e Bend back the lockwasher tabs (arrows) . . .

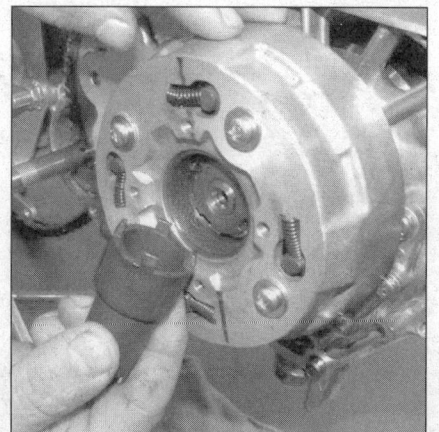

11.10f . . . then unscrew the nut using a special tool

11.10g Remove the nut, cone washer and lockwasher

11.10h The OUT SIDE mark on the cone washer faces away from the engine

11.10i Pull the clutch off the crankshaft

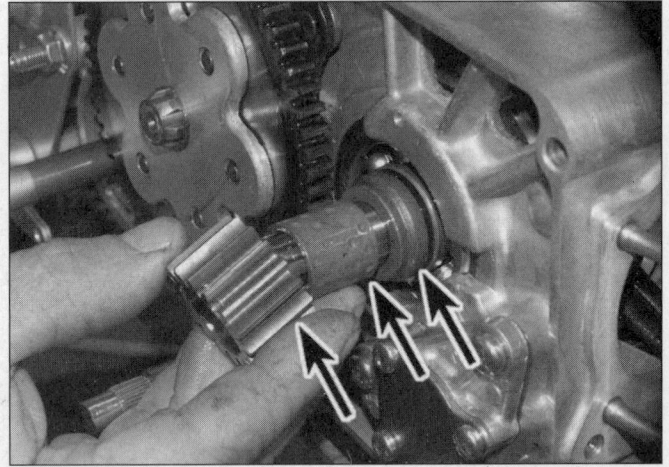

11.10j Remove the primary drive gear (left arrow) and bushing (center arrow); to remove the spacer (right arrow), you'll need to remove the primary driven gear

requires a special tool, available from aftermarket suppliers such as Motion Pro.

Disassembly

Refer to illustrations 11.11a through 11.11k and 11.12

11   Refer to the accompanying illustrations to remove the clutch com-

ponents **(see illustrations)**.

12   Check the primary drive gear for obvious damage such as chipped or broken teeth. Replace it if any of these problems are found. If neces-

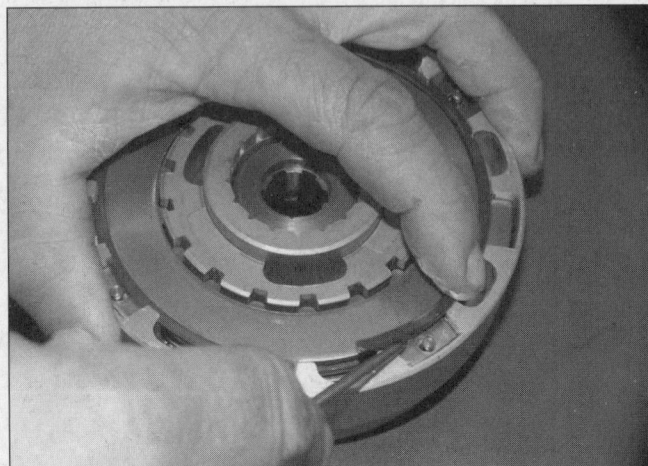

11.11a Pry out the retaining ring . . .

11.11b . . . and remove the clutch center, together with the plates . . .

11.11c . . . then separate the plates from the cluch center

11.11d The plates go in this order (bottom to top): metal with inner tabs, friction with outer tabs, friction with inner tabs and metal with outer tabs

11.11e The bottom plate has friction material on the bottom side

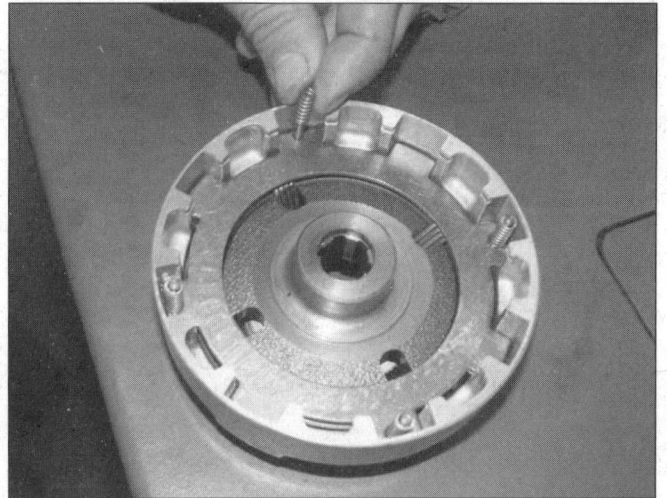

11.11f Remove the free springs from the clutch plate . . .

11.11g . . . and remove the clutch plate from the housing

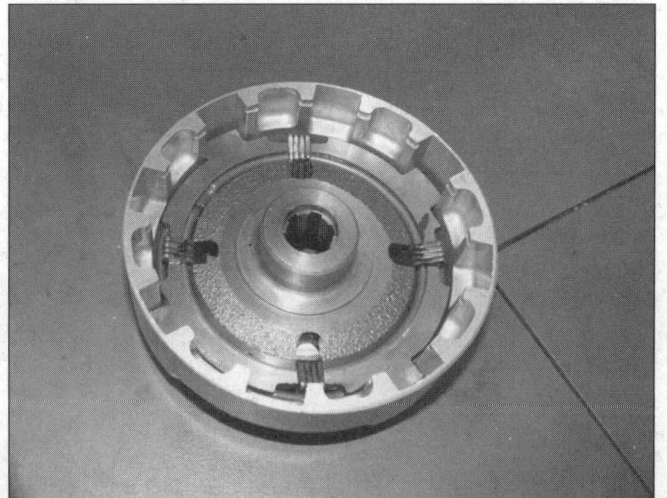

11.11h The clutch weight, center ring and drive plate fit in the housing like this

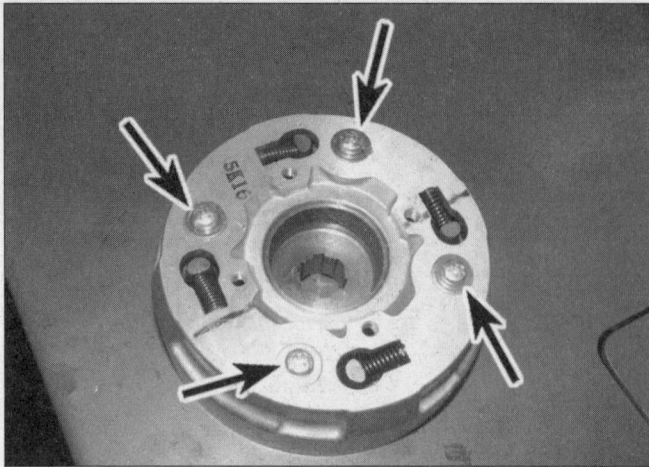

11.11i Loosen the clutch housing screws (arrows) evenly; they're spring loaded

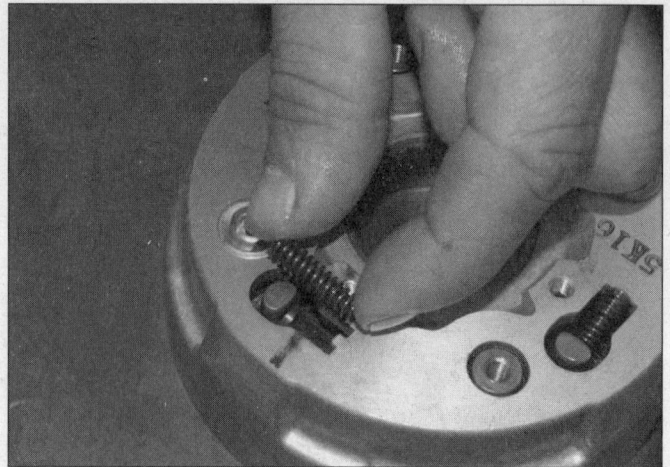

11.11j Remove the damper springs

sary, remove the snap-ring and take the gear off the shaft **(see illustration)**. **Note:** *The spacer on the end of the transmission shaft can't be removed unless the primary drive gear is removed first.*

13   Measure the inside and outside diameters of the clutch center guide and the inside diameter of the primary drive gear and compare them to the values listed in Chapter 2C. Replace any parts worn beyond the limits.

14   Spin the bearings in the crankcase cover and clutch lifter and check for rough or noisy movement. Replace them if problems are found, referring to crankcase bearing replacement procedures in Chapter 2C.

15   Refer to Chapter 2C to inspect the clutch springs and plates.

Assembly and installation

16   Assembly and installation are the reverse of the removal steps, with the following additions:

  a) Use a new snap-ring on the primary driven gear.
  b) Lubricate the clutch center guide, primary drive gear and primary driven gear with clean engine oil.
  c) When installing the primary drive gear on the clutch center, align its teeth with the slots in the clutch center.
  d) Align the tab on the inner lockwasher with the notch in the clutch housing.
  e) Install the outer lockwasher with its OUT SIDE mark facing away from the engine.

  f) Tighten the clutch locknut to the torque listed in this Chapter's Specifications. If necessary, tighten it further to align its notch with the tab on the inner lockwasher, then bend the lockwasher tab into the slot.
  g) Use a new gasket on the clutch outer cover and tighten its screws evenly to the torque listed in this Chapter's Specifications.
  h) Install the ball retainer on the lifter cam with its cutout side facing the lifter lever.

17   Fill the engine with oil (see Chapter 1).

12 Oil pump - removal, disassembly, reassembly and installation

Note: *The oil pump can be removed with the engine in the frame.*

Removal

Refer to illustrations 12.2a, 12.2b, 12.2c and 12.3

1   Refer to Section 11 and remove the right-side engine cover and clutch.

2   To check the pump for wear, remove its cover for access to the rotors **(see illustrations)**. The cover doesn't have a gasket, so you won't need a new one. Refer to Chapter 2C for inspection procedures.

3   To remove the pump completely, remove the mounting screws,

11.11k Lift the drive plate assembly off the clutch housing

11.12 Remove the snap-ring (arrow) and take the primary driven gear off the shaft

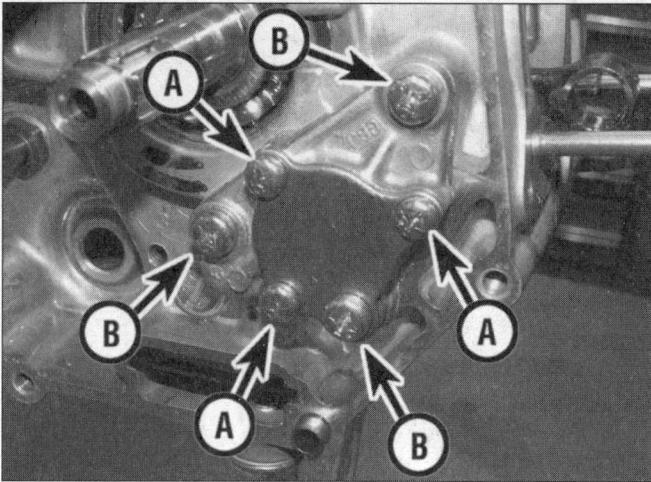

12.2a Here are the oil pump cover screws (A) and mounting screws (B)

12.2b To inspect the rotors, remove the cover plate . . .

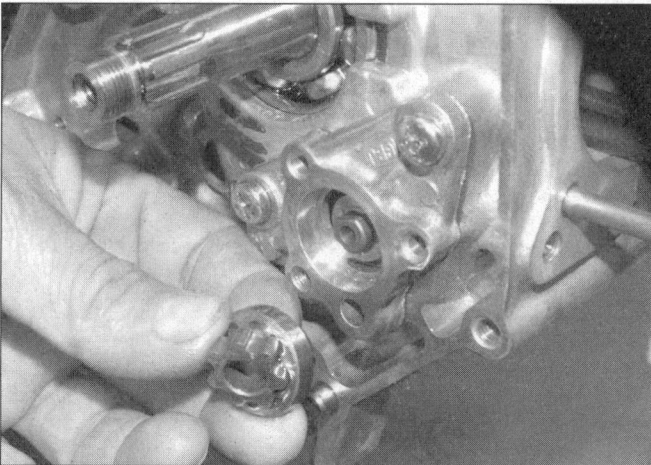

12.2c . . . and take the rotors out - the flat on the shaft engages the flat in the inner rotor

12.3 Remove the pump and gasket - on installation, be sure the slot in the pump shaft engages the tang in the engine

then take the pump and gasket off of the engine and remove the rotor shaft **(see illustration)**.

Installation

4   Installation is the reverse of removal, with the following additions:
a) *Fill the pump with a small amount (0.5 to 1.0 cc) of clean engine oil.*
b) *Use a new oil pump gasket.*
c) *Tighten the oil pump mounting screws to the torque listed in this Chapter's Specifications.*

13 External shift mechanism - removal, inspection and installation

Shift pedal

1   These procedures are basically the same as for 80 and 100 models (see Chapter 2A).

External shift linkage

Removal

Refer to illustrations 13.4, 13.5a, 13.5b, 13.6a, 13.6b, 13.7 and 13.8

2   Remove the shift pedal as described above.

3   Remove the right crankcase cover and clutch (see Section 11).
4   Unbolt the stopper arm, then remove the arm and its spring **(see illustration)**.

13.4 Pull the stopper arm (arrow) down, clear of the cam plate, and unbolt it from the engine

13.5a Pull the gearshift arm down until it clears the cam plate, then pull the gearshift spindle out of the engine

13.5b The gearshift spindle spring is installed like this

5   Pull down the stopper arm and disengage the shift shaft pawls from the shift drum **(see illustration)**. Pull the shift shaft out of the crankcase **(see illustration)**.
6   Remove the bolt from the shift drum center and take the drum center off the drum **(see illustrations)**.
7   Remove the dowel pins from the shift drum **(see illustration)**.
8   Check the return spring pin for wear, damage, or looseness **(see illustration)**. If it's loose, unscrew it and screw it back in, using non-permanent thread locking agent on the threads. If it's worn or damaged, replace it.

Inspection

9   Check the shift shaft for bends and damage to the splines. If the shaft is bent, you can attempt to straighten it, but if the splines are damaged it will have to be replaced. Pry the return spring apart, then slide it and the shift arm down the shaft. Check the condition of the shift arm and the pawl spring. Replace them if they're worn, cracked or distorted. If the arm, spring and shaft are good, reassemble them.
10   Make sure the return spring pin isn't loose **(see illustration 13.5)**. If it is, unscrew it, apply a non-hardening locking compound to the threads, then reinstall it and tighten it securely.

Installation

11   Install the dowel pins in the shift drum **(see illustration 13.7)**. Install the drum center on the shift drum and tighten its bolt to the torque listed in this Chapter's Specifications.
12   Slide the shift shaft into the engine, taking care not to damage the

seal as the splines pass through it. Pull down the stopper arm, slide the shaft all the way in and make sure the pawls engage the shift drum dowel pins.
13   Position the spring on the stopper arm, then install the stopper arm on the engine and tighten its bolt to the torque listed in this Chapter's Specifications **(see illustration 13.4)**. Make sure the stopper arm spring is correctly installed and that the roller end of the stopper arm engages a notch in the drum center.
14   The remainder of installation is the reverse of the removal steps.
15   Check the engine oil level and add some, if necessary (see Chapter 1).

14   Crankcase - disassembly and reassembly

1   To examine and repair or replace the crankshaft, connecting rod, bearings, kickstarter and transmission components, the crankcase must be split into two parts.

Disassembly

Refer to illustrations 14.10a, 14.10b, 14.13 and 14.14

2   Remove the engine from the vehicle (see Section 5).
3   Remove the carburetor (see Chapter 3).
4   Remove the alternator rotor (see Chapter 4).
5   Remove the clutch (see Section 11).
6   Remove the external shift mechanism (see Section 13).

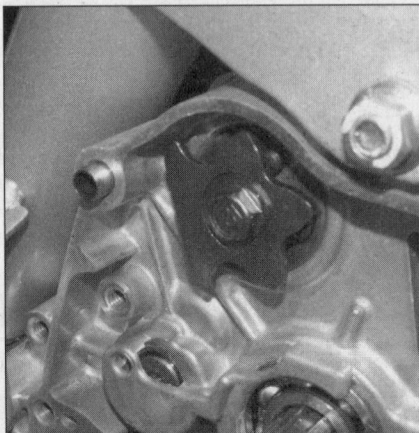

13.6a Unbolt the cam plate . . .

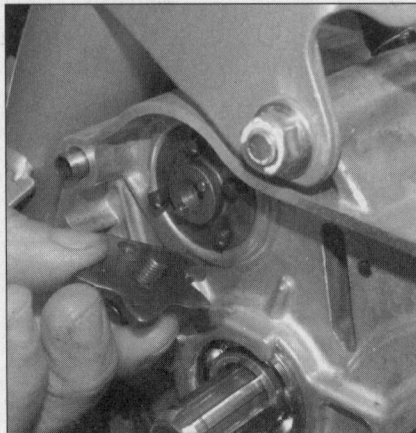

13.6b . . . and remove it from the shift drum

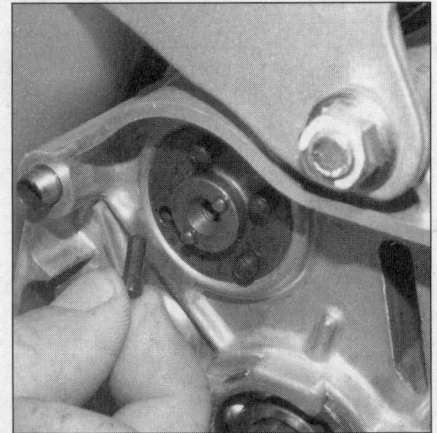

13.7 Remove the dowel pins from the shift drum

13.8 Check the return spring pin for wear, damage or looseness

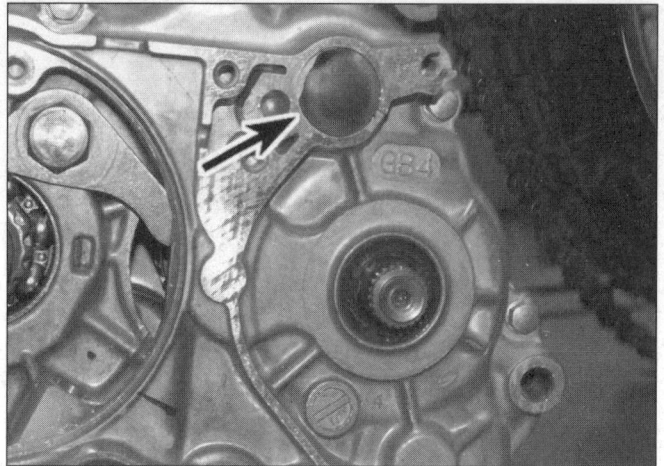

14.10a Remove the rubber cover from the shift drum bolt . . .

7   Remove the oil pump (see Section 12).
8   Remove the valve cover, rocker assembly and camshaft, cylinder head, cylinder, cam chain tensioner and piston (see Sections 6, 7, 8, 9, 10 and Chapter 2C).
9   Remove the snap-ring, retainer and spring from the kickstarter shaft (see Section 15).
10   Pry the rubber cap off of the shift drum bolt, then remove the bolt **(see illustrations)**.
11   If you haven't already done so, remove the crankcase breather hose and cam chain.
12   Check carefully to make sure there aren't any remaining components that attach the halves of the crankcase together.
13   Loosen the crankcase bolts evenly in two or three stages **(see illustration)**.
14   Carefully pry the crankcase apart and lift the right half off the left half **(see illustration)**. Don't pry against the mating surfaces or they'll develop leaks.
15   Locate the two crankcase dowels and remove the gasket **(see illustration 14.14)**.
16   Refer to Sections 16 and 17 and Chapter 2C for information on the internal components of the crankcase.

Reassembly

17   Remove all traces of old gasket and sealant from the crankcase mating surfaces with a sharpening stone or similar tool. Be careful not to let any fall into the case as this is done and be careful not to damage the mating surfaces.

14.10b . . . and remove the bolt and its washer

18   Check to make sure the two dowel pins are in place in their holes in the mating surface of the left crankcase half **(see illustration 14.14)**.
19   Pour some engine oil over the transmission and kickstarter gears, the right crankshaft bearing and the shift drum. Don't get any oil on the crankcase mating surface.
20   Install a new gasket on the crankcase mating surface.

14.13 Remove the crankcase bolts (arrows) . . .

14.14 . . . and lift the right case half off the left half and locate the dowels (arrows)

15.2 Mark the position of the kickstarter pedal, then remove its pinch bolt and take the pedal off

15.4a Note how the retainer spring is installed, then remove the snap-ring . . .

21   Carefully place the right crankcase half onto the left crankcase half. While doing this, make sure the transmission shafts, shift drum, crankshaft and kickstarter fit into their bearings in the right crankcase half.

22   Install the crankcase bolts and tighten them so they are just snug. Then tighten them evenly in two or three stages until they are secure, but don't overtighten them and strip out the threads.

23   Tighten the shift drum bolt to the torque listed in this Chapter's Specifications and install its rubber cap.

24   Turn the transmission mainshaft to make sure it turns freely. Also make sure the crankshaft turns freely.

25   The remainder of assembly is the reverse of disassembly.

---

15   Kickstarter - removal, inspection and installation

Removal

Pedal

Refer to illustration 15.2

1   The kickstarter pedal is accessible from outside the engine. The spindle spring and retainer can be reached by removing the right crankcase cover. The engine must be removed and the crankcase disassembled to remove the kickstarter mechanism.

2   Look for a punch mark on the end of the kickstarter spindle **(see illustration)**. If you can't see one, make your own to align with the slit in the pedal. Loosen the pinch bolt and slide the pedal off the spindle.

Spring and retainer

Refer to illustrations 15.4a and 15.4b

3   Remove the right crankcase cover (see Section 11).

4   Remove the snap-ring that secures the retainer to the kickstarter spindle **(see illustration)**. Pry the hooked end of the return spring off its resting place on the crankcase **(see illustration)**, then slide the retainer and spring off the spindle.

Ratchet mechanism

Refer to illustrations 15.6, 15.7a, 15.7b and 15.7c

5   Refer to Section 14 and separate the crankcase halves.

6   Remove the thrust washer from the kickstarter spindle and lift the spindle out of the crankcase **(see illustration)**.

7   Remove the snap-ring and take the spring and ratchet off the spindle **(see illustration)**. Remove the snap-ring behind the ratchet, then remove the thrust washer and pinion gear **(see illustration)**.

Inspection

8   Check all parts for wear or damage, paying special attention to the teeth on the ratchet and the matching teeth on the pinion gear. Replace worn or damaged parts.

9   Check for wear inside the pinion gear and on the outside of the spindle where the pinion rides. If either is worn, replace the worn part.

15.4b . . . pry the spring away from the crankcase and remove the retainer

15.6 Lift the spindle out of the case - on installation, align the spring tab with the case notch (lower arrow) and be sure the thrust washer is installed (upper arrow)

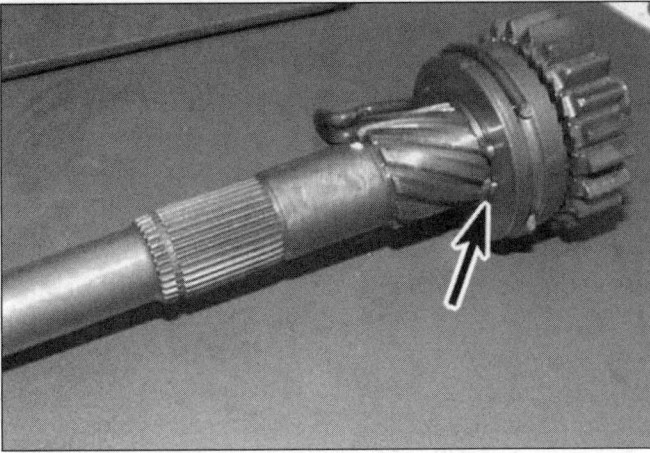

15.7a Remove the snap-ring (left arrow) and slide the starter ratchet with friction spring off the spindle (right arrow)

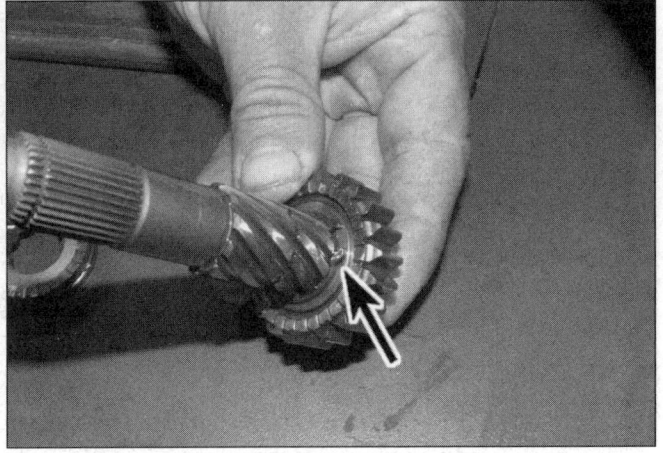

15.7b Remove a second snap-ring and the starter pinion gear

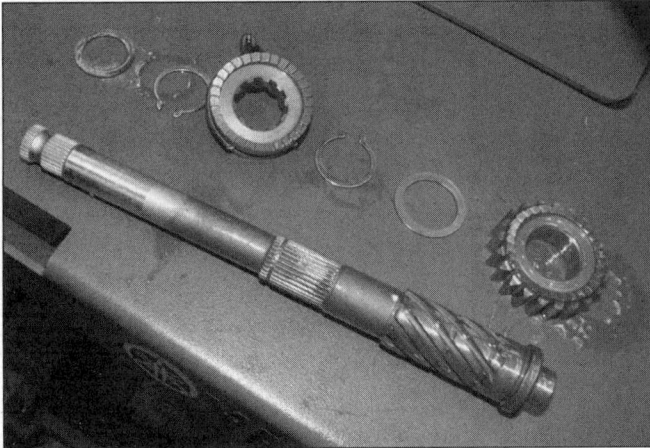

15.7c Kickstarter details

Installation

Ratchet mechanism

10   Apply moly-based grease to the splines on the spindle and ratchet. Install the pinion gear, snap-ring, thrust washer, ratchet, friction spring and remaining snap-ring on the spindle.

11   Install the spindle in the crankcase, making sure the end of the friction spring fits into the cast groove in the crankcase (see illustration 15.6).

12   Refer to Section 14 and reassemble the crankcase halves.

Spring and collar

13   Engage the spring with the slot in the retainer and slip them onto the spindle (see illustration 15.4b).

14   Temporarily install the kickstarter pedal on the spindle. Use it as handle, turning it counterclockwise, to align the spring ends and engage the retainer with its stop on the crankcase (see illustration 15.4a). Once they are positioned correctly, remove the pedal so the right crankcase cover can be installed.

Pedal

15   Slip the pedal onto the kickstarter spindle, aligning the marks. Install the pinch bolt and tighten it securely.

16   Shift drum, forks and transmission shafts - removal and installation

Removal

Refer to illustrations 16.2a and 16.2b

1   Refer to Section 14 and disassemble the crankcase halves.

2   Note how the forks fit in the gear grooves, then pull out the fork shaft and transmission shafts together (see illustrations).

3   Disengage the forks from the gears and separate the shafts.

16.2a Lift the shift drum and forks and both transmission shafts out of the crankcase as a unit

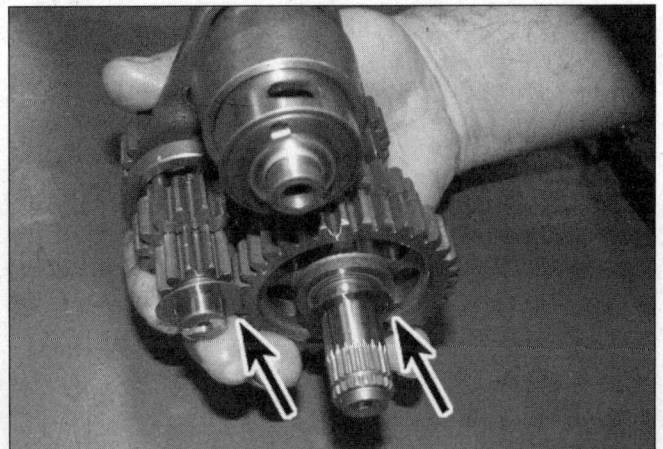

16.2b Remove the thrust washers (arrows) from the transmission shafts

17.1a The shift forks are secured to the shift drum by clips and dowels (arrows) (one dowel hidden)

17.1b Pull out each clip . . .

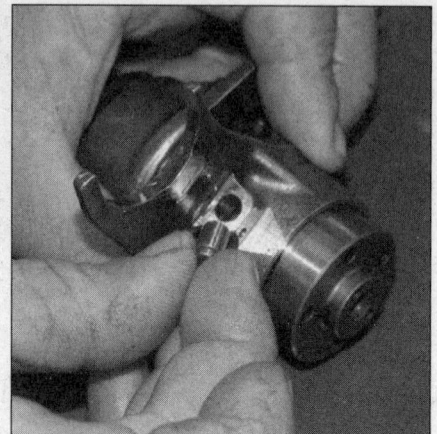

17.1c . . . and remove the dowel, then lift the fork off the shift drum

17.1d Shift drum and fork details

17.4a Transmission mainshaft details

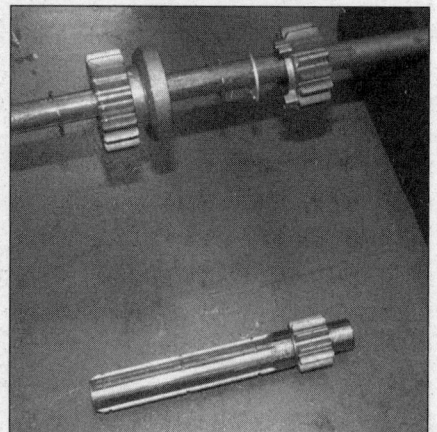

17.4b Transmission countershaft details

Installation

4   Installation is the reverse of the removal steps.

17 Shift drum, forks and transmission shafts - disassembly and reassembly

Note: *When disassembling the transmission shafts, place the parts on a long rod or thread a wire through them to keep them in order and facing in the proper direction.*

Shift drum and forks

Refer to illustrations 17.1a, 17.1b, 17.1c and 17.1d

1   Pull out the guide pin clips, then remove the guide pins and slip the forks off the drum **(see illustrations)**.
2   Refer to Chapter 2C for inspection procedures.
3   Assembly is the reverse of the disassembly steps.

Transmission shafts

Refer to illustrations 17.4a, 17.4b and 17.4c

4   Remove the snap-rings that hold the gears and thrust washers on the shafts and disassemble them. Place the parts in order on a rod or dowel so they can be reassembled in the correct order **(see illustrations)**.
5   Refer to Chapter 2C for inspection procedures.

6   Assembly is the reverse of the disassembly steps. Install the snap-rings with their rounded edges facing toward the component they secure (the sharp edge faces away from the component). Check that the gears mesh correctly before installing the shafts in the crankcase **(see illustration 17.4c)**.

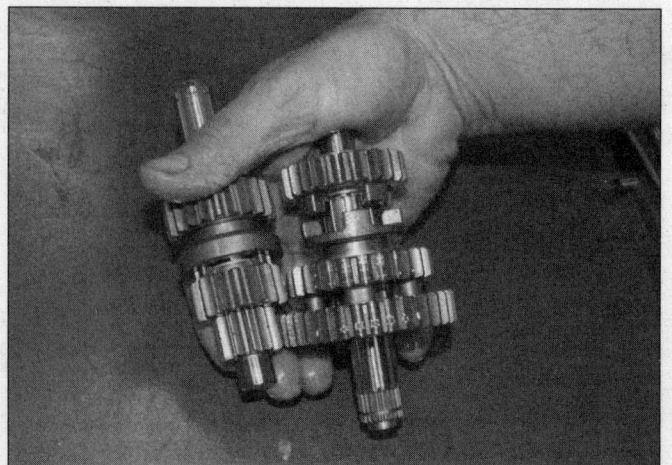

17.4c The shafts should mesh like this when installed

Chapter 2 Part C
General engine overhaul procedures

Contents

Specifications

Note: *Refer to Chapter 2 Part A or Part B for additional specifications.*

80 and 100 models

Cylinder compression
XR80R
  1993-1997 .... 98.1-1373 kPa (143-199 psi)
  1998 and later .... 1176 kPa (177 psi)
XR100R .... 1128 +/- 147 kPa (164 +/- 21 psi)
CRF80F, CRF100F .... 1177 kPa (171 psi)

Rocker arms
Rocker arm inside diameter
  Standard .... 10.000 to 10.015 mm (0.3937 to 0.3943 inch)
  Limit .... 10.1 mm (0.40 inch)
Rocker shaft outside diameter
  Standard .... 9.978 to 9.987 mm (0.3930 to 0.3931 inch)
  Limit .... 9.91 mm (0.39 inch)
Shaft-to-arm clearance
  Standard .... 0.013 to 0.037 mm (0.0005 to 0.0014 inch)
  Limit .... 0.08 mm (0.003 inch)

Camshaft
Lobe height
XR80R, CRF80F
  Intake
    Standard .... 28.017 to 28.197 mm (1.1030 to 1.1102 inches)
    Limit .... 27.95 mm (1.100 inches)
  Exhaust
    Standard .... 27.835 to 278.015 mm (1.0959 to 1.1030 inches)
    Limit .... 27.75 mm (1.092 inches)
XR100R, CRF100F
  Intake
    Standard (1985 through 1997) .... 27.840 to 28.020 mm (1.0960 to 1.1031 inch)
    Standard (1998 and later) .... 27.860 to 28.040 mm (1.0968 to 1.1039 inch)
  Exhaust
    Standard .... 27.776 to 27.950 mm (1.0935 to 1.1004 inches)
    Limit .... 27.70 mm (1.091 inches)

Camshaft (continued)

Journal diameter
  Standard .... 19.950 to 19.968 mm (0.7854 to 0.7861 inch)
  Limit... 19.90 mm (0.783 inch)
Bearing journal inside diameter
  Standard .... 20.008 to 20.063 mm (0.7877 to 0.7899 inch)
  Limit... 20.15 mm (0.793 inch)
Camshaft runout
  XR80R, XR10R .... Not specified
  CRF80F, CRF100F .... 0.03 mm (0.001 inch)

Cylinder head, valves and valve springs

Cylinder head warpage limit .... 0.10 mm (0.004 inch)
Valve stem runout... Not specified
Valve stem diameter
  Intake
    Standard .... 5.450 to 5.465 mm (0.2145 to 0.2151 inch)
    Limit .... 5.42 mm (0.213 inch)
  Exhaust
    Standard .... 5.430 to 5.445 mm (0.2145 to 0.2151 inch)
    Limit .... 5.40 mm (0.212 inch)
Valve guide inside diameter (intake and exhaust)
  Standard .... 5.475 to 5.485 mm (0.2155 to 0.2159 inch)
  Limit .... 5.50 mm (0.217 inch)
Stem to guide clearance
  Intake
    Standard .... 0.010 to 0.035 mm (0.0004 to 0.0013 inch)
    Limit .... 0.08 mm (0.003 inch)
  Exhaust
    Standard .... 0.030 to 0.055 mm (0.0012 to 0.0022 inch)
    Limit .... 0.10 mm (0.004 inch)
Valve seat width (intake and exhaust)
  Standard
    XR80R, XR100R .... 1.0 mm (0.04 inch)
    CRF80F, CRF100F .... 1.7 mm (0.06 inch)
  Limit
    XR80R, XR100R .... 1.5 mm (0.06 inch)
    CRF80F, CRF100F .... 2.1 mm (0.08 inch)
Valve spring free length
  Inner spring
    Standard .... 28.05 mm (1.10 inches)
    Limit .... 27.6 mm (1.09 inches)
  Outer spring
    Standard .... 34.80 mm (1.37 inches)
    Limit .... 33.7 mm (1.33 inches)

Cylinder

Bore diameter
  XR80R
    Standard .... 47.50 to 47.51 mm (1.8700 to 1.8704 inches)
    Limit .... 47.6 mm (1.874 inches)
  XR100R
    Standard .... 53.00 to 53.01 mm (2.0866 to 2.0870 inches)
    Limit .... 53.1 mm (2.091 inches)
Taper and out-of-round limits... 0.10 mm (0.004 inch)
Surface warpage limit .... 0.10 mm (0.004 inch)

Piston and rings

Piston diameter
  XR80R
    Standard .... 47.465 to 47.490 mm (1.8686 to 1.8697 inches)
    Limit .... 47.40 mm (1.866 inches)
  XR100R, CRF100F
    Standard (XR100R) .... 52.970 to 52.990 mm (2.0854 to 2.0862 inches)
    Standard (CRF100F) .... 52.960 to 52.990 mm (2.0850 to 2.0862 inches)
Piston diameter measuring point (above bottom of piston)
  XR80R .... 7 mm (0.28 inch)
  XR100R .... 10 mm (0.40 inch)

Piston-to-cylinder clearance
  Standard .... 0.01 to 0.04 mm (0.0004 to 0.0016 inch)
  Limit.. 0.10 mm (0.004 inch)
Piston pin bore in piston
  XR80R
    Standard .... 13.002 to 13.008 mm (0.5119 to 0.5121 inch)
    Limit.. 13.04 mm (0.513 inch)
  XR100R
    Standard .... 14.002 to 14.008 mm (0.5513 to 0.5515 inch)
    Limit.. 14.04 mm (0.553 inch)
Piston pin bore in connecting rod
  XR80R
    Standard .... 13.016 to 13.034 mm (0.5124 to 0.5131 inch)
    Limit.. 13.04 mm (0.513 inch)
  XR100R
    Standard .... 14.012 to 14.030 mm (0.5517 to 0.5524 inch)
    Limit.. 14.05 mm (0.553 inch)
Piston pin outer diameter
  XR80R
    Standard .... 12.994 to 13.000 mm (0.5116 to 0.5118 inch)
    Limit.. 12.96 mm (0.510 inch)
  XR100R
    Standard .... 13.994 to 14.000 mm (0.5509 to 0.5512 inch)
    Limit.. 13.96 mm (0.550 inch)
Piston pin-to-piston clearance
  Standard .... 0.002 to 0.014 mm (0.0001 to 0.0006 inch)
  Limit .... 0.02 mm (0.001 inch)
Piston pin-to-connecting rod clearance
  Standard .... 0.016 to 0.040 mm (0.0006 to 0.0016 inch)
  Limit.. 0.09 mm (0.003 inch)
Ring side clearance
  Top
    Standard (XR80R) .... 0.015 to 0.050 mm (0.0006 to 0.0020 inch)
    Standard (XR100R) .... 0.015 to 0.045 mm (0.0006 to 0.0018 inch)
    Limit.. 0.10 mm (0.004 inch)
  Second
    Standard .... 0.015 to 0.045 mm (0.0006 to 0.0018 inch)
    Limit.. 0.10 mm (0.004 inch)
  Oil (1985 through 1997 only)
    Standard .... 0.035 to 0.180 mm (0.0014 to 0.0071 inch)
    Limit.. Not specified
Ring end gap
  1985 through 1997
    Top and second
      Standard.. 0.15 to 0.35 mm (0.006 to 0.014 inch)
      Limit.. 0.5 mm (0.02 inch)
    Oil
      Standard.. 0.20 to 0.90 mm (0.01 to 0.03 inch)
      Limit.. 1.1 mm (0.043 inch)
  1998 and 1999 XR80R
    Top and second
      Standard.. 0.15 to 0.35 mm (0.006 to 0.014 inch)
      Limit.. 0.5 mm (0.02 inch)
    Oil
      Standard.. 0.3 to 0.9 mm (0.012 to 0.035 inch)
      Limit.. 1.1 mm (0.043 inch)
  1998 and 1999 XR100R
    Top and second
      Standard.. 0.15 to 0.45 mm (0.006 to 0.018 inch)
      Limit.. 0.5 mm (0.02 inch)
    Oil
      Standard.. 0.3 to 0.9 mm (0.012 to 0.035 inch)
      Limit.. 1.1 mm (0.043 inch)
  2000 and later XR100R, CRF100F
    Top and second
      Standard.. 0.05 to 0.20 mm (0.002 to 0.008 inch)
      Limit.. 0.4 mm (0.015 inch)
    Oil
      Standard.. 0.2 to 0.7 mm (0.008 to 0.027 inch)
      Limit.. 0.9 mm (0.035 inch)

Clutch

Clutch spring free length	
1985 through 1997	
Standard	26.1 mm (1.03 inches)
Limit	24.1 mm (0.95 inch)
1998 and later XR80R, CRF80F	
Standard	27.6 mm (1.09 inches)
Limit	25.5 mm (1.00 inch)
1998 and later XR100R, CRF100F	
Standard	31.9 mm (1.25 inches)
Limit	29.5 mm (1.16 inches)
Friction plate thickness	
1985 through 1997 all, 1998 through 2003 CR80R	
Standard	2.8 to 2.9 mm (0.110 to 0.114 inch)
Limit	2.5 mm (0.10 inch)
1998 through 2003 XR100R, all CRF100F	
Standard	2.92 to 3.08 mm (0.115 to 0.121 inch)
Limit	2.7 mm (0.11 inch)
CRF80F	
Standard	2.9 to 3.0 mm (0.114 to 0.118 inch)
Limit	2.5 mm (0.10 inch)
Friction and metal plate warpage limit	0.20 mm (0.008 inch)

Oil pump

Outer rotor to body clearance	
Standard	0.15 to 0.21 mm (0.006 to 0.008 inch)
Limit	0.40 mm (0.016 inch)
Inner to outer rotor clearance	
Standard	0.15 mm (0.006 inch) or less
Limit	0.20 mm (0.008 inch)
Side clearance (rotors to straightedge, gasket in place)	
1985 through 1997 models	
Standard	0.15 to 0.21 mm (0.006 to 0.008 inch)
Limit	0.25 mm (0.010 inch)
1998 and later	
Standard	0.02 to 0.07 mm (0.001 to 0.003 inch)
Limit	0.25 mm (0.010 inch)

Kickstarter

Shaft outside diameter	
Standard	17.959 to 17.980 mm (0.7070 to 0.7078 inch)
Limit	17.88 mm (0.704 inch)
Pinion gear inside diameter	
Standard	18.020 to 18.041 mm (0.7094 to 0.7103 inch)
Limit	18.06 mm (0.711 inch)

Shift drum and forks

Fork inside diameter	
Standard	12.000 to 12.018 mm (0.4724 to 0.4731 inch)
Limit	12.05 mm (0.474 inch)
Fork shaft outside diameter	
Standard	11.976 to 11.994 mm (0.4715 to 0.4722 inch)
Limit	11.96 mm (0.553 inch)
Fork ear thickness	
Standard	4.93 to 5.00 mm (0.194 to 0.197 inch)
Limit	4.70 mm (0.19 inch)
Shift drum groove width limit (1985 through 1987 only)	7.16 mm (0.282 inch)

Transmission

Gear inside diameters	
Mainshaft fourth and fifth	
Standard	17.016 to 17.034 mm (0.6699 to 0.6706 inch)
Limit	17.05 mm (0.671 inch)
Countershaft first (XR80R, CRF80F)	
Standard	17.022 to 17.033 mm (0.6701 to 0.6710 inch)
Limit	17.06 mm (0.672 inch)
Countershaft first (XR100R, CRF100F)	
Standard	20.622 to 20.643 mm (0.8119 to 0.8127 inch)
Limit	20.66 mm (0.814 inch)
Countershaft second	
Standard	19.520 to 19.541 mm (0.7685 to 0.7693 inch)
Limit	19.56 mm (0.770 inch)

Countershaft third (XR80R, CRF80F)
    Standard .... 17.016 to 17.034 mm (0.6699 to 0.6706 inch)
    Limit .... 17.05 mm (0.671 inch)
Countershaft third (XR100R, CRF100F)
    Standard .... 18.016 to 18.034 mm (0.7093 to 0.7100 inch)
    Limit .... 18.05 mm (0.711 inch)
Countershaft first gear collar diameter (XR100R only)
    Standard .... 20.559 to 20.580 mm (0.8094 to 0.8102 inch)
    Limit .... 20.54 mm (0.809 inch)
Shaft diameters
  Mainshaft
    Standard .... 16.966 to 16.984 mm (0.6680 to 0.6687 inch)
    Limit .... 16.95 mm (0.667 inch)
  Countershaft dimension A
    Standard .... 19.459 to 19.480 mm (0.7661 to 0.7669 inch)
    Limit .... 19.44 mm (0.765 inch)
  Countershaft dimension B (XR80R, CRF80F)
    Standard .... 16.966 to 16.984 mm (0.6680 to 0.6687 inch)
    Limit .... 16.95 mm (0.667 inch)
  Countershaft dimension B (XR100R, CRF100F)
    Standard .... 17.966 to 17.984 mm (0.7073 to 0.7080 inch)
    Limit .... 17.95 mm (0.707 inch)
  Countershaft dimension C
    Standard .... 16.966 to 16.984 mm (0.6680 to 0.6687 inch)
    Limit .... 16.95 mm (0.667 inch)

Crankshaft

Connecting rod side clearance
  Standard .... 0.10 to 0.35 mm (0.0039 to 0.0138 inch)
  Limit .... 0.60 mm (0.024 inch)
Connecting rod big end radial clearance
  Standard .... 0 to 0.008 mm (0 to 0.0003 inch)
  Limit .... 0.01 mm (0.0004 inch)
Runout limit
  Right end .... 0.085 mm (0.0033 inch)
  Left end .... 0.070 mm (0.0027 inch)

50 and 70 models

Cylinder compression
XR70R .... 1079 kPa (156 psi)
XR50R, CRF50F, CRF70F .... 981 to 1177 kPa (142 to 171)

Rocker arms
Rocker arm inside diameter
  Standard .... 10.000 to 10.015 mm (0.3937 to 0.3943 inch)
  Limit .... 10.1 mm (0.40 inch)
Rocker shaft outside diameter
  XR50R, XR70R
    Standard .... 9.978 to 9.987 mm (0.3928 to 0.3931 inch)
    Limit .... 9.91 mm (0.39 inch)
  CRF50F, CRF70F
    Standard .... 9.972 to 9.987 mm (0.3926 to 0.3931 inch)
    Limit .... 9.91 mm (0.39 inch)
Shaft-to-arm clearance
  XR50R, CRF50F, XR70R .... Not specified
  CRF70F
    Standard .... 0.013 to 0.043 mm (0.0005 to 0.0017 inch)
    Limit .... 0.08 mm (0.003 inch)

Camshaft
Lobe height
  XR50R, CRF50F
    Intake
      Standard .... 20.003 to 20.123 mm (0.7875 to 0.7922 inches)
      Limit .... 19.66 mm (0.774 inches)
    Exhaust
      Standard .... 19.994 to 20.114 mm (0.7872 to 0.7919 inches)
      Limit .... 19.65 mm (0.774 inches)

Camshaft (continued)

XR70R
Intake
Standard .... 27.945 mm (1.1002 inches)
Limit .... 27.55 mm (1.085 inches)
Exhaust
Standard .... 26.076 mm (1.0266 inches)
Limit .... 25.69 mm (1.011 inches)
CRF70F
Intake
Standard .... 27.885 to 28.005 mm (1.0978 to 1.1026 inches)
Limit .... 27.55 mm (1.085 inches)
Exhaust
Standard .... 26.016 to 26.136 mm (1.0242 to 1.0290 inches)
Limit .... 25.69 mm (1.011 inches)
Journal diameter .... Not applicable
Camshaft runout .... Not specified

Cylinder head, valves and valve springs

Cylinder head warpage limit .... 0.05 mm (0.002 inch)
Valve stem runout .... Not specified
Valve stem diameter
CRF50F
Intake
Standard .... 4.975 to 4.985 mm (0.1959 to 0.1963 inch)
Limit .... 4.92 mm (0.194 inch)
Exhaust
Standard .... 4.955 to 4.970 mm (0.1951 to 0.1957 inch)
Limit .... 4.92 mm (0.194 inch)
XR50R, XR70R (intake and exhaust)
Standard .... 4.970 to 4.985 mm (0.1957 to 0.1963 inch)
Limit .... 4.92 mm (0.194 inch)
CRF70F
Intake
Standard .... 4.975 to 4.990 mm (0.1959 to 0.1965 inch)
Limit .... 4.92 mm (0.194 inch)
Exhaust
Standard .... 4.955 to 4.970 mm (0.1951 to 0.1957 inch)
Limit .... 4.92 mm (0.194 inch)
Valve guide inside diameter (intake and exhaust)
Standard .... 5.000 to 5.012 mm (0.1969 to 0.1973 inch)
Limit .... 5.03 mm (0.198 inch)
Stem to guide clearance
XR50R, CRF50F
Intake
Standard .... 0.015 to 0.042 mm (0.0006 to 0.0017 inch)
Limit .... 0.08 mm (0.003 inch)
Exhaust
Standard .... 0.030 to 0.057 mm (0.0012 to 0.0022 inch)
Limit .... 0.10 mm (0.004 inch)
XR70R, CRF70F
Intake
Standard .... 0.010 to 0.037 mm (0.0004 to 0.0015 inch)
Limit .... 0.08 mm (0.003 inch)
Exhaust
Standard .... 0.030 to 0.057 mm (0.0012 to 0.0022 inch)
Limit .... 0.10 mm (0.004 inch)
Valve seat width (intake and exhaust)
Standard .... 1.0 to 1.3 mm (0.04 to 0.05 inch)
Limit .... 2.0 mm (0.08 inch)
Valve spring free length (50 models)
Standard .... 33.34 mm (1.313 inches)
Limit .... 31.8 mm (1.25 inches)
Valve spring free length (70 models)
Inner spring
Standard .... 32.78 mm (1.291 inches)
Limit .... 31.2 mm (1.23 inches)
Outer spring
Standard .... 35.55 mm (1.400 inches)
Limit .... 34.0 mm (1.34 inches)

Cylinder

Bore diameter
  XR50R, CRF50F
    Standard .... 39.005 to 39.015 mm (1.5356 to 1.5360 inches)
    Limit .... 30.05 mm (1.537 inches)
  XR70R, CRF70F
    Standard .... 47.005 to 47.015 mm (1.8506 to 1.8510 inches)
    Limit .... 47.05 mm (1.852 inches)
Taper and out-of-round limits.. 0.10 mm (0.004 inch)
Surface warpage limit... 0.05 mm (0.002 inch)

Piston and rings

Piston diameter
  XR50R, CRF50F
    Standard .... 38.975 to 38.995 mm (1.5344 to 1.5352 inches)
    Limit .... 38.90 mm (1.531 inches)
  XR70R, CRF70F
    Standard .... 46.980 to 46.995 mm (1.896 to 1.8502 inches)
Piston diameter measuring point (above bottom of piston)
  XR50R, CRF50F .... 8 mm (0.31 inch)
  XR70R, CRF70F .... 10 mm (0.4 inch)
Piston-to-cylinder clearance
  XR50R, CRF50F, XR70R
    Standard .... 0.01 to 0.04 mm (0.0004 to 0.0016 inch)
    Limit .... 0.15 mm (0.006 inch)
  CRF70F
    Standard .... 0.01 to 0.035 mm (0.0004 to 0.0014 inch)
    Limit .... 0.15 mm (0.006 inch)
Piston pin bore in piston
    Standard .... 13.002 to 13.008 mm (0.5119 to 0.5121 inch)
    Limit .... 13.06 mm (0.514 inch)
Piston pin bore in connecting rod
  XR50R, CRF50F
    Standard .... 13.016 to 13.034 mm (0.5124 to 0.5131 inch)
    Limit .... 13.08 mm (0.515 inch)
  XR70R, CRF70F
    Standard .... 13.013 to 13.043 mm (0.5123 to 0.5135 inch)
    Limit .... 13.10 mm (0.516 inch)
Piston pin outer diameter
    Standard.. 12.994 to 13.000 mm (0.5116 to 0.5118 inch)
    Limit .... 12.98 mm (0.511 inch)
Piston pin-to-piston clearance
    Standard.. 0.002 to 0.014 mm (0.0001 to 0.0006 inch)
    Limit .... 0.08 mm (0.003 inch)
Piston pin-to-connecting rod clearance
  XR50R, CRF50F
    Standard .... 0.016 to 0.040 mm (0.0006 to 0.0016 inch)
    Limit .... 0.12 mm (0.005 inch)
  CRF70F
    Standard .... 0.002 to 0.014 mm (0.0001 to 0.0006 inch)
    Limit .... 0.08 mm (0.003 inch)
Ring side clearance
  Top and second
    Standard .... 0.015 to 0.050 mm (0.0006 to 0.0020 inch)
    Limit .... 0.12 mm (0.005 inch)
  Oil .... Not specified
Ring end gap
  XR50R, CRF50F
    Top
      Standard.. 0.05 to 0.15 mm (0.002 to 0.006 inch)
      Limit... 0.5 mm (0.02 inch)
    Second
      Standard.. 0.05 to 0.20 (0.002 to 0.008 inch)
      Limit... 0.5 mm (0.02 inch)
    Oil
      Standard.. 0.30 to 0.90 mm (0.01 to 0.03 inch)
      Limit... 1.1 mm (0.043 inch)

Piston and rings (continued)
XR70R
    Top and second
        Standard.. 0.05 to 0.20 mm (0.006 to 0.014 inch)
        Limit... 0.5 mm (0.02 inch)
    Oil
        Standard.. 0.2 to 0.9 mm (0.008 to 0.035 inch)
        Limit... 1.1 mm (0.043 inch)
CRF70F
    Top and second
        Standard.. 0.10 to 0.25 mm (0.004 to 0.010 inch)
        Limit... 0.5 mm (0.02 inch)
    Oil
        Standard.. 0.20 to 0.80 mm (0.01 to 0.03 inch)
        Limit... 1.1 mm (0.043 inch)

Clutch
Clutch spring free length
    XR50R, CRF50F
        Standard .... 22.4 mm (0.88 inches)
        Limit .... 19.4 mm (0.76 inch)
    XR70R
        Standard .... 17.3 mm (0.68 inches)
        Limit .... 16.4 mm (0.65 inch)
    CRF70F
        Standard .... 19.1 mm (0.75 inches)
        Limit .... 17.9mm (0.70 inches)
Friction plate thickness
    XR50R, CRF50F, CRF70F (without tabs)
        Standard .... 2.52 to 2.68 mm (0.099 to 0.106 inch)
        Limit .... 2.3 mm (0. inch)
    XR50R, CRF50F, CRF70F (with tabs)
        Standard .... 3.32 to 3.48 mm (0.131 to 0.137 inch)
        Limit .... 3.0 mm (0.12 inch)
    XR70R (without tabs)
        Standard .... 2.52 to 2.68 mm (0.099 to 0.106 inch)
        Limit .... 2.3 mm (0. inch)
    XR70R (with tabs)
        Standard .... 3.35 to 3.45 mm (0.132 to 0.136 inch)
        Limit .... 3.0 mm (0.12 inch)
Friction and metal plate warpage limit................................ 0.20 mm (0.008 inch)
Center guide diameter (all models)
    Inside .... 16.988 to 17.006 mm (0.6688 to 0.6695 inch)
    Outside .... 20.930 to 20.950 mm (0.8249 to 0.8248 inch)
Crankshaft diameter at center guide .... 16.966 to 16.984 mm (0.6680 to 0.6687 inch)

Oil pump
XR50R, CRF50F
    Outer rotor to body clearance
        Standard .... 0.2 to 0.7 mm (0.001 to 0.003 inch)
        Limit .... 0.12 mm (0.005 inch)
    Inner to outer rotor clearance
        Standard .... 0.15 mm (0.006 inch) or less
        Limit .... 0.20 mm (0.008 inch)
    Side clearance (rotors to straightedge, gasket in place)
        Standard .... 0.10 to 0.15 mm (0.004 to 0.006 inch)
        Limit .... 0.20 mm (0.008 inch)
XR70R
    Outer rotor to body clearance
        Standard .... 0.10 to 0.21 mm (0.004 to 0.008 inch)
        Limit .... 0.27 mm (0.011 inch)
    Inner to outer rotor clearance
        Standard .... 0.15 mm (0.006 inch) or less
        Limit .... 0.20 mm (0.008 inch)
    Side clearance (rotors to straightedge, gasket in place)
        Standard .... 0.03 to 0.08 mm (0.001 to 0.003 inch)
        Limit .... 0.12 mm (0.005 inch)

CRF70F
   Outer rotor to body clearance
      Standard .... 0.15 to 0.21 mm (0.006 to 0.008 inch)
      Limit .... 0.20 mm (0.008 inch)
   Inner to outer rotor clearance
      Standard .... 0.15 mm (0.006 inch) or less
      Limit .... 0.20 mm (0.008 inch)
   Side clearance (rotors to straightedge, gasket in place)
      Standard .... 0.03 to 0.09 mm (0.001 to 0.002 inch)
      Limit .... 0.20 mm (0.008 inch)

Shift drum and forks
   Fork inside diameter
      Standard .... 34.075 to 34.100 mm (1.3415 to 1.3425 inch)
      Limit .... 34.14 mm (1.344 inch)
   Fork finger thickness
      Standard .... 4.86 to 4.94 mm (0.191 to 0.194 inch)
      Limit .... 4.60 mm (0.181 inch)
   Shift drum outside diameter
      Standard .... 33.950 to 33.975 mm (1.3366 to 1.3376 inch)
      Limit .... 33.93 mm (1.336 inch)

Transmission
Gear inside diameters
   Mainshaft second
      Standard .... 17.016 to 17.10 mm (0.6699 to 0.6706 inch)
      Limit .... 17.05 mm (0.671 inch)
   Countershaft first (1999 and earlier XR70R)
      Standard .... 20.020 to 20.053 mm (0.7882 to 0.7895 inch)
      Limit .... 20.10 mm (0.791 inch)
   Countershaft first (XR50R, CRF50F, CRF70F, 2000 and later XR70R)
      Standard .... 23.020 to 23.053 mm (0.9063 to 0.9076 inch)
      Limit .... 23.10 mm (0.909 inch)
   Countershaft third
      Standard .... 20.020 to 20.053 mm (0.7882 to 0.7895 inch)
      Limit .... 20.10 mm (0.791 inch)
Shaft diameters
   Mainshaft (at second gear) (1999 and earlier XR70R)
      Standard .... 16.983 to 16.986 mm (0.6686 to 0.6687 inch)
      Limit .... 16.95 mm (0.667 inch)
   Mainshaft (at second gear) (2000 and later XR70R)
      Standard .... 16.984 to 16.986 mm (0.6686 to 0.6687 inch)
      Limit .... 16.95 mm (0.667 inch)
   Mainshaft (at second gear) (XR50R, CRF50F, CRF70F)
      Standard .... 16.966 to 16.984 mm (0.6680 to 0.6687 inch)
      Limit .... 16.95 mm (0.667 inch)
Bushing diameters (countershaft first gear)
   1999 and earlier XR70R
      Inside
         Standard.. 17.000 to 17.018 mm (0.6693 to 0.6700 inch)
         Limit.. 17.08 mm (0.672 inch)
      Outside
         Standard.. 19.979 to 20.000 mm (0.9047 to 0.9055 inch)
         Limit.. 19.93 mm (0.785 inch)
   2000 and later XR70R, XR50R, CRF50F, CRF70F
      Inside
         Standard.. 20.000 to 20.021 mm (0.7874 to 0.7882 inch)
         Limit.. 20.08 mm (0.791 inch)
      Outside
         Standard.. 22.979 to 23.000 mm (0.9047 to 0.9055 inch)
         Limit.. 22.93 mm (0.903 inch)
Countershaft diameter (at countershaft first)
   1999 and earlier XR70R
      Standard .... 16.966 to 16.986 mm (0.6680 to 0.6687 inch)
      Limit .... 16.94 mm (0.667 inch)
   2000 and later XR70R, XR50R, CRF50F, CRF70F
      Standard .... 19.959 to 19.980 mm (0.7858 to 0.7866 inch)
      Limit .... 19.94 mm (0.785 inch)

Crankshaft

Connecting rod side clearance	
Standard	0.10 to 0.35 mm (0.0039 to 0.0138 inch)
Limit	0.60 mm (0.024 inch)
Connecting rod big end radial clearance	
Standard	0 to 0.012 mm (0 to 0.0005 inch)
Limit	0.05 mm (0.002 inch)
Runout limit	0.10 mm (0.004 inch)

1   General information

Included in this portion of Chapter 2 are general inspection and overhaul procedures. The information includes advice concerning preparation for an overhaul and the purchase of replacement parts, as well as inspection procedures which will tell you if a part must be conditioned or replaced.

The Specifications included in this Part are only those necessary for the inspection and overhaul procedures which follow. Refer to earlier parts of Chapter 2 for additional Specifications.

2   Major engine repair - general note

1   It is not always easy to determine when or if an engine should be completely overhauled, as a number of factors must be considered.
2   High mileage is not necessarily an indication that an overhaul is needed, while low mileage, on the other hand, does not preclude the need for an overhaul. Frequency of servicing is probably the single most important consideration. An engine that has regular and frequent oil and filter changes, as well as other required maintenance, will most likely give many miles of reliable service. Conversely, a neglected engine, or one which has not been broken in properly, may require an overhaul very early in its life.
3   Exhaust smoke and excessive oil consumption are both indications that piston rings and/or valve guides are in need of attention. Make sure oil leaks are not responsible before deciding that the rings and guides are bad. Refer to Chapter 1 and perform a cylinder compression check to determine for certain the nature and extent of the work required.
4   If the engine is making obvious knocking or rumbling noises, the connecting rod and/or main bearings are probably at fault.
5   Loss of power, rough running, excessive valve train noise and high fuel consumption rates may also point to the need for an overhaul, especially if they are all present at the same time. If a complete tune-up does not remedy the situation, major mechanical work is the only solution.
6   An engine overhaul generally involves restoring the internal parts to the specifications of a new engine. During an overhaul the piston rings are replaced and the cylinder walls are bored and/or honed. If a rebore is done, then a new piston is also required. The crankshaft and connecting rod are permanently assembled, so if one of these components needs to be replaced both must be. Generally the valves are serviced as well, since they are usually in less than perfect condition at this point. While the engine is being overhauled, other components such as the carburetor and the starter motor can be rebuilt also. The end result should be a like-new engine that will give as many trouble-free miles as the original.
7   Before beginning the engine overhaul, read through all of the related procedures to familiarize yourself with the scope and requirements of the job. Overhauling an engine is not all that difficult, but it is time consuming. Plan on the vehicle being tied up for a minimum of two (2) weeks. Check on the availability of parts and make sure that any necessary special tools, equipment and supplies are obtained in advance.
8   Most work can be done with typical shop hand tools, although a number of precision measuring tools are required for inspecting parts to determine if they must be replaced. Often a dealer service department

3.5 A compression gauge with a threaded fitting for the spark plug hole is preferred over the type that requires hand pressure to maintain the seal

or repair shop will handle the inspection of parts and offer advice concerning reconditioning and replacement. As a general rule, time is the primary cost of an overhaul so it doesn't pay to install worn or substandard parts.
9   As a final note, to ensure maximum life and minimum trouble from a rebuilt engine, everything must be assembled with care in a spotlessly clean environment.

3   Cylinder compression - check

Refer to illustration 3.5
1   Among other things, poor engine performance may be caused by leaking valves, incorrect valve clearances, a leaking head gasket, or worn piston, rings and/or cylinder wall. A cylinder compression check will help pinpoint these conditions and can also indicate the presence of excessive carbon deposits in the cylinder head.
2   The only tools required are a compression gauge and a spark plug wrench. Depending on the outcome of the initial test, a squirt-type oil can may also be needed.
3   Start the engine and allow it to reach normal operating temperature, then remove the spark plug (see Chapter 1, if necessary). Work carefully - don't strip the spark plug hole threads and don't burn your hands.
4   Disable the ignition by disconnecting the primary (low tension) wires from the coil (see Chapter 4). Be sure to mark the locations of the wires before detaching them.
5   Install the compression gauge in the spark plug hole **(see illustration)**. Hold or block the throttle wide open.
6   Crank the engine over a minimum of four or five revolutions (or until the gauge reading stops increasing) and observe the initial movement of the compression gauge needle as well as the final total gauge reading. Compare the results to the value listed in this Chapter's Specifications.

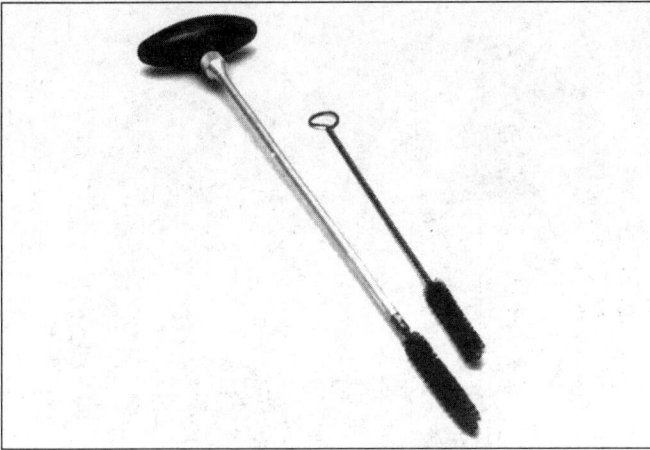

4.2 A selection of brushes is required for cleaning holes and passages in the engine components

4.3 An engine stand can be made from short lengths of lumber and lag bolts or nails

7 If the compression built up quickly and evenly to the specified amount, you can assume the engine upper end is in reasonably good mechanical condition. Worn or sticking piston rings and worn cylinders will produce very little initial movement of the gauge needle, but compression will tend to build up gradually as the engine spins over. Valve and valve seat leakage, or head gasket leakage, is indicated by low initial compression which does not tend to build up.

8 To further confirm your findings, add a small amount of engine oil to the cylinder by inserting the nozzle of a squirt-type oil can through the spark plug hole. The oil will tend to seal the piston rings if they are leaking.

9 If the compression increases significantly after the addition of the oil, the piston rings and/or cylinder are definitely worn. If the compression does not increase, the pressure is leaking past the valves or the head gasket. Leakage past the valves may be due to insufficient valve clearances, burned, warped or cracked valves or valve seats or valves that are hanging up in the guides.

10 If compression readings are considerably higher than specified, the combustion chamber is probably coated with excessive carbon deposits. It is possible (but not very likely) for carbon deposits to raise the compression enough to compensate for the effects of leakage past rings or valves. Refer to Chapter 2A or 2B, remove the cylinder head and carefully decarbonize the combustion chamber.

4 Engine disassembly and reassembly - general information

Refer to illustrations 4.2 and 4.3

1 Before disassembling the engine, clean the exterior with a degreaser and rinse it with water. A clean engine will make the job easier and prevent the possibility of getting dirt into the internal areas of the engine.

2 In addition to the precision measuring tools mentioned earlier, you will need a torque wrench, a valve spring compressor, oil gallery brushes **(see illustration)**, a piston ring removal and installation tool and a piston ring compressor. Some new, clean engine oil of the correct grade and type, some engine assembly lube (or moly-based grease) and a tube of RTV (silicone) sealant will also be required.

3 An engine support stand made from short lengths of 2 x 4's bolted together will facilitate the disassembly and reassembly procedures **(see illustration)**. If you have an automotive-type engine stand, an adapter plate can be made from a piece of plate, some angle iron and some nuts and bolts.

4 When disassembling the engine, keep "mated" parts together (including gears, drum shifter pawls, etc.) that have been in contact with each other during engine operation. These "mated" parts must be reused or replaced as an assembly.

5 Engine/transmission disassembly should be done in the following general order with reference to the appropriate Sections.

Remove the valve cover and rocker assembly
Remove the cam chain tensioner and camshaft
Remove the cylinder head
Remove the cylinder
Remove the piston
Remove the clutch
Remove the oil pump
Remove the external shift mechanism
Remove the alternator rotor
Separate the crankcase halves
Remove the shift drum/forks
Remove the transmission shafts/gears
Remove the crankshaft and connecting rod

6 Reassembly is accomplished by reversing the general disassembly sequence.

5 Rocker arms and camshaft - inspection

Refer to illustrations 5.1, 5.2, 5.4, 5.5a and 5.5b

1 Check the rocker arms for wear at the cam contact surfaces and at the tips of the valve adjusting screws **(see illustration)**. Try to twist the rocker arms from side-to-side on the shafts. If they're loose on the shafts or if there's visible wear, remove them as described below.

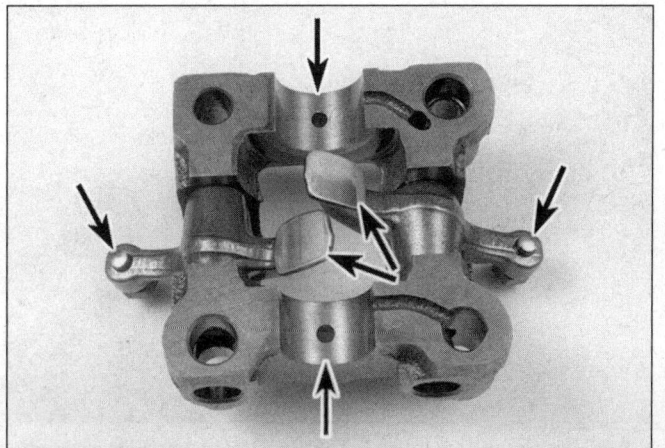

5.1 Inspect the valve adjuster tips, the camshaft bearing surfaces and the camshaft contact surfaces on the rocker arms (arrows)

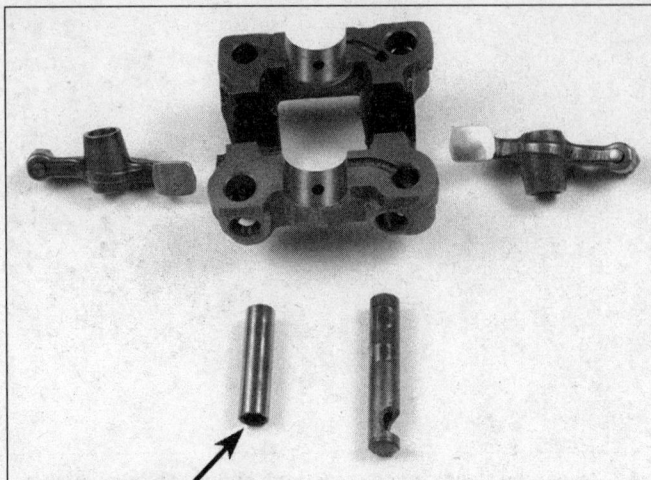

5.2 Insert a bolt into the threaded end of the exhaust rocker shaft to pull it out (arrow); be sure to face the threaded end out on reassembly

5.4 Inspect the camshaft bearing surfaces in the cylinder head

2   Thread an 8mm bolt into the exhaust rocker shaft and pull it out of the rocker assembly **(see illustration)**. **Note:** *On 50 models, the fuel tank front mounting bolt is the correct size to use for this.* Push the intake rocker shaft out and remove the rocker arms.

3   Measure the outer diameter of each rocker shaft and the inner diameter of the rocker arms with a micrometer and compare the measurements to the values listed in this Chapter's Specifications. If rocker arm-to-shaft clearance is excessive, replace the rocker arm or shaft, whichever is worn.

4   Inspect the cam bearing surfaces of the head and the rocker assembly **(see illustration 5.1 and the accompanying illustration)**. Look for score marks, deep scratches and evidence of spalling (a pitted appearance).

5   Check the camshaft lobes for heat discoloration (blue appearance), score marks, chipped areas, flat spots and spalling **(see illustration)**. Measure the height of each lobe with a micrometer **(see illustration)** and compare the results to the minimum lobe height listed in this Chapter's Specifications. If damage is noted or wear is excessive, the camshaft must be replaced. **Note:** *Before replacing camshafts or the cylinder head because of damage, check with local machine shops specializing in motorcycle engine work. In the case of the camshaft, it may be possible for cam lobes to be welded, reground and hardened, at a cost far lower than that of a new camshaft. If the bearing surfaces in*

the cylinder head or cover are damaged, it may be possible for them to be bored out to accept bearing inserts. Due to the cost of a new cylinder head it is recommended that all options be explored before condemning it as trash! Also, be sure to check the condition of the rocker arms, as described above.

6   Except in cases of oil starvation, the camshaft chain wears very little. If the chain has stretched excessively, which makes it difficult to maintain proper tension, replace it with a new one. To remove the chain from the crankshaft sprocket, it's necessary to disassemble the crankcase halves (see Chapter 2A or 2B).

7   Check the sprocket for wear, cracks and other damage, replacing it if necessary. If the sprocket is worn, the chain is also worn, and possibly the sprocket on the crankshaft. If wear this severe is apparent, the entire engine should be disassembled for inspection.

8   On 80 and 100 models, check the chain guides for wear or damage. If they are worn or damaged, replace them. To remove the exhaust side (front) chain guide, you'll need to remove the cylinder head. To remove the intake side guide, you'll need to remove the cylinder.

6   Valves/valve seats/valve guides - servicing

1   Because of the complex nature of this job and the special tools and equipment required, servicing of the valves, the valve seats and the valve

5.5a Check the cam lobes for wear - here's a good example of damage which will require replacement (or repair) of the camshaft

5.5b Measure the height of the cam lobes with a micrometer

7.4 Clean all gasket material from the cylinder mating surface

7.7a Install a valve spring compressor and compress the valve springs, then remove the keepers, the valve spring retainer, springs, spring seat and valve

guides (commonly known as a valve job) is best left to a professional.

2   The home mechanic can, however, remove and disassemble the head, do the initial cleaning and inspection, then reassemble and deliver the head to a dealer service department or properly equipped repair shop for the actual valve servicing. Refer to Section 7 for those procedures.

3   The dealer service department will remove the valves and springs, recondition or replace the valves and valve seats, replace the valve guides, check and replace the valve springs, spring retainers and keepers (as necessary), replace the valve seals with new ones and reassemble the valve components.

4   After the valve job has been performed, the head will be in like-new condition. When the head is returned, be sure to clean it again very thoroughly before installation on the engine to remove any metal particles or abrasive grit that may still be present from the valve service operations. Use compressed air, if available, to blow out all the holes and passages.

7   Cylinder head and valves - disassembly, inspection and reassembly

1   As mentioned in the previous Section, valve servicing and valve guide replacement should be left to a dealer service department or vehicle repair shop. However, disassembly, cleaning and inspection of the valves and related components can be done (if the necessary special tools are available) by the home mechanic. This way no expense is incurred if the inspection reveals that service work is not required at this time.

2   To properly disassemble the valve components without the risk of damaging them, a valve spring compressor is absolutely necessary. If the special tool is not available, have a dealer service department or vehicle repair shop handle the entire process of disassembly, inspection, service or repair (if required) and reassembly of the valves.

Disassembly

Refer to illustrations 7.4, 7.7a and 7.7b

3   Remove the intake manifold from the cylinder head (see Chapter 3).

4   Before the valves are removed, scrape away any traces of gasket material from the head gasket sealing surface **(see illustration)**. Work slowly and do not nick or gouge the soft aluminum of the head. Gasket removing solvents, which work very well, are available at most motorcycle shops and auto parts stores.

5   Carefully scrape all carbon deposits out of the combustion chamber area. A hand held wire brush or a piece of fine emery cloth can be used once most of the deposits have been scraped away. Do not use a

wire brush mounted in a drill motor, or one with extremely stiff bristles, as the head material is soft and may be eroded away or scratched by the wire brush.

6   Before proceeding, arrange to label and store the valves along with their related components so they can be kept separate and reinstalled in the same valve guides they are removed from (plastic bags work well for this).

7   Compress the valve spring(s) on the first valve with a spring compressor, then remove the keepers and the retainer from the valve assembly **(see illustration)**. Do not compress the spring(s) any more than is absolutely necessary. Carefully release the valve spring compressor and remove the spring(s), spring seat and valve from the head. If the valve binds in the guide (won't pull through), push it back into the head and deburr the area around the keeper groove with a very fine file or whetstone **(see illustration)**.

8   Repeat the procedure for the remaining valves. Remember to keep the parts for each valve together so they can be reinstalled in the same location.

9   Once the valves have been removed and labeled, pull off the valve stem seals with pliers and discard them (the old seals should never be reused).

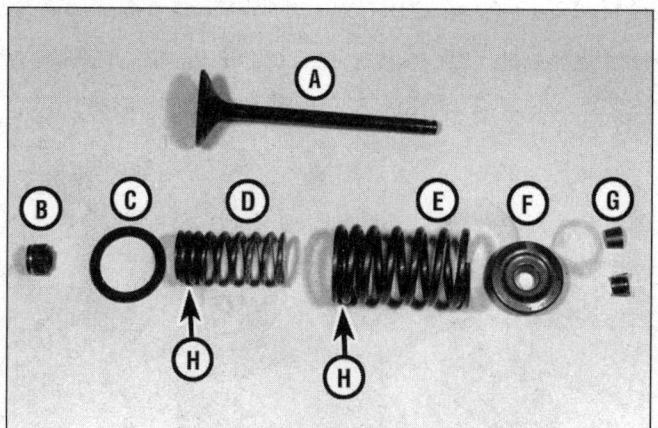

7.7b Valve and related components

A Valve stem	E Outer valve spring
B Oil seal	F Valve spring retainer
C Spring seat	G Keepers
D Inner valve spring	H Tightly wound coils

7.14 Check the gasket surface for flatness with a straightedge and feeler gauge

7.15 Measuring valve seat width

10   Next, clean the cylinder head with solvent and dry it thoroughly. Compressed air will speed the drying process and ensure that all holes and recessed areas are clean.

11   Clean all of the valve springs, keepers, retainers and spring seats with solvent and dry them thoroughly. Do the parts from one valve at a time so that no mixing of parts between valves occurs.

12   Scrape off any deposits that may have formed on the valve, then use a motorized wire brush to remove deposits from the valve heads and stems. Again, make sure the valves do not get mixed up.

Inspection

Refer to illustrations 7.14, 7.15, 7.16, 7.17, 7.18, 7.19a and 7.19b

13   Inspect the head very carefully for cracks and other damage. If cracks are found, a new head will be required. Check the cam bearing surfaces for wear and evidence of seizure. Check the camshaft for wear as well (see Section 5).

14   Using a precision straightedge and a feeler gauge, check the head gasket mating surface for warpage. Lay the straightedge lengthwise, across the head and diagonally (corner-to-corner), intersecting the head bolt holes, and try to slip a feeler gauge under it, on either side of the combustion chamber **(see illustration)**. The feeler gauge thickness should be the same as the cylinder head warpage limit listed in this Chapter's Specifications. If the feeler gauge can be inserted between the head and the straightedge, the head is warped and must either be machined or, if warpage is excessive, replaced with a new one.

15   Examine the valve seats in each of the combustion chambers. If

they are pitted, cracked or burned, the head will require valve service that is beyond the scope of the home mechanic. Measure the valve seat width **(see illustration)** and compare it to this Chapter's Specifications. If it is not within the specified range, or if it varies around its circumference, valve service work is required.

16   Clean the valve guides to remove any carbon buildup, then measure the inside diameters of the guides (at both ends and the center of the guide) with a small hole gauge and a micrometer **(see illustration)**. Record the measurements for future reference. The guides are measured at the ends and at the center to determine if they are worn in a bell-mouth pattern (more wear at the ends). If they are, guide replacement is an absolute must.

17   Carefully inspect each valve face for cracks, pits and burned spots. Check the valve stem and the keeper groove area for cracks **(see illustration)**. Rotate the valve and check for any obvious indication that it is bent. Check the end of the stem for pitting and excessive wear. The presence of any of the above conditions indicates the need for valve servicing.

18   Measure the valve stem diameter **(see illustration)**. If the diameter is less than listed in this Chapter's Specifications, the valves will have to be replaced with new ones. Also check the valve stem for bending. Set the valve in a V-block with a dial indicator touching the middle of the stem. Rotate the valve and look for a reading on the gauge (which indicates a bent stem). If the stem is bent, replace the valve.

19   Check the end of each valve spring for wear and pitting. Measure the free length **(see illustration)** and compare it to this Chapter's Spec-

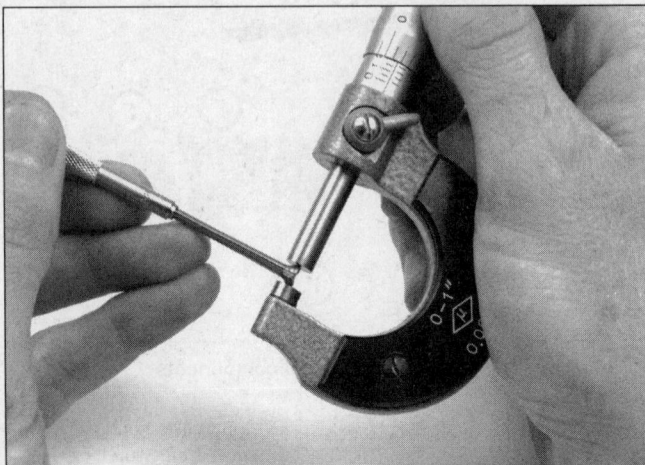

7.16 Measure the valve guide inside diameter with a hole gauge, then measure the gauge with a micrometer

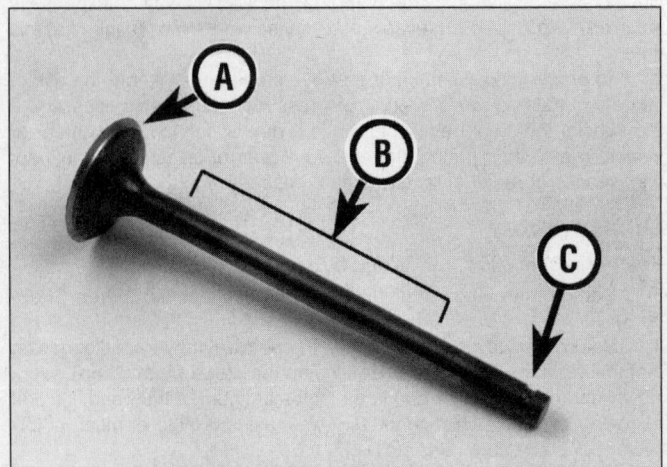

7.17 Check the valve face (A), stem (B) and keeper groove (C) for wear and damage

7.18 Measuring valve stem diameter

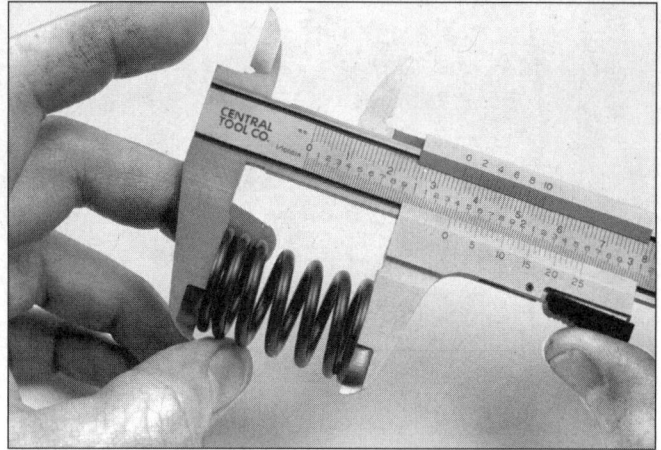

7.19a Measuring the free length of a valve spring

ifications. Any springs that are shorter than specified have sagged and should not be reused. Stand the spring on a flat surface and check it for squareness **(see illustration)**.

20   Check the spring retainers and keepers for obvious wear and cracks. Any questionable parts should not be reused, as extensive damage will occur in the event of failure during engine operation.

21   If the inspection indicates that no service work is required, the valve components can be reinstalled in the head.

Reassembly

Refer to illustrations 7.23, 7.24a, 7.24b, 7.26 and 7.27

22   If the valve seats have been ground, the valves and seats should be lapped before installing the valves in the head to ensure a positive seal between the valves and seats. This procedure requires coarse and fine valve lapping compound (available at auto parts stores) and a valve lapping tool. If a lapping tool is not available, a piece of rubber or plastic hose can be slipped over the valve stem (after the valve has been installed in the guide) and used to turn the valve.

23   Apply a small amount of coarse lapping compound to the valve face **(see illustration)**, then slip the valve into the guide. **Note:** *Make sure the valve is installed in the correct guide and be careful not to get any lapping compound on the valve stem.*

24   Attach the lapping tool (or hose) to the valve and rotate the tool between the palms of your hands. Use a back-and-forth motion rather than a circular motion. Lift the valve off the seat and turn it at regular intervals to distribute the lapping compound properly. Continue the lapping procedure until the valve face and seat contact area is of uniform

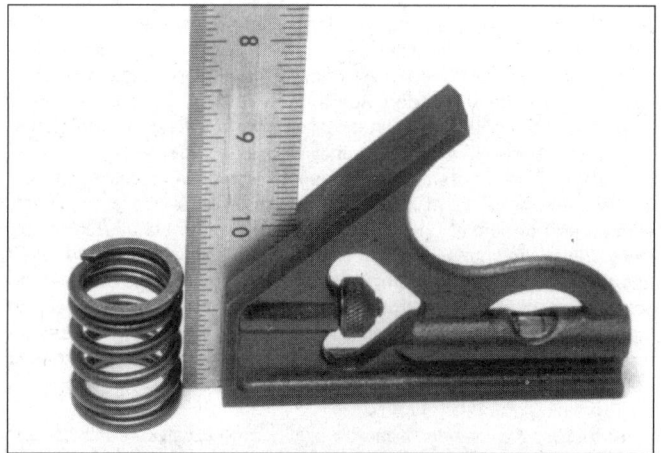

7.19b Checking the valve springs for squareness

width and unbroken around the entire circumference of the valve face and seat **(see illustrations)**. Once this is accomplished, lap the valves again with fine lapping compound.

25   Carefully remove the valve from the guide and wipe off all traces of lapping compound. Use solvent to clean the valve and wipe the seat area thoroughly with a solvent soaked cloth. Repeat the procedure for the remaining valves.

7.23 Apply the lapping compound very sparingly, in small dabs, to the valve face only

7.24a After lapping, the valve face should exhibit a uniform, unbroken contact pattern (arrow) . . .

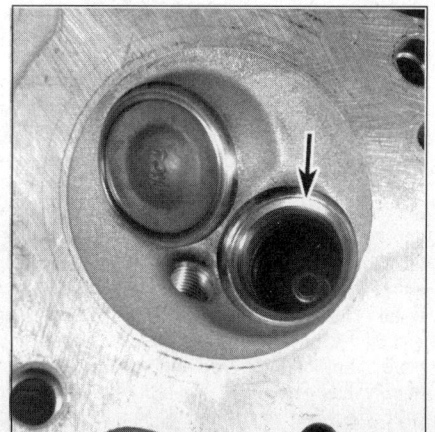

7.24b . . . and the seat (arrow) should be the specified width with a smooth, unbroken appearance

7.26 Push the oil seal onto the valve guide (arrow)

7.27 A small dab of grease will help hold the keepers in place on the valve while the spring compressor is released

26   Lay the spring seat in place in the cylinder head, then install a new valve stem seal on both guides (except XR100R) or just on the exhaust valve guide (XR100R) **(see illustration)**. Use an appropriate size deep socket to push the seals into place until they are properly seated. Don't twist or cock them, or they will not seal properly against the valve stems. Also, don't remove them again or they will be damaged.

27   Coat the valve stems with assembly lube or moly-based grease, then install one of them into its guide. Next, install the spring seat, springs and retainers, compress the springs and install the keepers. **Note:** *Install the springs with the tightly wound coils at the bottom (next to the spring seat).* When compressing the springs with the valve spring compressor, depress them only as far as is absolutely necessary to slip the keepers into place. Apply a small amount of grease to the keepers **(see illustration)** to help hold them in place as the pressure is released from the springs. Make certain that the keepers are securely locked in their retaining grooves.

28   Support the cylinder head on blocks so the valves can't contact the workbench top, then very gently tap each of the valve stems with a soft-faced hammer. This will help seat the keepers in their grooves.

29   Once all of the valves have been installed in the head, check for proper valve sealing by pouring a small amount of solvent into each of the valve ports. If the solvent leaks past the valve(s) into the combustion chamber area, disassemble the valve(s) and repeat the lapping procedure, then reinstall the valve(s) and repeat the check. Repeat the procedure until a satisfactory seal is obtained.

8   Cylinder - inspection

Refer to illustration 8.1

Caution: *Don't attempt to separate the liner from the cylinder.*

1   Check the top surface of the cylinder for warpage, using the same method as for the cylinder head (see Section 11). Measure along the sides and diagonally across the stud holes **(see illustration)**.

2   Check the cylinder walls carefully for scratches and score marks.

3   Using the appropriate precision measuring tools, check the cylinder's diameter at the top, center and bottom of the cylinder bore, parallel to the crankshaft axis. Next, measure the cylinder's diameter at the same three locations across the crankshaft axis. Compare the results to this Chapter's Specifications. If the cylinder walls are tapered, out-of-round, worn beyond the specified limits, or badly scuffed or scored, have the cylinder rebored and honed by a dealer service department or a motorcycle repair shop. If a rebore is done, an oversize piston and rings will be required as well. **Note:** *Honda supplies pistons in two oversizes.*

4   As an alternative, if the precision measuring tools are not available, a dealer service department or repair shop will make the measurements and offer advice concerning servicing of the cylinder.

5   If it's in reasonably good condition and not worn to the outside

of the limits, and if the piston-to-cylinder clearance can be maintained properly (see Section 9), then the cylinder does not have to be rebored; honing is all that is necessary.

6   To perform the honing operation you will need the proper size flexible hone with fine stones as shown in *Maintenance techniques, tools and working facilities* at the front of this book, or a "bottle brush" type hone, plenty of light oil or honing oil, some shop towels and an electric drill motor. Hold the cylinder in a vise (cushioned with soft jaws or wood blocks) when performing the honing operation. Mount the hone in the drill motor, compress the stones and slip the hone into the cylinder. Lubricate the cylinder thoroughly, turn on the drill and move the hone up and down in the cylinder at a pace which will produce a fine crosshatch pattern on the cylinder wall with the crosshatch lines intersecting at approximately a 60-degree angle. Be sure to use plenty of lubricant and do not take off any more material than is absolutely necessary to produce the desired effect. Do not withdraw the hone from the cylinder while it is running. Instead, shut off the drill and continue moving the hone up and down in the cylinder until it comes to a complete stop, then compress the stones and withdraw the hone. Wipe the oil out of the cylinder. Remember, do not remove too much material from the cylinder wall. If you do not have the tools, or do not desire to perform the honing operation, a dealer service department or motorcycle repair shop will generally do it for a reasonable fee.

7   Next, the cylinder must be thoroughly washed with warm soapy water to remove all traces of the abrasive grit produced during the honing operation. Be sure to run a brush through the bolt holes and flush them with running water. After rinsing, dry the cylinder thoroughly and apply a coat of light, rust-preventative oil to all machined surfaces.

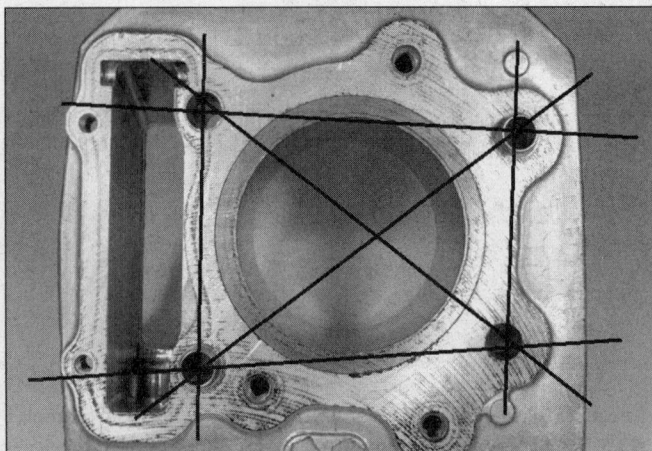

8.1 Check the cylinder top surface for warpage in the directions shown

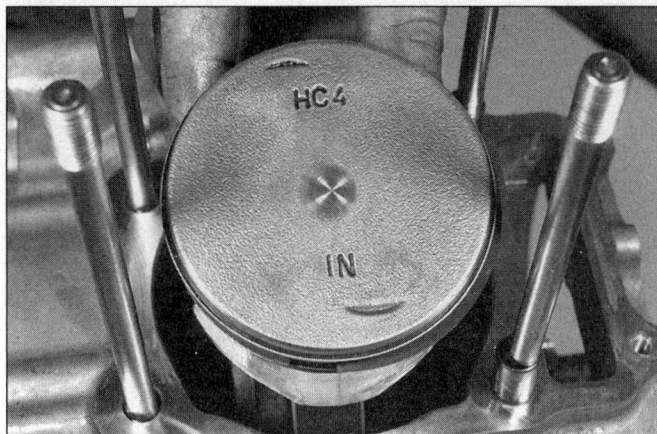

9.3a The IN mark on top of the piston faces the intake (rear) side of the engine

9.3b Wear eye protection and pry the circlip out of its groove with a pointed tool

9 Piston - removal, inspection and installation

1   The piston is attached to the connecting rod with a piston pin that is a slip fit in the piston and rod.

2   Before removing the piston from the rod, stuff a clean shop towel into the crankcase hole, around the connecting rod. This will prevent the circlips from falling into the crankcase if they are inadvertently dropped.

Removal

Refer to illustrations 9.3a, 9.3b, 9.4a and 9.4b

3   The piston should have an IN mark on its crown that goes toward the intake (rear) side of the engine **(see illustration)**. If this mark is not visible due to carbon buildup, scribe an arrow into the piston crown before removal. Support the piston and pry the circlip out with a pointed tool **(see illustration)**.

4   Push the piston pin out from the opposite end to free the piston from the rod **(see illustration)**. You may have to deburr the area around the groove to enable the pin to slide out (use a triangular file for this procedure). If the pin won't come out, you can fabricate a piston pin removal tool from a long bolt, a nut, a piece of tubing and washers **(see illustration)**.

Inspection

Refer to illustrations 9.6, 9.13, 9.14 and 9.16

5   Before the inspection process can be carried out, the piston must be cleaned and the old piston rings removed.

6   Using a piston ring removal and installation tool, carefully remove

9.4a Push the piston pin partway out, then pull it the rest of the way

the rings from the piston **(see illustration)**. Do not nick or gouge the piston in the process.

7   Scrape all traces of carbon from the top of the piston. A hand-held wire brush or a piece of fine emery cloth can be used once the majority of the deposits have been scraped away. Do not, under any circumstances, use a wire brush mounted in a drill motor to remove deposits from the piston; the piston material is soft and will be eroded away by the wire brush.

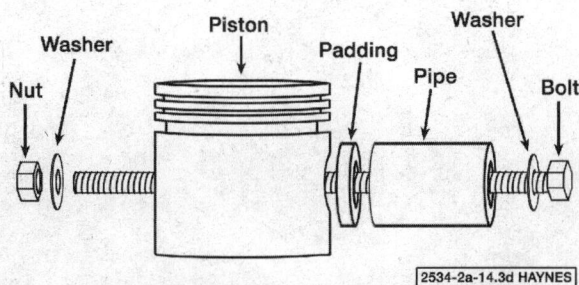

Nut · Washer · Piston · Padding · Pipe · Washer · Bolt

2534-2a-14.3d HAYNES

9.4b The piston pin should come out with hand pressure - if it doesn't, this removal tool can be fabricated from readily available parts

9.6 Remove the piston rings with a ring removal and installation tool

9.13 Measure the piston ring-to-groove clearance with a feeler gauge

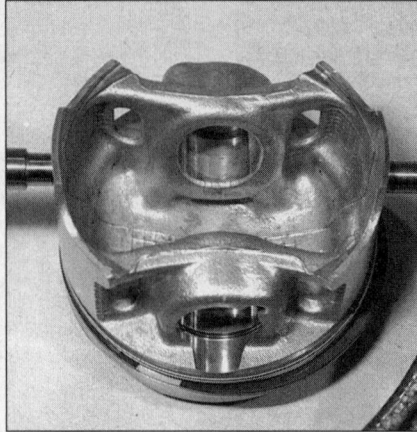

9.14 Measure the piston diameter with a micrometer

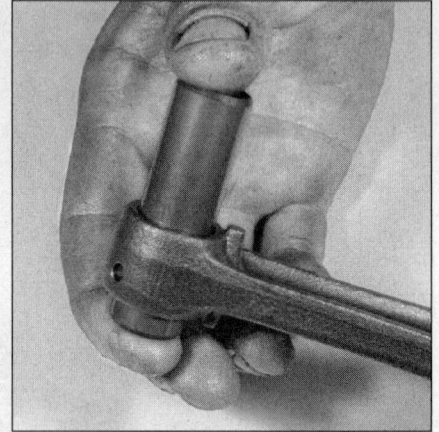

9.16 Slip the piston pin into the rod and try to rock it back-and-forth to check for looseness

8   Use a piston ring groove cleaning tool to remove any carbon deposits from the ring grooves. If a tool is not available, a piece broken off the old ring will do the job. Be very careful to remove only the carbon deposits. Do not remove any metal and do not nick or gouge the sides of the ring grooves.

9   Once the deposits have been removed, clean the piston with solvent and dry them thoroughly. Make sure the oil return holes below the oil ring grooves are clear.

10   If the piston is not damaged or worn excessively and if the cylinder is not rebored, a new piston will not be necessary. Normal piston wear appears as even, vertical wear on the thrust surfaces of the piston and slight looseness of the top ring in its groove. New piston rings, on the other hand, should always be used when an engine is rebuilt.

11   Carefully inspect each piston for cracks around the skirt, at the pin bosses and at the ring lands.

12   Look for scoring and scuffing on the thrust faces of the skirt, holes in the piston crown and burned areas at the edge of the crown. If the skirt is scored or scuffed, the engine may have been suffering from overheating and/or abnormal combustion, which caused excessively high operating temperatures. The oil pump should be checked thoroughly. A hole in the piston crown, an extreme to be sure, is an indication that abnormal combustion (pre-ignition) was occurring. Burned areas at the edge of the piston crown are usually evidence of spark knock (detonation). If any of the above problems exist, the causes must be corrected or the damage will occur again.

13   Measure the piston ring-to-groove clearance (side clearance) by laying a new piston ring in the ring groove and slipping a feeler gauge in beside it **(see illustration)**. Check the clearance at three or four locations around the groove. Be sure to use the correct ring for each groove; they are different. If the clearance is greater than specified, a new piston will have to be used when the engine is reassembled.

14   Check the piston-to-bore clearance by measuring the bore (see Section 8) and the piston diameter **(see illustration)**. Measure the piston across the skirt on the thrust faces at a 90-degree angle to the piston pin, at the specified distance up from the bottom of the skirt. Subtract the piston diameter from the bore diameter to obtain the clearance. If it is greater than specified, the cylinder will have to be rebored and a new oversized piston and rings installed. If the appropriate precision measuring tools are not available, the piston-to-cylinder clearance can be obtained, though not quite as accurately, using feeler gauge stock. Feeler gauge stock comes in 12-inch lengths and various thicknesses and is generally available at auto parts stores. To check the clearance, slip a piece of feeler gauge stock of the same thickness as the specified piston clearance into the cylinder along with appropriate piston. The cylinder should be upside down and the piston must be positioned exactly as it normally would be. Place the feeler gauge between the piston and cylinder on one of the thrust faces (90-degrees to the piston pin bore). The piston should slip through the cylinder (with the feeler gauge in

place) with moderate pressure. If it falls through, or slides through easily, the clearance is excessive and a new piston will be required. If the piston binds at the lower end of the cylinder and is loose toward the top, the cylinder is tapered, and if tight spots are encountered as the piston/feeler gauge is rotated in the cylinder, the cylinder is out-of-round. Be sure to have the cylinder and piston checked by a dealer service department or a repair shop to confirm your findings before purchasing new parts.

15   Apply clean engine oil to the pin, insert it into the piston and check for freeplay by rocking the pin back-and-forth. If the pin is loose, a new piston and possibly a new pin must be installed.

16   Repeat Step 15, this time inserting the piston pin into the connecting rod **(see illustration)**. If the pin is loose, measure the pin diameter and the pin bore in the rod (or have this done by a dealer or repair shop). A worn pin can be replaced separately; if the rod bore is worn, the rod must be replaced.

17   Refer to Section 10 and install the rings on the piston.

Installation

Refer to illustration 9.18

18   Install the piston with its IN mark toward the intake side (rear) of the engine. Lubricate the pin and the rod bore with moly-based grease. Install a new circlips in the groove on one side of the piston (don't reuse the old circlips). Push the pin into position from the opposite side and install another new circlip. Compress the circlips only enough for them to fit in the piston. Make sure the clips are properly seated in the grooves **(see illustration)**.

9.18 Make sure both piston pin circlips are securely seated in the piston grooves

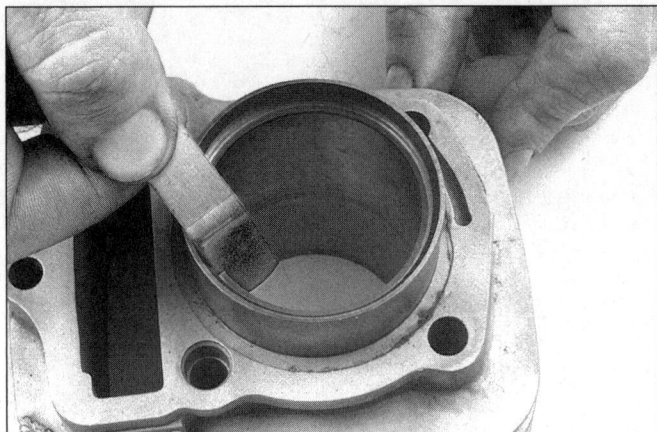

10.2 Check the piston ring end gap with a feeler gauge at the bottom of the cylinder

10.4 If the end gap is too small, clamp a file in a vise and file the ring ends (from the outside in only) to enlarge the gap slightly

10 Piston rings - installation

Refer to illustrations 10.2, 10.4, 10.7a, 10.7b and 10.7c

1   Before installing the new piston rings, the ring end gaps must be checked.

2   Insert the top (No. 1) ring into the bottom of the cylinder and square it up with the cylinder walls by pushing it in with the top of the piston. The ring should be about one-half inch above the bottom edge of the cylinder. To measure the end gap, slip a feeler gauge between the ends of the ring **(see illustration)** and compare the measurement to the Specifications.

3   If the gap is larger or smaller than specified, double check to make sure that you have the correct rings before proceeding.

4   If the gap is too small, it must be enlarged or the ring ends may come in contact with each other during engine operation, which can cause serious damage. The end gap can be increased by filing the ring ends very carefully with a fine file **(see illustration)**. When performing this operation, file only from the outside in.

5   Repeat the procedure for the second compression ring and oil ring.

6   Once the ring end gaps have been checked/corrected, the rings can be installed on the piston.

7   The oil control ring (lowest on the piston) is installed first. It is composed of three separate components. Slip the spacer into the groove, then install the upper side rail **(see illustrations)**. Do not use a piston ring installation tool on the oil ring side rails as they may be damaged. Instead, place one end of the side rail into the groove between

10.7a Installing the oil ring expander - make sure the ends don't overlap

the spacer expander and the ring land. Hold it firmly in place and slide a finger around the piston while pushing the rail into the groove (taking care not to cut your fingers on the sharp edges). Next, install the lower side rail in the same manner.

8   After the three oil ring components have been installed, check to make sure that both the upper and lower side rails can be turned smoothly in the ring groove.

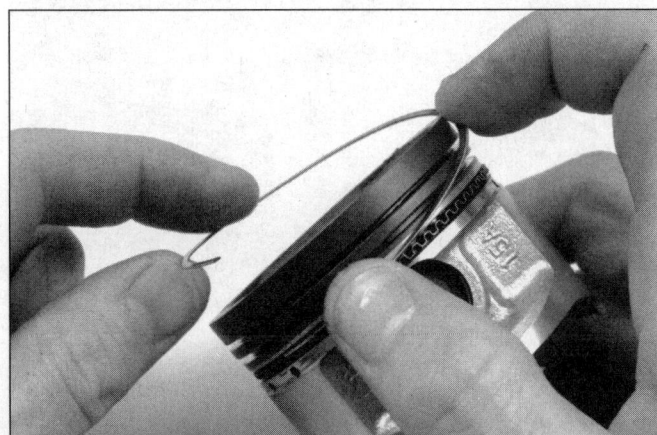

10.7b Installing an oil ring side rail - don't use a ring installation tool to do this

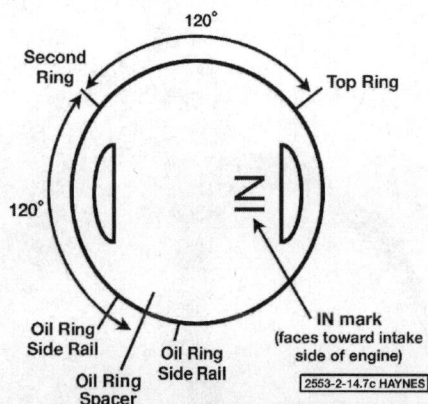

10.7c Ring details

11.1 Clutch inspection points (80 and 100 models)

A) Pressure plate posts
B) Pressure plate friction
    surface
C) Clutch housing slots
D) Clutch housing bearing
    surface
E) Gear teeth

9   Install the no. 2 (middle) ring next. It can be readily distinguished from the top ring by its cross-section shape **(see illustration 10.7c)**. Do not mix the top and middle rings.
10   To avoid breaking the ring, use a piston ring installation tool and make sure that the identification mark is facing up **(see illustration 10.7c)**. Fit the ring into the middle groove on the piston. Do not expand the ring any more than is necessary to slide it into place.
11   Finally, install the no. 1 (top) ring in the same manner. Make sure the identifying mark is facing up. Be very careful not to confuse the top and second rings.
12   Once the rings have been properly installed, stagger the end gaps, including those of the oil ring side rails **(see illustration 10.7c)**.

11   Clutch - inspection

Refer to illustrations 11.1, 11.3, 11.4, 11.5 and 11.7

1   If you're working on an 80 or 100 model, check the bolt posts and the friction surface on the pressure plate for damaged threads, scoring or wear **(see illustration)**. Replace the pressure plate if any defects are found.

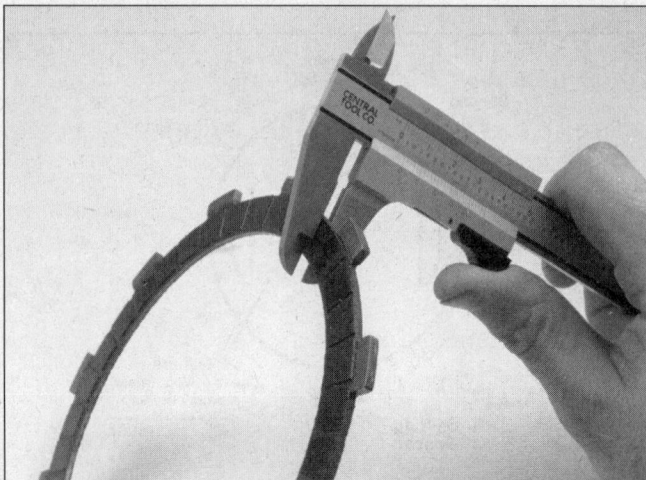

11.3 Measure the clutch spring free length

2   Check the edges of the slots in the clutch housing for indentations made by the friction plate tabs **(see illustration 11.1)**. If the indentations are deep they can prevent clutch release, so the housing should be replaced with a new one. If the indentations can be removed easily with a file, the life of the housing can be prolonged to an extent. Also, check the driven gear teeth for cracks, chips and excessive wear and the springs on the back side (if equipped) for breakage. If the gear is worn or damaged or the springs are broken, the clutch housing must be replaced with a new one. Check the bearing surface in the center of the clutch housing for score marks, scratches and excessive wear.
3   Measure the free length of the clutch springs **(see illustration)** and compare the results to this Chapter's Specifications. If the springs have sagged, or if cracks are noted, replace them with new ones as a set.
4   If the lining material of the friction plates smells burnt or if it is glazed, new parts are required. If the metal clutch plates are scored or discolored, they must be replaced with new ones. Measure the thickness of the friction plates **(see illustration)** and replace with new parts any friction plates that are worn.
5   Lay the metal plates, one at a time, on a perfectly flat surface (such as a piece of plate glass) and check for warpage by trying to slip a feeler gauge between the flat surface and the plate **(see illustration)**. The feeler gauge should be the same thickness as the maximum warp listed in this Chapter's Specifications. Do this at several places around the plate's circumference. If the feeler gauge can be slipped under the plate, it is warped and should be replaced with a new one.

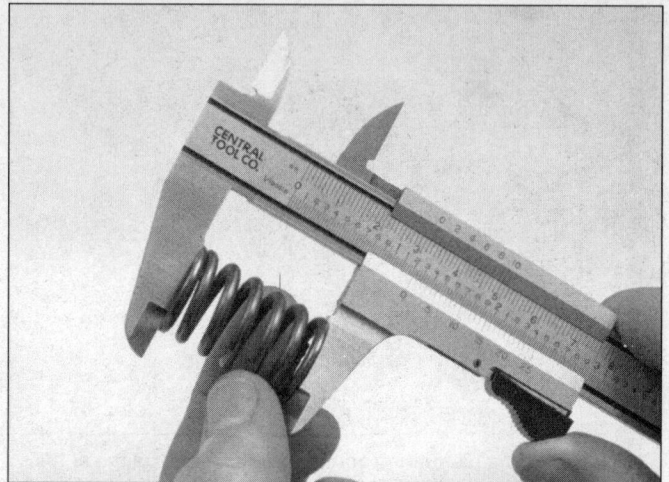

11.4 Measure the thickness of the friction plates

11.5 Check the metal plates for warpage

11.7 Check the ball bearing in the center of the lifter plate for roughness, looseness or noise

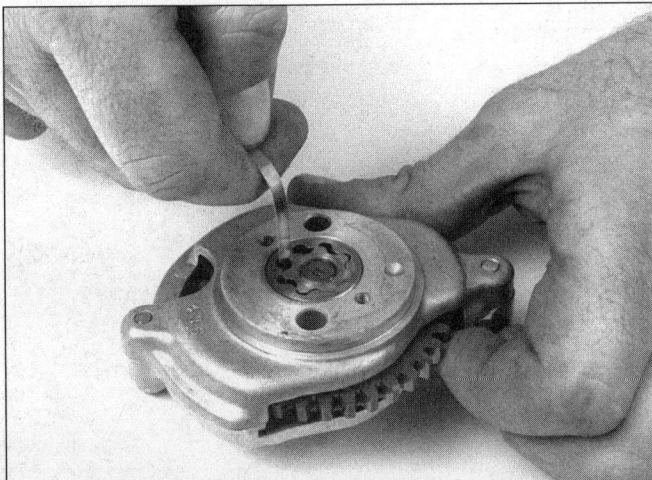

12.3a Measure the clearance between the outer rotor and body . . .

6   Check the tabs on the friction plates for excessive wear and mush-roomed edges. They can be cleaned up with a file if the deformation is not severe. Check the friction plates for warpage as described in Step 14.

7   If you're working on an 80 or 100 model, check the clutch lifter plate for wear and damage. Rotate the inner race of the bearing and check for roughness, looseness or excessive noise (**see illustration**).

8   Check the splines of the clutch center for wear or damage and replace the clutch center if problems are found.

12 Oil pump - inspection

Refer to illustrations 12.3a, 12.3b and 12.4

1   Remove and disassemble the oil pump (see Chapter 2A or 2B).

2   Wash all the components in solvent, then dry them off. If you're working on an 80 or 100 model, don't remove the gasket yet, since you'll need it in place for a later clearance measurement. Check the pump body, the rotors, the gear and the covers for scoring and wear. If any damage or uneven or excessive wear is evident, replace the pump. If you are rebuilding the engine, it's a good idea to install a new oil pump.

3   Place the rotors in the pump body. Measure the clearance between the outer rotor and body, and between the inner and outer rotors, with a

feeler gauge (**see illustrations**).

4   Place a straightedge across the pump body and rotors and mea-sure the gap with a feeler gauge (**see illustration**).

5   If any of the measurements in Step 3 or 4 is beyond the limits listed in this Chapter's Specifications, replace the pump with a new one.

13 Crankcase components - inspection and servicing

Refer to illustrations 13.3a and 13.3b

1   Separate the crankcase and remove the following:

a) *Kickstarter*
b) *Transmission shafts and gears*
c) *Crankshaft, cam chain and main bearings*
d) *Shift drum and forks*

2   Clean the crankcase halves thoroughly with new solvent and dry them with compressed air. All oil passages should be blown out with compressed air and all traces of old gasket should be removed from the mating surfaces. **Caution:** *Be very careful not to nick or gouge the crankcase mating surfaces or leaks will result.* Check both crankcase halves very carefully for cracks and other damage.

3   Check the bearings in the case halves. If they don't turn smoothly, replace them. The smaller ball bearings aren't accessible from the out-

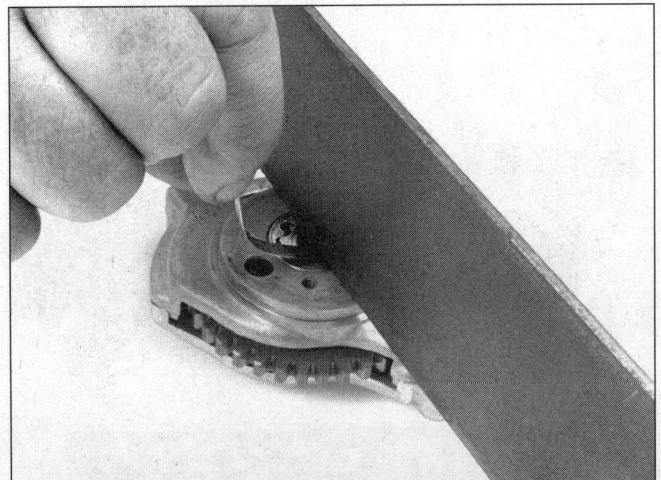

12.3b . . . between the inner and outer rotors . . .

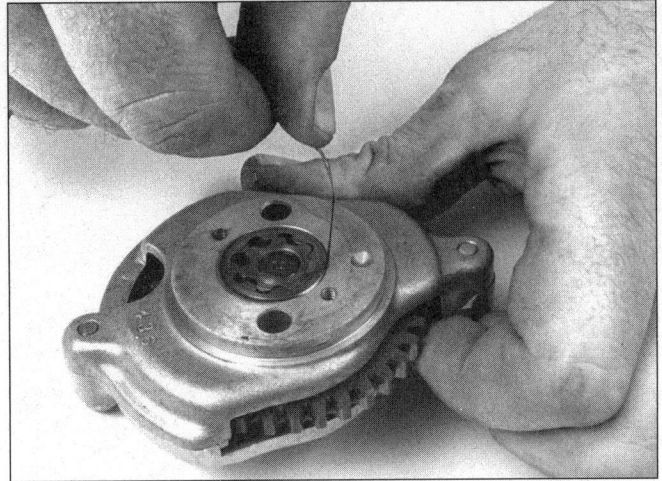

12.4 . . . and between the rotors and a straightedge laid across the pump body (with the gasket in place)

13.3a Bearings that aren't accessible from both sides can be removed with a blind hole puller

13.3b Drive the bearings in with a bearing driver or socket; bearings accessible from both sides can be removed and installed with a bearing driver or socket

side, so a blind hole puller will be needed for removal **(see illustration)**. Drive the remaining bearing out with a bearing driver or a socket having an outside diameter slightly smaller than that of the bearing outer race. Before installing the bearings, allow them to sit in the freezer overnight, and about fifteen-minutes before installation, place the case half in an oven, set to about 200-degrees F, and allow it to heat up. The bearings are an interference fit, and this will ease installation. **Warning:** *Before heating the case, wash it thoroughly with soap and water so no explosive fumes are present. Also, don't use a flame to heat the case.* Install the ball bearings with a socket or bearing driver that bears against the bearing outer race **(see illustration)**.

4   If any damage is found that can't be repaired, replace the crankcase halves as a set.

5   Assemble the case halves (see Chapter 2A or 2B) and check to make sure the crankshaft and the transmission shafts turn freely.

14 Shift drum and forks - inspection

Refer to illustrations 14.3 and 14.5

1   Wash all of the components in clean solvent and dry them off.

2   Inspect the shift fork grooves in the gears. If a groove is worn or scored, replace the affected gear (see Chapter 2A or 2B) and inspect its corresponding shift fork.

3   Check the shift forks for distortion and wear, especially at the fork

fingers **(see illustration)**. Measure the thickness of the fork fingers and compare your findings with this Chapter's Specifications. If they are discolored or severely worn they are probably bent. Inspect the guide pins for excessive wear and distortion and replace any defective parts with new ones.

4   Measure the inside diameter of the forks and the outside diameter of the fork shaft and compare to the values listed in this Chapter's Specifications. Replace any parts that are worn beyond the limits. Check the shift fork shaft for evidence of wear, galling and other damage. Make sure the shift forks move smoothly on the shaft. If the shaft is worn or bent, replace it with a new one.

5   Check the edges of the grooves in the drum for signs of excessive wear **(see illustration)**. Measure the width of the grooves and compare it with the limit listed in this Chapter's Specifications. If any groove is worn beyond the limit, replace the shift drum.

6   Spin the shift drum bearing with fingers and replace it if it's rough, loose or noisy.

15 Transmission shafts - inspection

Refer to illustration 15.10

1   Wash all of the components in clean solvent and dry them off.

2   Inspect the shift fork grooves in the countershaft fifth gear, counter-

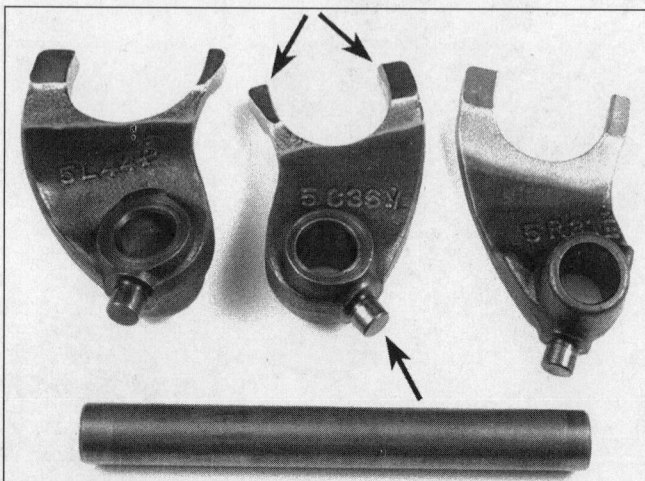

14.3 The fork fingers and pins (arrows) are common wear points

14.5 Check the shift drum grooves for wear

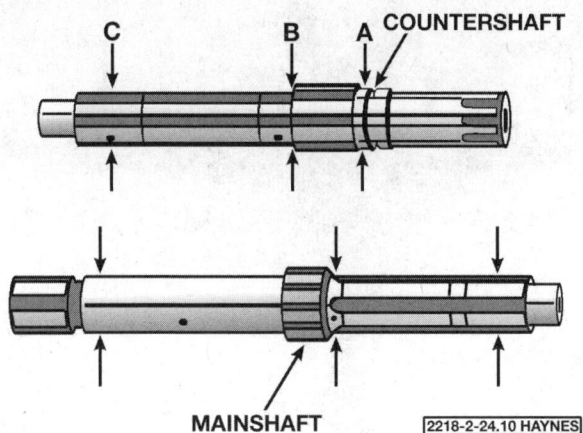

15.10 Measure the transmission shaft diameters at these points

16.2a If you haven't already done so, disengage the cam chain from the sprocket (80 and 100 shown) on the crankshaft . . .

shaft fourth gear and mainshaft third gear. If a groove is worn or scored, replace the affected gear and inspect its corresponding shift fork.

3   Check the gear teeth for cracking and other obvious damage. Check the bushing or surface in the inner diameter of the freewheeling gears for scoring or heat discoloration. Measure the inside diameters of the gears and compare them to the values listed in this Chapter's Specifications. Replace parts that are damaged or worn beyond the limits.

4   Inspect the engagement dogs and dog holes on gears so equipped for excessive wear or rounding off. Replace the paired gears as a set if necessary.

5   If you're working on an 80 or 100 model, measure the transmission shaft diameters at the points shown (see illustration). If they're worn beyond the limits listed in this Chapter's Specifications, replace the shaft(s).

6   If you're working on an XR100R, measure the outer diameter of the countershaft first gear collar. Replace it if it's worn beyond the limit listed in this Chapter's Specifications.

7   Inspect the thrust washers. Honda doesn't specify wear limits, but they should be replaced if they show any visible wear or scoring. It's a good idea to replace them whenever the transmission is disassembled.

8   Check the transmission shaft bearings in the crankcase for roughness, looseness or noise and replace them if necessary (see Section 13).

9   Discard the snap-rings and use new ones on reassembly.

16 Crankshaft - removal, inspection and installation

Removal

Refer to illustrations 16.2a and 16.2b

1   Remove the engine and separate the crankcase halves (Sections 5 and 13).

2   Disengage the cam chain from its sprocket and lift the crankshaft out of the left crankcase half (see illustrations). The ball bearing will come out with the crankshaft.

Inspection

Refer to illustrations 16.3, 16.4, 16.5 and 16.6

3   Measure the side clearance between connecting rod and crankshaft with a feeler gauge (see illustration). If it's more than the limit listed in this Chapter's Specifications, replace the crankshaft and connecting rod as an assembly.

4   Set up the crankshaft in V-blocks with a dial indicator contacting the big end of the connecting rod (see illustration). Move the connecting rod up-and-down against the indicator pointer and compare the reading to the value listed in this Chapter's Specifications. If it's beyond the limit, replace the crankshaft and connecting rod as an assembly.

16.2b . . . and lift the crankshaft out of the engine (80 and 100 shown)

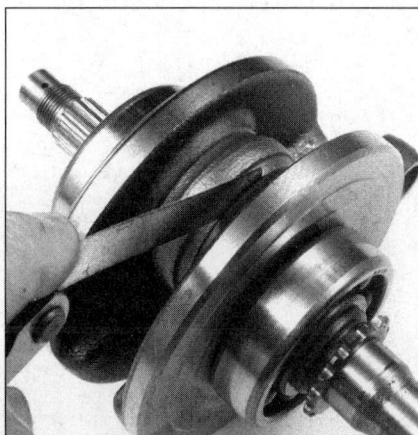

16.3 Check the connecting rod side clearance with a feeler gauge

16.4 Check the connecting rod radial clearance with a dial indicator

16.5 Check the cam chain sprocket for worn or damaged teeth and the ball bearings for roughness, looseness or noisy rotation

16.6 Place a V-block on each side of the crankshaft and measure runout with a dial indicator at the ends (arrows)

5   Check the crankshaft, sprocket and bearings for visible wear or damage, such as chipped teeth or scoring **(see illustration)**. Rotate the ball bearings and check them for roughness, looseness or noise. If any of these conditions are found, replace the crankshaft and connecting rod as an assembly.
6   Set the crankshaft in a pair of V-blocks, with a dial indicator contacting each end **(see illustration)**. Rotate the crankshaft and note the runout. If the runout at either end is beyond the limit listed in this Chapter's Specifications, replace the crankshaft and connecting rod as an assembly.

Installation
7   Position the cam chain in its tunnel and install the crankshaft in the left crankcase half, passing it through the cam chain **(see illustrations 16.2a and 16.2b)**.
8   The remainder of installation is the reverse of the removal steps.

17   Initial start-up after overhaul

1   Make sure the engine oil level is correct, then remove the spark plug from the engine. Unplug the primary wires from the coil.
2   Turn on the key switch and crank the engine over with the kickstarter several times to build up oil pressure. Reinstall the spark plug and connect the wires.
3   Make sure there is fuel in the tank, then operate the choke.
4   Start the engine and allow it to run at a moderately fast idle. Let the engine continue running until it reaches operating temperature.
5   Check carefully for oil leaks and make sure the transmission and controls, especially the brakes, function properly before road testing the machine. Refer to Section 18 for the recommended break-in procedure.
6   Upon completion of the road test, and after the engine has cooled down completely, recheck the valve clearances (see Chapter 1).

18   Recommended break-in procedure

1   Any rebuilt engine needs time to break-in, even if parts have been installed in their original locations. For this reason, treat the machine gently for the first few miles to make sure oil has circulated throughout the engine and any new parts installed have started to seat.
2   Even greater care is necessary if the cylinder has been rebored or a new crankshaft has been installed. In the case of a rebore, the engine will have to be broken in as if the machine were new. This means greater use of the transmission and a restraining hand on the throttle for the first few operating days. There's no point in keeping to any set speed limit - the main idea is to vary the engine speed, keep from lugging (laboring) the engine and to avoid full-throttle operation. These recommendations can be lessened to an extent when only a new crankshaft is installed.
3   If a lubrication failure is suspected, stop the engine immediately and try to find the cause. If an engine is run without oil, even for a short period of time, irreparable damage will occur.

Chapter 3
Fuel and exhaust systems

Contents

Specifications

General

Fuel type .... Unleaded or low lead gasoline subject to local regulations; minimum octane 91 RON (87 pump octane)

Carburetor

Identification mark

XR80R

1985 and 1986	PC10D
1987 through 1999	PC20B
2000	PC20F
2001 through 2003	PC20J

XR80F

2004 through 2005	PC20M
2006 through 2007	PC20P

XR100R, CRF100F

1985 and 1986	PD36D
1987 through 1997	PD80C
1998 through 2000 (except California)	PD80C
1998 through 2000 California	PDC3D
2001through 2005	PDC3L
2006 and 2007	PDCBF
2008 and later	PDCBL

XR70R	PB12H

XR50R, CRF50F

2004 and 2005	PA42A
2006 through 2007	PA42B
2008 through 2012	PA42C
2013 and later	PA42G

CRF70F

2004 and 2005	PB12H
2006 through 2013	PA42J

Jet sizes and settings

1985 through 1997 XR80R, XR100R

Main jet

Standard (sea level to 1800 meters/6000 feet)

1985 and 1986 XR80R	92
1987 through 1997 XR80R, all XR100R	95

High altitude (above 1500 meters/5000 feet)

1985 and 1986 XR80R	88
1987 through 1997 XR80R, all XR100R	90

Slow jet

XR80R	35
XR100R	38

Jet needle clip position

1985 and 1986 XR80R	Fourth groove from top
1987 through 1997 XR80R	Second groove from top
XR100R	Third groove from top

XR80R air screw setting (turns out from lightly seated position)
   Sea level to 1800 meters (6000 feet)
      1985 and 1986.. 1-1/2
      1987 through 1997.. 1-3/4
   Above 1500 meters (5000 feet)
      1985 and 1986.. 2-1/2
      1987 through 1997.. 2-3/4
XR100R pilot screw setting (turns out from lightly seated position)
   Sea level to 1800 meters (6000 feet)
      1985 and 1986.. 2-5/8
      1987 through 1997.. 1-3/4
   Above 1500 meters (5000 feet)
      1985 and 1986.. 1-5/8
      1987 through 1997.. 1-3/4
Float level
   XR80R... 21.5 mm (0.85 inch)
   XR100R... 12.5 mm (0.49 inch)

1998 through 2003 XR80R, XR100R

Main jet
   XR80R... 95
   XR100R
      1998 through 2000.. 95
      2001 through 2003.. 98
Slow jet
   XR80R... 35
   XR100R
      1998 through 2000 except California.............................. 38 X 38
      1998 through 2000 California .... 35 X 35
      2000 through 2003.. 35 X 35
Jet needle clip position
   1998 and 1999 XR80R.. Second groove from top
   2000 through 2003 XR80R .... Third groove from top
   XR100R... Third groove from top
XR80R air screw setting (turns out from lightly seated position)
   1998 and 1999 .... 1-3/4
   2000 through 2003
      Initial opening... 2-1/8
      Final opening 1/2
XR100R pilot screw setting (turns out from lightly seated position)
   1998 through 2000
      Initial opening... 1-3/4
      Final opening 1/2
   2001 through 2003
      Initial opening... 2-3/8
      Final opening 1/2
Float level
   XR80R... 21.5 mm (0.85 inch)
   XR100R... 12.5 mm (0.49 inch)

2004 and later CRF80F, CRF100F

Main jet
   Standard (sea level to 1500 meters/5000 feet)
      CRF80F 95
      CRF100F 98
   High altitude (1000 to 2500 meters/3000 to 8000 feet)
      CRF80F 90
      CRF100F 92
Slow jet
   CRF80F... 35
   CRF100F... 35 X 35
Jet needle clip position .... Third groove from top
CRF80F air screw setting (turns out from lightly seated position)
   Initial opening 2-1/8
   Final opening.. 1/2
   High altitude setting... 1/2 turn out from factory preset
CRF100F pilot screw setting (turns out from lightly seated position)
   Initial opening 2-3/8
   Final opening.. 3/4 turn in from factory preset
   High altitude setting...
Float level
   CRF80F... 21.5 mm (0.85 inch)
   CRF100F... 12.5 mm (0.49 inch)

XR70R

Main jet..	62
Slow jet..	38
Jet needle clip position	Third groove from top
Air screw setting (turns out from lightly seated position)	
Initial opening	1-1/2
Final opening	
1997 through 1999..	Highest idle speed
2000 and later...	1/4
Float level	10.7 mm (0.42 inch)

XR50R, CRF50F

Main jet..	58
Slow jet..	35 X 35
Jet needle clip position	Second groove from top
Air screw setting (turns out from lightly seated position)	
Initial opening	1-1/2
Final opening..	1/4
Float level	12.7 mm (0.5 inch)

CRF70F

Main jet	
Standard..	62
High altitude	60
Slow jet...	38 X 38
Jet needle clip position (2004 and 2005 only)	Third groove from top
Air screw setting (turns out from lightly seated position)	
Initial opening	1-1/2
Final opening..	1/2
High altitude	
Float level	10.7 mm (0.42 inch)

Torque settings

Exhaust pipe to cylinder head nuts	
80 and 100 models..	10 to 14 Nm (84 to 120 inch-lbs)
XR70R..	Not specified
XR50R, CRF50F	Not specified
CRF70F..	12 Nm (108 inch-lbs)
Exhaust system mounting bolt(s) to frame	
XR80R, XR100R...	24 to 30 Nm (17 to 22 ft-lbs)
CRF80F, CRF100F	26 Nm (20 ft-lbs)
XR70R..	26 Nm (20 ft-lbs)
XR50R, CRF50F	26 Nm (20 ft-lbs)
CRF70F..	32 Nm (23 ft-lbs)

1 General information

The fuel system consists of the fuel tank, fuel tap, filter screen, carburetor and connecting lines, hoses and control cables.

The carburetor used on these vehicles is a slide unit, in which the slide acts as the throttle valve. For cold starting, a choke valve is actuated by a lever mounted on the carburetor.

The exhaust system consists of a pipe and muffler/silencer with a spark arrester function.

Many of the fuel system service procedures are considered routine maintenance items and for that reason are included in Chapter 1.

2 Fuel tank - removal and installation

Warning: *Gasoline is extremely flammable, so take extra precautions when you work on any part of the fuel system. Don't smoke or allow open flames or bare light bulbs near the work area, and don't work in a garage where a gas-type appliance (such as a water heater or clothes dryer) is present. Since gasoline is carcinogenic, wear protective gloves when there's a possibility of being exposed to fuel, and, if you spill any fuel on your skin, rinse it off immediately with soap and water. Mop up any spills immediately and do not store fuel-soaked rags where they could ignite. When you perform any kind of work on the fuel system, wear safety glasses and have an extinguisher suitable for a class B type fire (flammable liquids) on hand.*

1   The fuel tank on all except XR50R and CRF50 models is secured to the frame by two bolts at the front or sides and a rubber strap at the rear. The XR50R and CRF50F fuel tank is secured by two bolts, one at the front and one at the rear.

Removal

Refer to illustrations 2.3, 2.4a, 2.4b and 2.5

2   Remove the seat (see Chapter 7).

3   On all except XR50R and CRF50F models, unhook the strap from the rear of the tank **(see illustration)**.

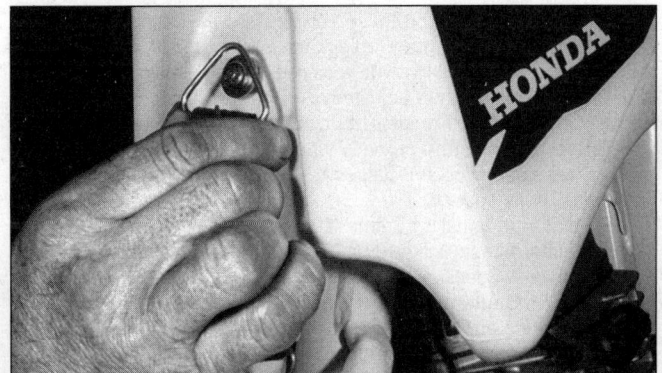

2.3 Unhook the retaining strap from the tank (except CRF50F)

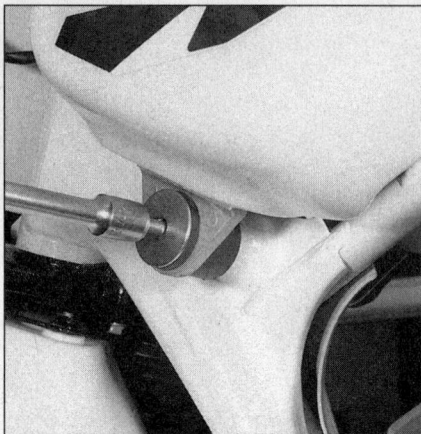

2.4a On all except 50 models, remove the mounting bolts at the front (there's one on each side)

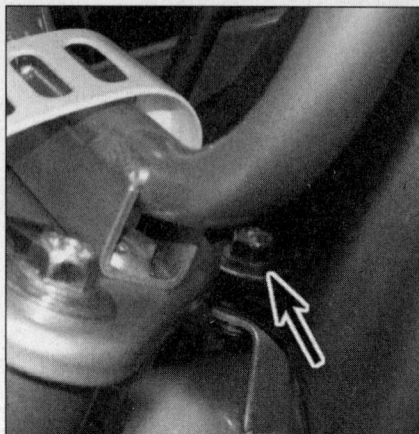

2.4b The fuel tank on 50 models is secured at the front and rear by bolts (front bolt shown)

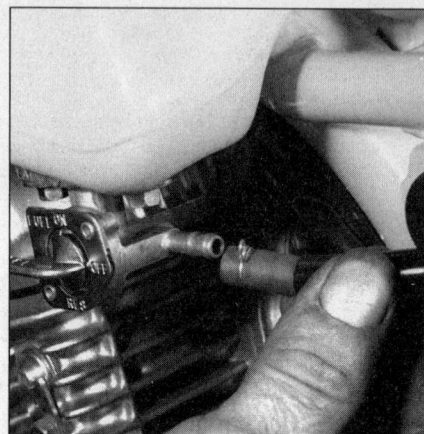

2.5 Disconnect the fuel line from the tap

4   Remove the fuel tank mounting bolts **(see illustrations)**.
5   Make sure the fuel tap is turned off, then disconnect the fuel line from the fuel tap **(see illustration)**.
6   Lift the fuel tank off the bike together with the fuel tap.

Installation

7   Before installing the tank, check the condition of the rubber mounting bushings at the front and the rubber strap at the rear - if they're hardened, cracked, or show any other signs of deterioration, replace them.
8   When installing the tank, reverse the removal procedure. Make sure the tank does not pinch any wires.

3   Fuel tank - cleaning and repair

1   All repairs to the fuel tank should be carried out by a professional who has experience in this critical and potentially dangerous work. Even after cleaning and flushing of the fuel system, explosive fumes can remain and ignite during repair of the tank.
2   If the fuel tank is removed from the vehicle, it should not be placed in an area where sparks or open flames could ignite the fumes coming out of the tank. Be especially careful inside garages where a natural gas-type appliance is located, because the pilot light could cause an explosion.

4   Idle fuel/air mixture adjustment

Normal adjustment

1   Idle fuel/mixture on these vehicles is preset at the factory and should not need adjustment unless the carburetor is overhauled or the mixture adjustment screw is replaced. On all except XR100R and CRF100F models, mixture adjustment is controlled by an air screw. On XR100R and CRF100F models, it's controlled by a pilot screw.
2   The engine must be properly tuned up before making the adjustment (valve clearances set to specifications, spark plug in good condition and properly gapped).
3   To make an initial adjustment, turn the air screw or pilot screw clockwise until it seats lightly, then back it out the number of turns listed in this Chapter's Specifications **(see illustration 20.3a, 20.3b or 20.3c in Chapter 1)**. **Caution:** *Turn the screw just far enough to seat it lightly. If it's bottomed hard, the screw or its seat may be damaged, which will make accurate mixture adjustments impossible.*
4   Warm up the engine to normal operating temperature (10 minutes

of stop-and-go riding will do). Shut it off and connect a tune-up tachometer, following the tachometer manufacturer's instructions.
5   Restart the engine and compare idle speed to the value listed in the Chapter 1 Specifications. Adjust it if necessary.

XR80R models

6   Turn the air screw in or out to obtain the highest possible idle speed.
7   Recheck idle speed on the tachometer and readjust it to the specified setting with the throttle stop screw.
8   Slowly turn the air screw clockwise until the idle speed drops 100 rpm.
9   If the air screw seats before the idle speed drops sufficiently, back it out one full turn, then repeat Steps 7 and 8.

XR100R models

10   Turn the pilot screw slowly clockwise until the engine stalls, then back it out one full turn.
11   Restart the engine and recheck the idle speed. Readjust it if necessary with the throttle stop screw.

1997 through 1999 XR70R models

12   Perform Steps 2 through 5 above.
13   Turn the air screw as needed to obtain the highest idle speed. If this is higher than the specified idle speed, reset it to the specified speed, referring to Chapter 1.
14   Rev the engine slightly. If the engine speed does not increase smoothly, repeat Step 13.

2000 through 2003 XR70R, CRF50F and CRF70F models

15   Perform Steps 2 through 5 above.
16   Turn the air screw as needed to obtain the highest idle speed. If this is higher than the specified idle speed, reset it to the specified speed, referring to Chapter 1.
17   Rev the engine two or three times and let it idle. If necessary, reset the idle to the speed listed in the Chapter 1 Specifications.
18   Turn the air screw slowly outward until idle speed drops 100 rpm from the specified speed. From this point, turn the air screw out to the final setting listed in this Chapter's Specifications.
19   Recheck the idle speed and readjust it if necessary.
20   If the engine runs roughly, misses or stalls, repeat the adjustment.

High altitude adjustment (XR70R, XR80/100R, CRF80/100F)

21   If the vehicle is normally used at altitudes from sea level to 6000 feet (1800 meters), use the normal main jet and pilot screw setting. If it's used regularly at altitudes above 5000 feet (1500 meters), the main

6.2 Unscrew the carburetor top and lift out the throttlevalve and jet needle

6.3a Loosen the clamping band screw (left arrow) and remove the mounting nuts (right arrow) - one of the nuts is hidden behind the intake manifold

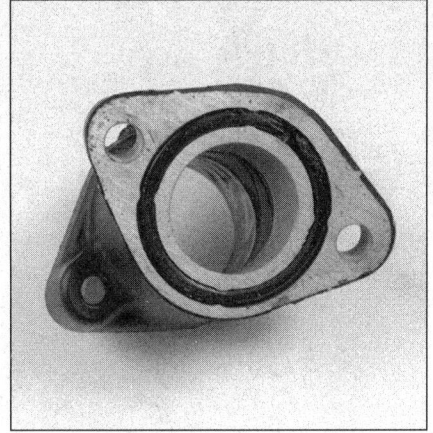

6.3b Replace the intake manifold O-ring if it's flattened, broken or deteriorated

jet and pilot screw setting must be changed to compensate for the thinner air. **Caution:** *Don't use the vehicle for sustained operation below 5000 feet (15 meters) with the main jet and pilot screw at the high altitude settings or the engine may overheat and be damaged.*

22   Refer to Section 7 and change the main jet to the high altitude jet listed in this Chapter's Specifications.

23   Set the air screw (70 and 80 models) or pilot screw (100 models) to the high altitude setting listed in this Chapter's Specifications.

24   With the vehicle at high altitude, refer to Chapter 1 and adjust the idle speed. If the engine runs roughly, misses or stalls, readjust fuel mixture with the air screw or pilot screw.

5   Carburetor overhaul - general information

1   Poor engine performance, hesitation, hard starting, stalling, flooding and backfiring are all signs that major carburetor maintenance may be required.

2   Keep in mind that many so-called carburetor problems are really not carburetor problems at all, but mechanical problems within the engine or ignition system malfunctions. Try to establish for certain that the carburetor is in need of maintenance before beginning a major overhaul.

3   Check the fuel tap and its strainer screen, the fuel lines, the intake manifold clamps, the O-ring between the intake manifold and cylinder head, the vacuum hoses, the air filter element, the cylinder compression, the spark plug and the ignition timing before assuming that a carburetor overhaul is required. If the bike has been unused for more than a month, refer to Chapter 1, drain the float chamber and refill the tank with fresh fuel.

4   Most carburetor problems are caused by dirt particles, varnish and other deposits which build up in and block the fuel and air passages. Also, in time, gaskets and O-rings shrink or deteriorate and cause fuel and air leaks which lead to poor performance.

5   When the carburetor is overhauled, it is generally disassembled completely and the parts are cleaned thoroughly with a carburetor cleaning solvent and dried with filtered, unlubricated compressed air. The fuel and air passages are also blown through with compressed air to force out any dirt that may have been loosened but not removed by the solvent. Once the cleaning process is complete, the carburetor is reassembled using new gaskets, O-rings and, generally, a new inlet needle valve and seat.

6   Before disassembling the carburetor, make sure you have a carburetor rebuild kit (which will include all necessary O-rings and other parts), some carburetor cleaner, a supply of rags, some means of blowing out the carburetor passages and a clean place to work.

6   Carburetor - removal and installation

Warning: *Gasoline is extremely flammable, so take extra precautions when you work on any part of the fuel system. Don't smoke or allow open flames or bare light bulbs near the work area, and don't work in a garage where a gas-type appliance (such as a water heater or clothes dryer) is present. Since gasoline is carcinogenic, wear protective gloves when there's a possibility of being exposed to fuel, and, if you spill any fuel on your skin, rinse it off immediately with soap and water. Mop up any spills immediately and do not store fuel-soaked rags where they could ignite. When you perform any kind of work on the fuel system, wear safety glasses and have an extinguisher suitable for a class B type fire (flammable liquids) on hand.*

Removal

Refer to illustrations 6.2, 6.3a and 6.3b

1   Remove the fuel tank (see Section 2).

2   Unscrew the carburetor top. Lift it off, pulling the throttle valve and jet needle out of the carburetor **(see illustration)**.

3   Loosen the clamping band on the air cleaner duct and the nuts on the intake manifold **(see illustration)**. Work the carburetor free of the duct and manifold, lift it off and remove the O-ring that goes between the manifold and carburetor **(see illustration)**.

4   Disconnect the vent and drain hoses from the carburetor.

5   Check the intake manifold tube for cracks, deterioration or other damage. If it has visible defects, or if there's reason to suspect its O-ring is leaking, remove it from the engine and inspect the gasket.

6   After the carburetor has been removed, stuff clean rags into the intake manifold (or the intake port in the cylinder head, if the tube has been removed) to prevent the entry of dirt or other objects.

Installation

7   Slip the clamping band onto the intake tube. Position the carburetor in the intake tube and slip its studs into the intake manifold holes. Tighten the nuts and clamping band screw securely.

8   Install the throttle valve in the carburetor body, making sure its groove aligns with the pin in the body.

9   Adjust the throttle freeplay (see Chapter 1).

10   The remainder of installation is the reverse of the removal steps.

7   Carburetor - disassembly, cleaning and inspection

Warning: *Gasoline is extremely flammable, so take extra precautions when you work on any part of the fuel system. Don't smoke or allow open flames or bare light bulbs near the work area, and don't work in a*

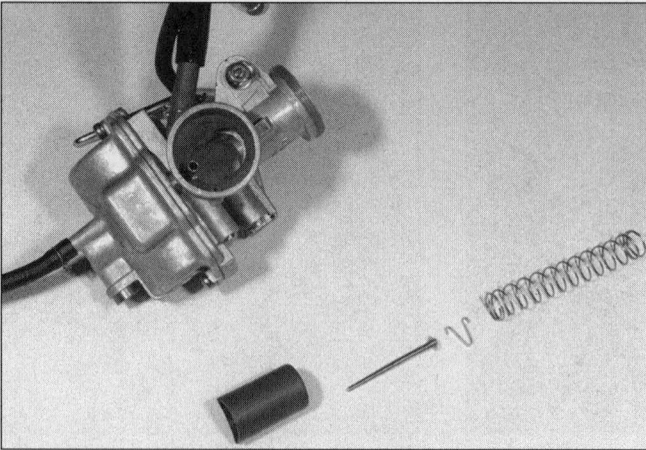

7.2 Remove the retainer and separate the jet needle and clip from the throttle valve

garage where a gas-type appliance (such as a water heater or clothes dryer) is present. Since gasoline is carcinogenic, wear protective gloves when there's a possibility of being exposed to fuel, and, if you spill any fuel on your skin, rinse it off immediately with soap and water. Mop up any spills immediately and do not store fuel-soaked rags where they could ignite. When you perform any kind of work on the fuel system,

wear safety glasses and have an extinguisher suitable for a class B type fire (flammable liquids) on hand.

Disassembly
Refer to illustration 7.2

1   Remove the carburetor from the machine as described in Section 6. Set it on a clean working surface.
2   Remove the clip and detach the throttle valve and jet needle from the carburetor top **(see illustration)**.

XR80R models
Refer to illustrations 7.3a through 7.3d

3   Refer to the accompanying illustrations to disassemble the carburetor.

XR100R models
Refer to illustrations 7.4a through 7.4d

4   Refer to the accompanying illustrations to disassemble the carburetor.

50 and 70 models
Refer to illustrations 7.5a through 7.5g

5   Refer to the accompanying **illustrations** to disassemble the carburetor. **Note:** *Removing the air screw on 2006 and later models requires a special tool. These are sometimes included in aftermarket jet kits and can also be purchased at motorcycle dealers or from aftermarket suppliers such as K&L or Motion Pro.*

7.3a Remove the float chamber screws and lift off the float chamber and its O-ring

7.3b Push out the float pivot pin (arrow) . . .

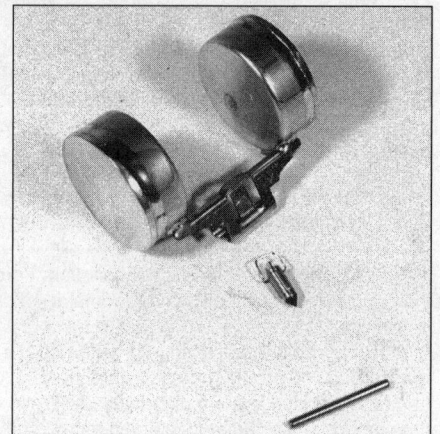

7.3c . . . then remove the float and needle valve

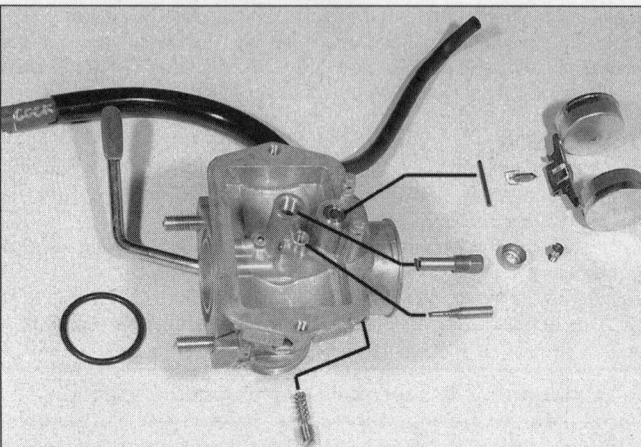

7.3d Unscrew the jets, the throttle stop screw and the air screw

7.4a On 2005 and later models, remove the plug covering the pilot screw. Remove the pilot screw and float chamber screw (arrows)

7.4b Lift off the float chamber and inspect its O-ring - remove the baffle and unscrew the main jet and needle jet holder (A); if the slow jet (B) has a screwdriver slot, unscrew it, but if not, don't try to remove it

7.4c Remove the needle jet from its bore, then push out the float pivot pin and remove the float

7.4d Unhook the needle valve clip from the floats

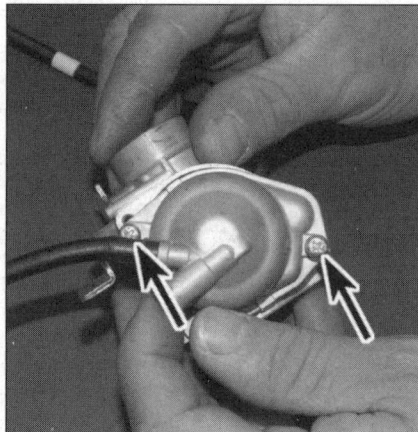

7.5a Remove the float chamber screws (arrows)

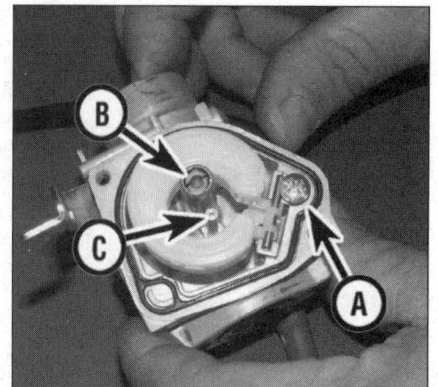

7.5b Remove the float screw (50 models, shown) or pull out the float pivot pin (70 models) . . .

a) Float screw
b) Main jet
c) Slow jet (removable on 70 models)

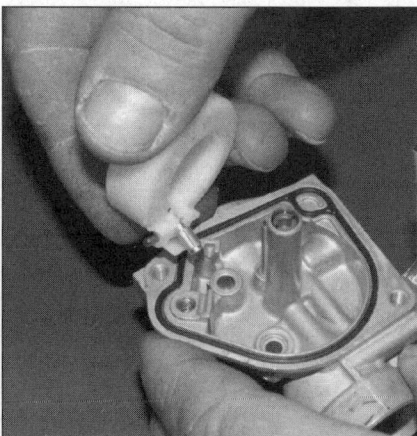

7.5c . . . and lift off the float, together with the needle valve - don't separate the needle valve from the float unless it needs to be replaced

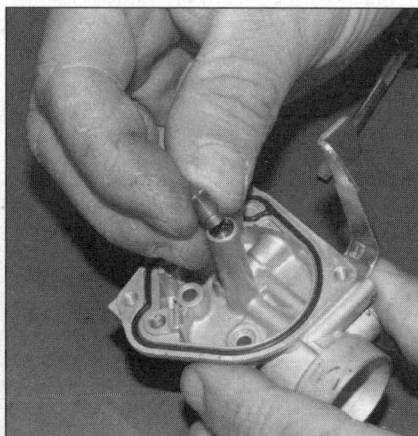

7.5d Unscrew the main jet; If you're working on a 70 model, unscrew the slow jet as well

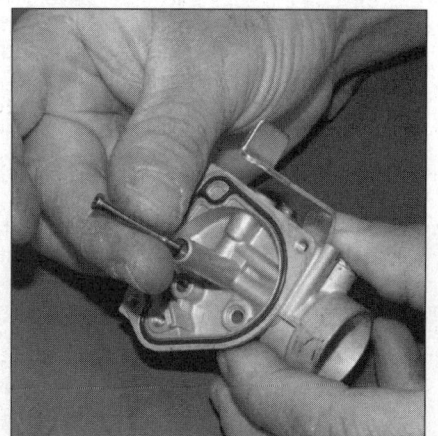

7.5e Pull out the needle jet holder and needle jet (one piece on 50 models, two pieces on 70 models)

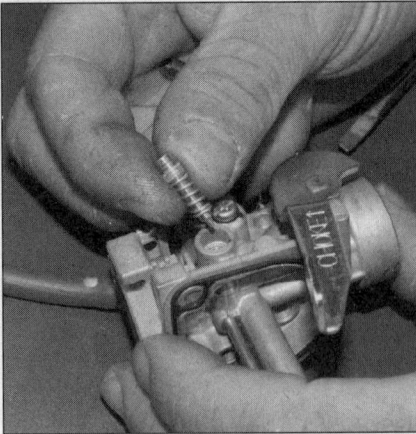

7.5f Remove the air screw - on 2006 and later models, it has an O-ring and requires a special tool

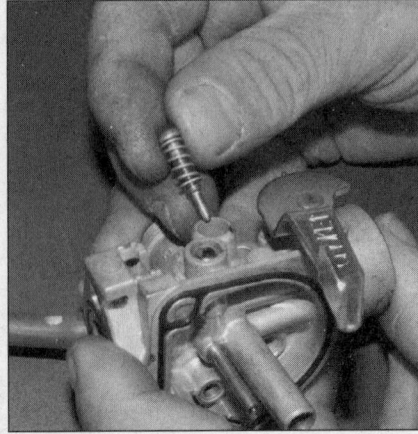

7.5g Remove the throttle stop screw and spring

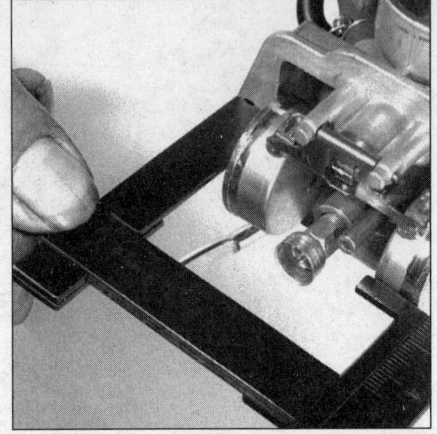

8.4 Float height can be measured with a gauge like this one or a ruler

Cleaning

Caution: *Use only a carburetor cleaning solution that is safe for use with plastic parts (be sure to read the label on the container).*

6   Submerge the metal components in the carburetor cleaner for approximately thirty minutes (or longer, if the directions recommend it).

7   After the carburetor has soaked long enough for the cleaner to loosen and dissolve most of the varnish and other deposits, use a brush to remove the stubborn deposits. Rinse it again, then dry it with compressed air. Blow out all of the fuel and air passages in the main and upper body. **Caution:** *Never clean the jets or passages with a piece of wire or a drill bit, as they will be enlarged, causing the fuel and air metering rates to be upset.*

Inspection

8   Check the operation of the choke lever. If it doesn't move smoothly, replace it.

9   Check the tapered portion of the pilot screw for wear or damage. Replace the pilot screw if necessary.

10   Check the carburetor body, float chamber and carburetor top for cracks, distorted sealing surfaces and other damage. If any defects are found, replace the faulty component, although replacement of the entire carburetor will probably be necessary (check with your parts supplier for the availability of separate components).

11   Check the jet needle for straightness by rolling it on a flat surface (such as a piece of glass). Replace it if it's bent or if the tip is worn.

12   Check the tip of the fuel inlet valve needle. If it has grooves or scratches in it, it must be replaced. Push in on the rod in the other end of the needle, then release it - if it doesn't spring back, replace the valve needle.

13   Check the O-rings on the float chamber and the drain plug (in the float chamber). Replace them if they're damaged.

14   Check the floats for damage. This will usually be apparent by the presence of fuel inside one of the floats. If the floats are damaged, they must be replaced.

15   Insert the throttle valve in the carburetor body and see that it moves up-and-down smoothly. Check the surface of the throttle valve for wear. If it's worn excessively or doesn't move smoothly in the bore, replace the carburetor.

8   Carburetors - reassembly and float height check

Refer to illustration 8.4

Caution: *When installing the jets, be careful not to over-tighten them - they're made of soft material and can strip or shear easily.*

Note: *When reassembling the carburetor, be sure to use the new O-rings, gaskets and other parts supplied in the rebuild kit.*

1   Install the clip on the jet needle if it was removed. Place it in the needle groove listed in this Chapter's Specifications. Install the needle and clip in the throttle valve.

2   Install the pilot screw along with its spring, washer and O-ring, turning it in until it seats lightly. Now, turn the screw out the number of turns that was previously recorded.

3   Reverse the disassembly steps to install the jets.

4   Invert the carburetor. Attach the fuel inlet valve needle to the float. Set the float into position in the carburetor, making sure the valve needle seats correctly. Install the float pivot pin. To check the float height, hold the carburetor so the float hangs down, then tilt it back until the valve needle is just seated. Measure the distance from the float chamber gasket surface to the top of the float and compare your measurement to the float height listed in this Chapter's Specifications **(see illustration)**. Bend the float tang as necessary to change the adjustment.

5   Install the O-ring into the groove in the float chamber. Place the float chamber on the carburetor and install the screws, tightening them securely.

9   Air cleaner housing - removal and installation

Removal

All except XR50R and CRF50F

Refer to illustrations 9.3a and 9.3b

1   Remove the seat and both side covers (see Chapter 7).

9.3a Remove the two air cleaner case bolts on the left side of the bike (arrows) . . .

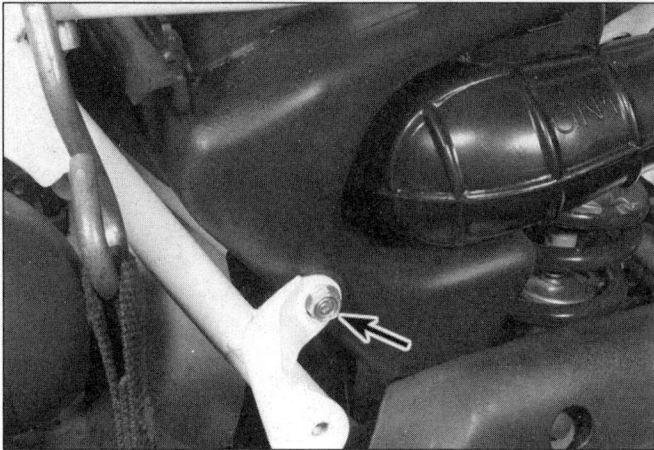

9.3b . . . and one on the right side (arrow)

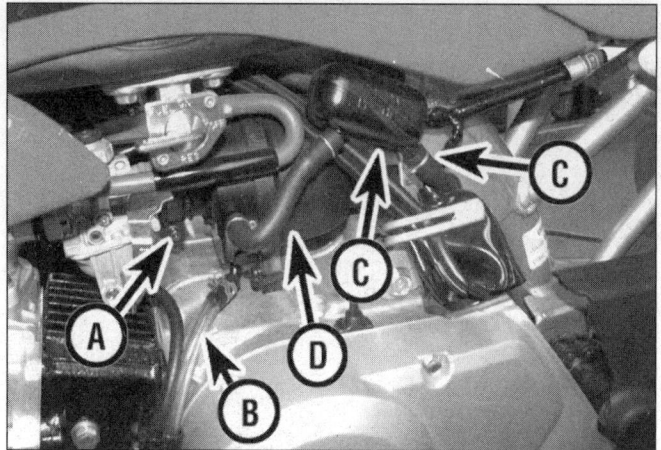

**9.4 Air cleaner housing details, 50 and 70 models
(CRF50F shown)**

a) *Clamp screw*
b) *Drain tube*
c) *Crankcase breather hoses*
d) *Crankcase emission storage tank*

2   Loosen the clamp and detach the connecting tube from the carburetor **(see illustration 6.3)**.
3   Remove the air cleaner housing bolts **(see illustrations)**. Lift the air cleaner housing out of the frame, together with the intake duct and carburetor connecting tube.

XR50R and CRF50F models

Refer to illustration 9.4
4   Loosen the clamp that secures the housing to the intake manifold and disconnect the crankcase breather tube **(see illustration)**.
5   Remove the bolt that secures the air cleaner housing to the frame **(see illustration 5.5b in Chapter 2B)**.
6   Pull the air clearer housing rearward to separate the duct form the intake manifold, then take it out of the motorcycle.

All models

7   Installation is the reverse of the removal steps.

---

10 Throttle cable - removal, installation and adjustment

Removal and installation

Refer to illustrations 10.4a, 10.4b and 10.4c
1   Remove the fuel tank (see Section 2) and unscrew the carburetor

top (see Section 6). **Note:** *On 1986 and later models, the throttle cable is replaced as a unit with the carburetor top.*
2   If you're working on a 1985 model, disconnect the throttle cable from the carburetor top.
3   If you're working on a 1986 or later model, detach the throttle valve spring from the carburetor top.
4   At the handlebar, loosen the throttle cable adjuster all the way (see Chapter 1). Separate the halves of the throttle cable housing and slip the end of the cable out of the pulley **(see illustrations)**.
5   Route the cable into place. Make sure it doesn't interfere with any other components and isn't kinked or bent sharply.
6   Lubricate the end of the cable with multi-purpose grease. Reverse the disconnection steps to connect the throttle cable to the twistgrip pulley.
7   Attach the cable to the carburetor top (1985 models) or install the spring (1986 and later models).
8   Operate the throttle and make sure it returns to the idle position by itself under spring pressure. **Warning:** *If the throttle doesn't return by itself, find and solve the problem before continuing with installation. A stuck throttle can lead to loss of control of the motorcycle.*

10.4a Remove the throttle housing screws; the punch mark in the handlebar (arrow) aligns with the parting line of the throttle housing halves upon installation

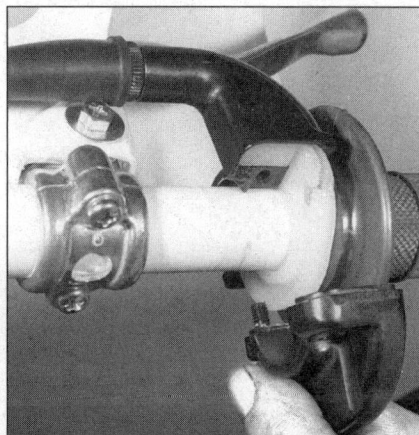

10.4b Separate the housing from the handlebar . . .

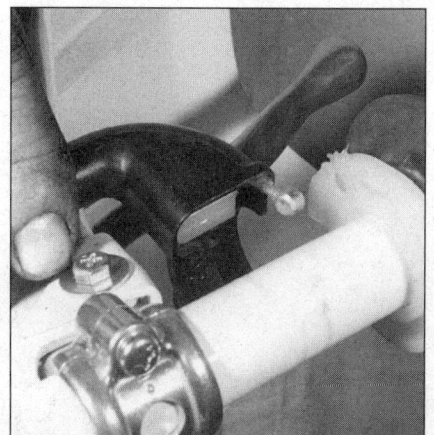

10.4c . . . and disengage the throttle cable from the grip

11.1 Remove the holder nuts (arrows) and slide the holder off the studs

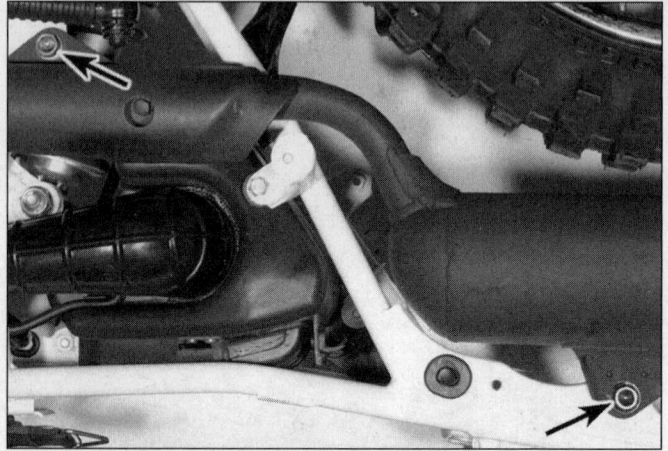

11.2 Remove the mounting bolts (arrows), pull the exhaust system forward to clear the engine and lift it off

Adjustment

9   Follow the procedure outlined in Chapter 1, *Throttle operation/grip freeplay - check and adjustment*, to adjust the cable.
10   Turn the handlebars back and forth to make sure the cable doesn't cause the steering to bind.
11   Once you're sure the cable operates properly, install the fuel tank.
12   With the engine idling, turn the handlebars through their full travel (full left lock to full right lock) and note whether idle speed increases. If it does, the cable is routed incorrectly. Correct this dangerous condition before riding the bike.

11   Exhaust system - removal and installation

Refer to illustrations 11.1 and 11.2
1   Remove the exhaust pipe holder nuts and slide the holder off the mounting studs **(see illustration)**.
2   Remove the muffler mounting bolts **(see illustration)**.

3   Pull the exhaust system forward, separate the pipe from the cylinder head and remove the system from the machine.
4   Installation is the reverse of removal, with the following additions:
a) *Be sure to install a new gasket at the cylinder head.*
b) *Tighten the muffler mounting bolts and holder nuts securely.*

12   Crankcase emission control system - inspection, removal and installation

1   Later models use a crankcase emission control system **(see illustration 9.4)**. Crankcase vapors are routed to the intake manifold through a storage tank for burning.
2   Check all parts for wear and damage. Check the hoses for deterioration. Replace any parts with visible problems.
3   To replace parts, disconnect the hoses. Install new ones, using new clamps if the old ones are weak or were damaged during removal.

Chapter 4
Ignition and electrical system

Contents

Specifications

Ignition coil resistance (at 20-degrees C/68-degrees F)
Primary resistance
Breaker point models .... 1.3 to 1.7 ohms
CDI models through 1997 .... 0.1 to 0.3 ohms
Secondary resistance
Breaker point models .... 7000 to 10,600 ohms
CDI models through 1997
With plug cap attached .... 6400 to 10,100 ohms
With plug cap detached .... 2700 to 3500 ohms
Spark plug cap resistance (breaker point models) .... 3700 to 6300 ohms
Condenser capacity .... 0.22 to 0.28 microfarads
Pulse generator resistance .... 50 to 200 ohms at 20-degrees C (68-degrees-F)
Stator coil resistance (breaker point models)
At TDC on compression stroke .... 0.57 to 0.71 ohms
At any other position .... 0 ohms
Exciter coil resistance (CDI models through 1997) .... 400 to 800 ohms
Pulse generator resistance (CDI models through 1997) .... 50 to 200 ohms

Tightening torques
Alternator nut
XR8R, 100R .... 60 to 70 Nm (43 to 51 ft-lbs)
CRF80F, CRF100F .... 64 Nm (47 ft-lbs)
50 and 70 models .... 41 Nm (30 ft-lbs)

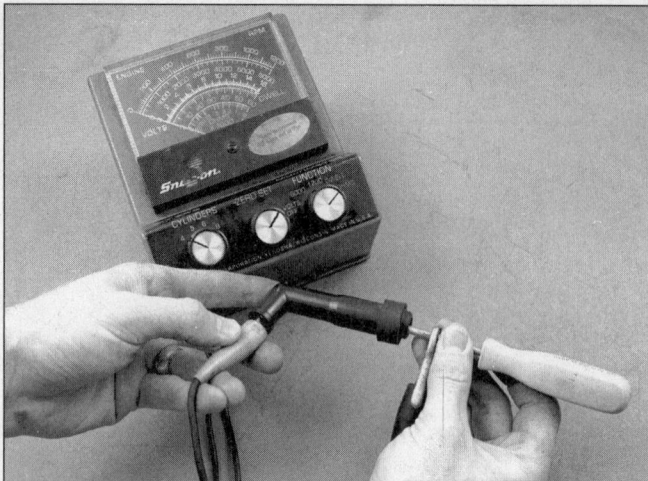

2.5 Unscrew the spark plug cap from the plug wire and measure its resistance with an ohmmeter

2.14 A simple spark gap testing fixture can be made from a block of wood, two nails, a large alligator clip, a screw and a piece of wire

1   General information

These motorcycles are equipped with one of two ignition system types: early models use a breaker point system and later models use a breakerless system. The system consists of the following components:

Breaker points (breaker point system)
Pulse generator and capacitive discharge ignition unit (CDI system)
Ignition coil
Spark plug
Engine kill (stop) switch
Primary and secondary circuit wiring

The breakerless ignition system functions on the same principle as a breaker point ignition system with the pulse generator and CDI unit performing the tasks previously associated with the breaker points and mechanical advance system. As a result, adjustment and maintenance of breakerless ignition components is eliminated (with the exception of spark plug replacement).

Because of their nature, the individual ignition system components can be checked but not repaired. If ignition system troubles occur, and the faulty component can be isolated, the only cure for the problem is to replace the part with a new one. Keep in mind that most electrical parts, once purchased, can't be returned. To avoid unnecessary expense, make very sure the faulty component has been positively identified before buying a replacement part.

2   Ignition system - check

Refer to illustrations 2.5 and 2.14
Warning: *Because of the very high voltage generated by the ignition system, extreme care should be taken when these checks are performed.*
1   If the ignition system is the suspected cause of poor engine performance or failure to start, a number of checks can be made to isolate the problem.
2   Make sure the ignition kill (stop) switch is in the Run or On position.

Engine will not start
3   Refer to Chapter 1 and disconnect the spark plug wire. Connect the wire to a spare spark plug and lay the plug on the engine with the threads contacting the engine. If necessary, hold the spark plug with an insulated tool. Crank the engine over and make sure a well-defined, blue spark occurs between the spark plug electrodes. **Warning:** *Don't remove the spark plug from the engine to perform this check, atomized fuel being pumped out of the open spark plug hole could ignite, causing severe injury!*
4   If no spark occurs, the following checks should be made:

5   Unscrew the spark plug cap from the plug wire and check the cap resistance with an ohmmeter **(see illustration)**. If the resistance is infinite, replace it with a new one.
6   Make sure all electrical connectors are clean and tight. Check all wires for shorts, opens and correct installation.
7   Check the battery voltage with a voltmeter. If the voltage is less than 12-volts, recharge the battery.
8   If you're working on a bike equipped with breaker points, inspect them (see Chapter 1).
9   On all models, refer to Section 8 and check the stator coil (breaker point models) or pulse generator and exciter coil (CDI models).
10   Refer to Section 3 and check the ignition coil primary and secondary resistance.
11   If you're working on a breaker point model and the preceding checks produce positive results but there is still no spark at the plug, refer to Section 4 and check the condenser.
12   If you're working on a CDI model and the preceding checks produce positive results but there is still no spark at the plug, refer to Section 11 and check the CDI unit.

Engine starts but misfires
13   If the engine starts but misfires, make the following checks before deciding that the ignition system is at fault.
14   The ignition system must be able to produce a spark across a seven millimeter (1/4-inch) gap (minimum). A simple test fixture **(see illustration)** can be constructed to make sure the minimum spark gap can be jumped. Make sure the fixture electrodes are positioned seven millimeters apart.
15   Connect one of the spark plug wires to the protruding test fixture electrode, then attach the fixture's alligator clip to a good engine ground.
16   Crank the engine over with the kill switch in the Run position and see if well-defined, blue sparks occur between the test fixture electrodes. If the minimum spark gap test is positive, the ignition coil is functioning properly. If the spark will not jump the gap, or if it is weak (orange colored), refer to Steps 5 through 11 of this Section and perform the checks described.

3   Ignition coil - check, removal and installation

Check
1   In order to determine conclusively that the ignition coil is defective, it should be tested by an authorized Honda dealer service department or other qualified repair shop which is equipped with the special electrical tester required for this check.

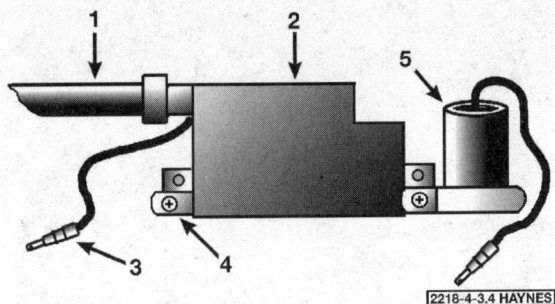

3.4 Ignition coil details (breaker point models)

1   Spark plug wire   4   Ground (mounting screw)
2   Ignition coil body   5   Condenser
3   Primary wire terminal

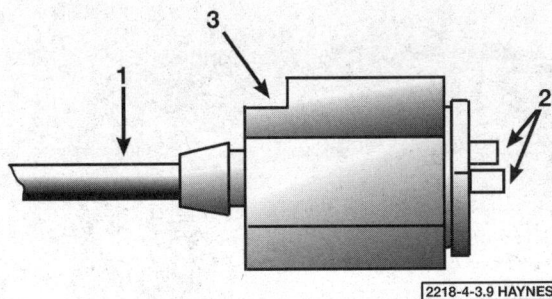

3.9 Ignition coil details (CDI models)

1   Spark plug wire   3   Ignition coil body
2   Primary terminals

2   However, the coil can be checked visually (for cracks and other damage) and the primary and secondary coil resistances can be measured with an ohmmeter. If the coil is undamaged, and if the resistances are as specified, it is probably capable of proper operation.
3   To check the coil for physical damage, it must be removed (see Step 9). To check the resistance, remove the fuel tank (see Chapter 3), unplug the primary circuit electrical connector(s) from the coil and remove the spark plug wire from the spark plug. Mark the locations of all wires before disconnecting them.

Breaker point models
Refer to illustration 3.4
4   To check the coil primary resistance, connect an ohmmeter between the primary terminal and ground **(see illustration)**.
5   Place the ohmmeter selector switch in the Rx1 position and compare the measured resistance to the value listed in this Chapter's Specifications.
6   If the coil primary resistance is as specified, unscrew the spark plug cap from the plug wire. Check the coil secondary resistance by connecting the ohmmeter leads between the spark plug wire terminal and ground **(see illustration 3.4)**. Compare the measured resistance to the value listed in this Chapter's Specifications.
7   Connect the ohmmeter to the ends of the spark plug cap and measure its resistance.
8   If the ignition coil or spark plug cap resistance measurements are not within specifications, replace the coil or cap.

CDI models
Refer to illustration 3.9
Note: *This procedure applies to CDI models through 1997. Testing the ignition coil on 1998 and later models requires a peak voltage tester and should be done by a dealer service department or other qualified shop.*

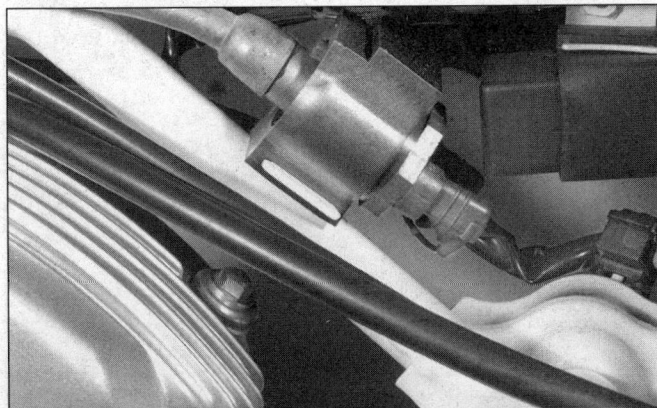

3.14 The ignition coil on some models is rubber-mounted to the frame; on others, it's bolted

9   Label the primary terminal wires, then disconnect them from the ignition coil primary terminals **(see illustration)**.
10 Connect an ohmmeter between the primary terminals. Set the ohmmeter selector switch in the Rx1 position and compare the measured resistance to the value listed in this Chapter's Specifications.
11 Connect the ohmmeter between the green wire's primary terminal and the spark plug cap. Place the ohmmeter selector switch in the Rx100 position and compare the measured resistance to the values listed in this Chapter's Specifications.
12 If the resistances are not as specified, unscrew the spark plug cap from the plug wire and check the resistance between the green wire's primary terminal and the end of the spark plug wire. If it's now within specifications, the spark plug cap is bad. If it's still not as specified, the coil is probably defective and should be replaced with a new one.

Removal and installation
Refer to illustration 3.14
13 To remove the coil, refer to Chapter 3 and remove the fuel tank, then disconnect the spark plug wire from the plug. After labeling them with tape to aid in reinstallation, unplug the coil primary circuit electrical connector(s).
14 On early models, remove the coil mounting screws, then lift the coil out. On later models, slip it off its mounting tab on the frame **(see illustration)**.
15 Installation is the reverse of removal. If you're working on a CDI model, make sure the primary circuit electrical connectors are attached to the proper terminals.

4   Condenser (breaker point models) - removal, check and installation

1   Refer to Chapter 3 and remove the fuel tank.
2   Disconnect the condenser electrical connector, then remove its mounting screw and detach it from the ignition coil **(see illustration 3.4)**.
3   Touch the end of the condenser wire to the condenser body to discharge it.
4   Checking the condenser capacity requires a special meter not normally possessed by do-it-yourselfers. The usual practice is to replace the condenser whenever the breaker points are replaced. If you have the special meter, connect it between the condenser body and the end of the wire. Compare the reading to the value listed in this Chapter's Specifications and replace the condenser if it's outside the range.

5   Alternator - check

Breaker point models
1   Refer to the valve clearance adjustment procedure in Chapter 1

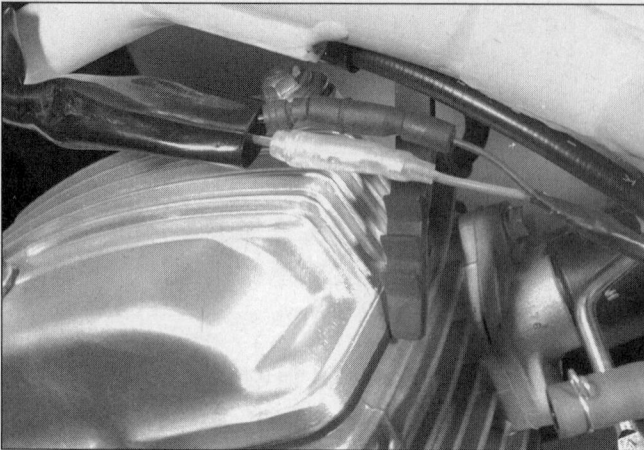

5.6 The alternator connectors on 80/100 CDI models are located above the engine

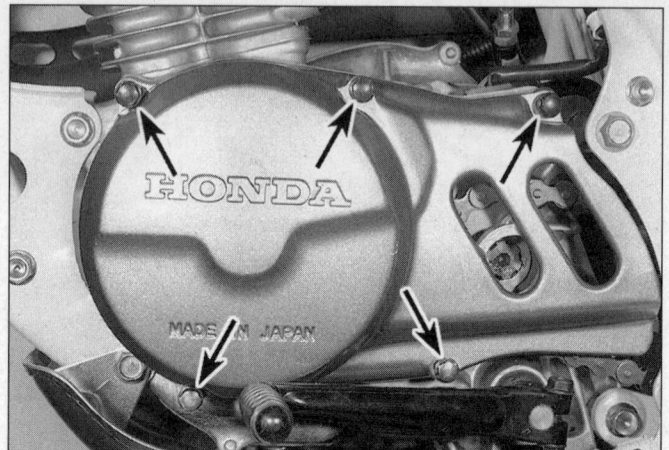

6.1a Remove the cover bolts (arrows), take off the cover and remove the gasket (here's the 80/100 cover) . . .

and position the cylinder at top dead center on its compression stroke.

2   Follow the alternator wire from the point where it exits the top of the left engine cover to its connector. Unplug the connector, then connect an ohmmeter between the disconnected end of the wire and ground (the alternator side, not the wiring harness side). Set the ohmmeter to Rx1 and compare the reading to the value listed in this Chapter's Specifications. If the resistance is above the specified range, try cleaning the breaker points (see Chapter 1).

3   If cleaning the points doesn't help, or if resistance is below the specified range, refer to Section 8 and replace the stator coil.

4   Turn the engine so the piston is no longer at top dead center (any other position is OK). Check the ohmmeter again and compare the reading to the value listed in this Chapter's Specifications. If the reading is not as specified, refer to Section 8 and replace the stator coil.

CDI models

Refer to illustration 5.6

Note: *This procedure applies to CDI models through 1997. Testing the alternator on 1998 and later models requires a peak voltage tester and should be done by a dealer service department or other qualified shop.*

5   Remove the fuel tank (see Chapter 3).

6   Locate the pulse generator connector in the blue-and-yellow wire on top of the engine **(see illustration)**.

7   Unplug the connector, then connect an ohmmeter between the disconnected end of the wire and ground (the alternator side, not the wiring harness side). Set the ohmmeter to Rx1 and compare the reading to the value listed in this Chapter's Specifications. If the resistance

is outside the specified range, refer to Section 10 and replace the pulse generator.

8   Locate the exciter coil connector in the red-and-black wire on top of the engine **(see illustration 5.6)**.

9   Unplug the connector, then connect an ohmmeter between the disconnected end of the wire and ground (the alternator side, not the wiring harness side). Set the ohmmeter to Rx100 and compare the reading to the value listed in this Chapter's Specifications. If the resistance is outside the specified range, refer to Section 9 and replace the exciter coil.

6   Alternator rotor - removal and installation

Note: *To remove the alternator rotor, the special Honda puller (part no. 07733-0010000 or 07933-0010000) or an aftermarket equivalent will be required. Don't try to remove the rotor without the proper puller, as it's almost sure to be damaged. Pullers are readily available from motorcycle dealers and aftermarket tool suppliers.*

Removal

Refer to illustrations 6.1a, 6.1b, 6.3, 6.4 and 6.6

1   Remove the left-side engine cover and gasket from the engine **(see illustrations)**.

2   Prevent the rotor from turning. If the engine is in the bike, you can place the transmission in gear and have an assistant hold the brakes

6.1b . . . and here's the 50/70 cover

6.3 Hold the rotor so it won't turn and remove the nut

6.4 Remove the rotor with a puller, don't try to do this with a makeshift tool

6.6 Look for the Woodruff key (arrow), if it isn't secure in its slot, set it aside for safekeeping

on. If the engine has been removed, use a strap wrench or rotor holding tool.

3   Remove the rotor nut **(see illustration)**.

4   Thread an alternator puller into the center of the rotor and use it to remove the rotor **(see illustration)**. If the rotor doesn't come off easily, tap sharply on the end of the puller to release the rotor's grip on the crankshaft end.

5   Pull the rotor off, together with the spark advancer on breaker point models.

6   Check the Woodruff key **(see illustration)**; if it's not secure in its slot, pull it out and set it aside for safekeeping. A convenient method is to stick the Woodruff key to one of the magnets inside the rotor, but be certain not to forget it's there, as serious damage to the rotor and stator coil or exciter coil will occur if the engine is run with anything stuck to the magnets.

Installation

Refer to illustration 6.11

7   Degrease the center of the rotor and the end of the crankshaft.

8   Make sure the Woodruff key is positioned securely in its slot. Take a look to make sure there isn't anything stuck to the inside of the rotor.

9   Align the rotor slit with the Woodruff key. Place the rotor on the crankshaft.

10   Install the rotor nut. Hold the rotor from turning with one of the methods described in Step 2 and tighten the nut to the torque listed in this Chapter's Specifications.

11   Make sure the wiring harness grommet is positioned in the crankcase, then install a new gasket (if equipped) on the engine **(see illustration)**.

12   Install the left engine cover. Tighten its bolts securely, but don't overtighten and strip the threads.

7   Spark advancer (breaker point models) - removal and installation

Refer to illustration 7.2

1   Remove the alternator rotor (see Section 6).

2   Remove two screws and detach the advancer from inside the rotor **(see illustration)**. Lift the advancer cam and advancer base from the rotor.

3   Installation is the reverse of the removal steps. Engage the grooves in the advancer cam with the tabs on the advancer base.

8   Stator coil (breaker point models) - removal and installation

Refer to illustrations 8.2 and 8.5

1   Remove the alternator rotor (see Section 6).

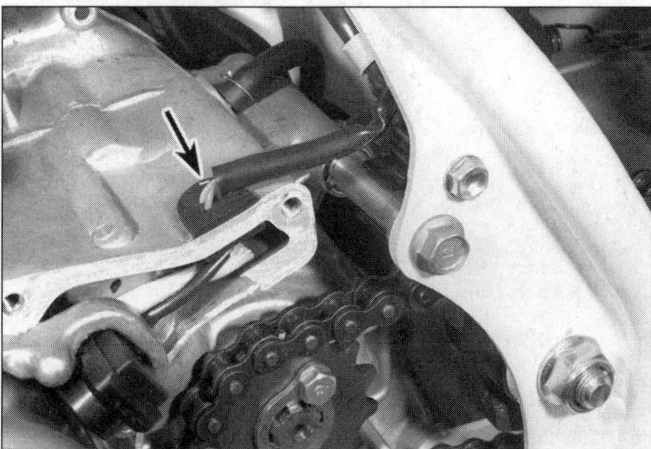

6.11 The wiring harness grommet fits in this notch behind the gasket (some models don't use a gasket)

7.2 The advancer is secured to the rotor by screws

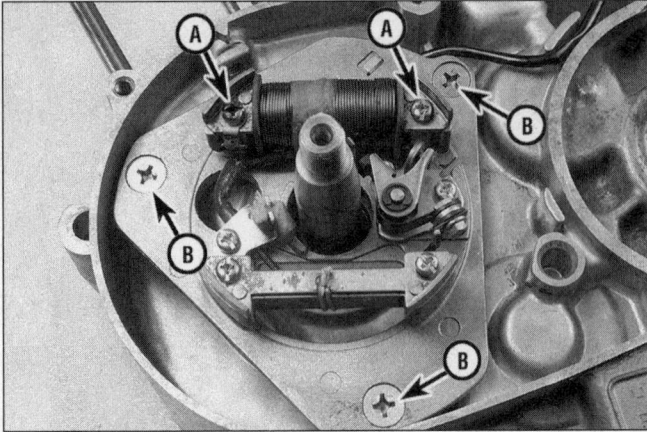

8.2 Loosen the stator coil screws (A) and remove the stator base screws (B); some models have only two stator base screws

8.5 Replace the stator base oil seal if there's any doubt about its condition

9.3 The exciter coil is secured by bolts (arrows)

9.4a On some models, the pulse generator bolts are accessible from the outside; if they aren't, as shown here (arrows), remove the stator base screws with an impact driver (some models have three screws) . . .

2   Loosen the stator coil screws **(see illustration)**. This will be easier to do while the stator base is bolted to the engine, especially if the screws are very tight. You may need to use an impact driver.

3   Follow the stator coil wire to its connector and unplug it. Remove the stator base screws and take the stator base off the engine.

4   Remove the stator coil screws and pull the wire through the stator base.

5   Inspect the oil seal in the stator base **(see illustration)**. If it shows signs of wear or has been leaking, pry it out of the stator base and drive in a new one with a seal driver or socket the same diameter as the seal.

6   Thread the stator coil wire through the stator base, then install the stator coil screws and tighten them slightly.

7   Install the stator base on the engine. Tighten the mounting screws and stator coil screws securely, but don't overtighten them and strip out the threads.

9   Exciter coil and pulse generator (CDI models)

Note: *On early models, the exciter coil and pulse generator can be replaced separately. On later models, they're supplied as a complete unit, so if one component is defective both must be replaced. If you're working on an early model and only plan to replace one component, ignore the steps that don't apply.*

80 and 100 models

Refer to illustrations 9.3, 9.4a and 9.4b

1   Remove the left engine cover (see Section 6) and the fuel tank (see Chapter 3).

2   Disconnect the exciter coil wire and pulse generator wire at the

9.4b . . . and turn the stator base around for access to the bolt heads

connector on top of the engine **(see illustration 5.6)**.

3   Remove the exciter coil bolts and take it off the engine **(see illustration)**.

4   If the pulse generator screws are accessible from outside, remove them. If they're installed with their heads toward the engine, you'll need to remove the stator base and turn it around for access to the screw heads **(see illustrations)**.

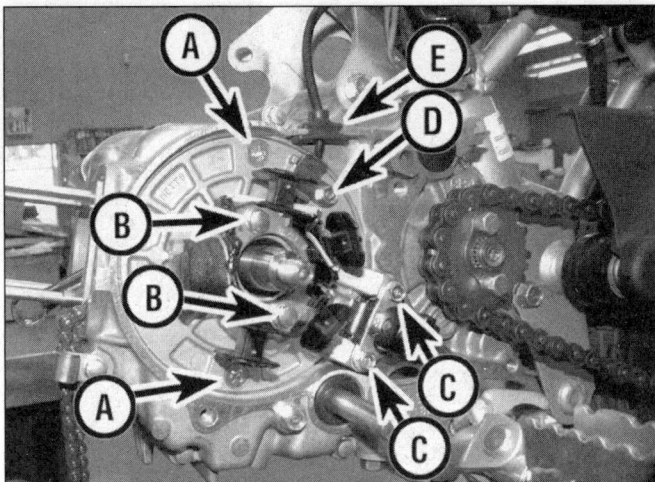

9.7 Alternator details (50 and 70 models)

a) Stator plate screws
b) Exciter coil bolts
c) Pulse generator bolts
d) Harness retainer bolt
e) Grommet

5   Installation is the reverse of the removal steps. Tighten the screws and bolts securely, but don't overtighten them and strip the threads.

50 and 70 models

Refer to illustrations 9.7, 9.8a, 9.8b and 9.9

6   Remove the left engine cover (see Section 6).
7   Remove the bolts and screws that secure the exciter coil, pulse generator and harness clamp **(see illustration)**.
8   Check around the edge of the stator plate and its oil seal for oil leaks. If leaks can be seen, remove the stator plate screws **(see illustration 9.7)**. Take the stator plate off and replace its O-ring **(see illustration)**. If the seal has been leaking, pry it out and press in a new one with a socket or bearing driver the same diameter as the seal **(see illustration)**.
9   Installation is the reverse of the removal steps. Use new O-rings to seal the stator plate screws **(see illustration)**.Tighten the screws and bolts securely, but don't overtighten them and strip the threads.

---

10 CDI unit, harness check - removal and installation

1   The CDI unit is tested by process of elimination (when all other possible causes of ignition problems have been checked and eliminated, the CDI unit is at fault).

9.9 Replace the screw hole O-rings (arrows) whenever the stator plate has been removed

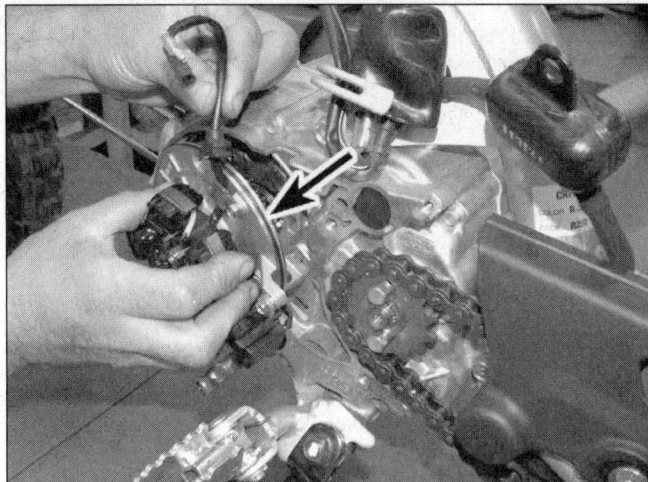

9.8a Remove the stator plate to replace its O-ring (arrow)

9.8b Check the stator plate seal and replace it if it has been leaking

Harness check

Refer to illustration 10.2

2   Disconnect the CDI unit electrical connectors **(see illustration)**. If necessary, remove the fuel tank (see Chapter 3).
3   Set an ohmmeter to the R x 1 position and connect it between the black/yellow and green wire terminals in the harness. It should give

10.2 The CDI unit is mounted on the frame

the same reading as for ignition coil primary resistance, listed in this Chapter's Specifications.

4   Set the ohmmeter at R x 100 and connect it between ground and the blue/yellow wire terminal in the harness. It should give the same reading as for the pulse generator resistance, listed in this Chapter's Specifications.

5   If the harness failed any of the preceding tests, check the affected wires for breaks or poor connections.

6   If the harness and all other system components tested good, the CDI unit may be defective. Before buying a new one, it's a good idea to substitute a known good CDI unit.

Removal and installation

7   Remove the fuel tank if you haven't already done so (see Chapter 3).

8   Locate the CDI unit (it's mounted under the main frame member near the coil) **(see illustration 10.2)**. Unplug its connector and work the unit out of its mounting band.

9   Installation is the reverse of the removal steps.

---

11   Kill switch - check, removal and installation

Refer to illustration 11.1

1   The kill switch works by grounding the ignition system. To test, follow the switch wires to the connector (black/white wire) and the mounting screw (black wire), then disconnect the wires **(see illustration)**.

2   Set an ohmmeter to the Rx1 position and connect it between the ends of the wires. When the button is not pressed, the ohmmeter should indicate infinite resistance (no continuity). When the button is pressed, the ohmmeter should indicate little or no resistance. If the ohmmeter readings are not as described, replace the switch.

3   To remove the switch from the handle, remove its mounting screw, open the clamp and take the switch off the handlebar.

4   Installation is the reverse of the removal steps.

---

12   Ignition switch - check and replacement

1   An ignition switch is used on 2001 and later models.

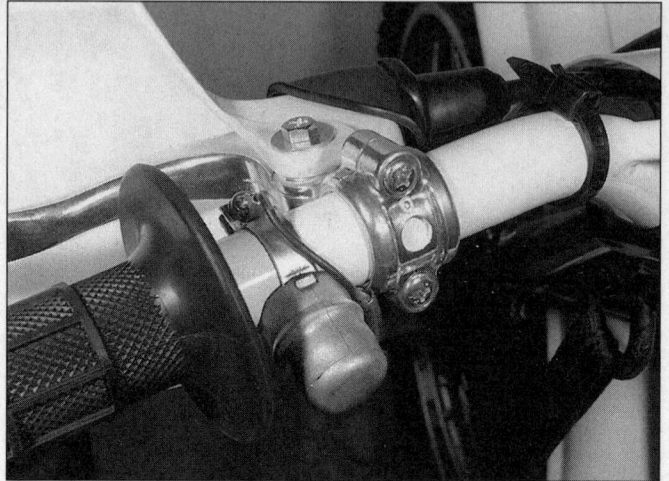

11.1 The kill switch is mounted on the left handlebar

Check

2   Remove the fuel tank (see Chapter 3).

3   Follow the wiring harness from the ignition switch to the connectors and disconnect them.

4   Connect an ohmmeter or continuity tester between the connectors in the switch side of the wiring harness.

5   With the switch in the On position, there should be continuity (the ohmmeter should indicate little or no resistance). With the switch in the Off position, there should be no continuity (the ohmmeter should indicate infinite resistance). If the switch doesn't perform as described, replace it.

Replacement

6   Perform Steps 2 and 3 above.

7   Squeeze the prongs on the sides of the switch and slip it out of the bracket.

8   Installation is the reverse of the removal Steps.

Chapter 5
Steering, suspension and final drive

Contents

Specifications

50 and 70 models

Front forks

Lubricant type	
XR50R, CRF50F	Multi-purpose grease
XR70R, CRF70F	Pro Honda Suspension Fluid SS-8 or equivalent
Lubricant capacity	
XR50R, CRF50F	
Slider outer guide groove	5 to 6 grams
Fork spring interior	14 grams
XR70R	78 +/- 2.5 cc (2.64 +/- 0.08 fl oz, 2.75 +/- 0.09 Imp oz)
CRF70F	74 +/- 1 cc (2.50 +/0 0.03 fl oz, 2.60 +/- 0.04 Imp oz)
Fluid level	
XR70R	123 mm (4.8 inches)
CRF70F	135 mm (3.5 inches)
Fork spring length	
XR50R	
Standard	160.8 mm (6.33 inches)
Limit	158.3 mm (6.23 inches)
CR50F	
2004 through 2012	
Standard	169.0 mm (6.65 inches)
Limit	166.5 mm (6.56 inches)
XR70R	
Standard	404.5 mm (15.93 inches)
Limit	396.4 mm (15.61 inches)
CRF70F	1985 through 2000
Standard	417.5 mm (16.44 inches)
Limit	409.2 mm (16.11 inches)
Fork tube bend limit (1/2 indicator reading)	0.2 mm (0.008 inch)

Drive chain

Drive chain slider wear limit	Wear limit guide worn away
Drive chain length limit	
XR50R, CRF50F (41 pins)	511 mm (20.1 inches)
XR70R, CRF70F (85 pins)	1101 mm (43-5/16 inches)

Tightening torques

Handlebar mounting nuts
XR50R, CRF50F .... 20 Nm (14 ft-lbs)
CRF70F .... 47 Nm (35 ft-lbs)
Handlebar bracket bolts (XR70R, CRF70F) .... 10 Nm (84 inch-lbs)
Front axle nut .... See Chapter 6
Upper triple clamp bolts .... Not applicable
Lower triple clamp bolts (XR70R, CRF70F) .... 32 Nm (24 ft-lbs)
Damper rod bolt (XR70R, CRF70F) .... 20 Nm (14 ft-lbs)
Fork cap bolt
XR50R, CRF50F .... Not specified
XR70R, CRF70F .... 23 Nm (17 ft-lbs)
Steering stem bearing adjusting nut .... See Chapter 1
Rear shock absorber mounting bolts and nuts .... 34 Nm (25 ft-lbs)
Swingarm pivot bolt
80 and 100 models .... 64 Nm (47 ft-lbs)
50 and 70 models .... 39 Nm (29 ft-lbs)
Engine sprocket bolts .... 12 Nm (108 inch-lbs)
Rear sprocket bolts/nuts .... 32 Nm (24 ft-lbs)

80 and 100 models

Front forks

Oil type .... Honda SS-8 suspension fluid or equivalent fork oil
Oil capacity
XR80R .... 83 +/- 2.5 cc (2.8 +/- 0.08 fl oz)
CRF80F .... 85 +/- 2.5 cc (2.9 +/- 0.08 fl oz)
XR100R
1985 through 2000 .... 88 +/- 2.5 cc (3.0 +/- 0.08 fl oz)
2001 through 2003 .... 86 +/- 2.5 cc (2.9 +/- 0.08 fl oz)
CRF100F .... 84 +/- 2.5 cc (2.8 +/- 0.08 fl oz)
Oil level (fork fully compressed and spring removed)
XR80R .... 184 mm (7.24 inches)
CRF80F .... 177 mm (6.97 inches)
XR100R
1985 through 2000 .... 205 mm (8.07 inches)
2001 through 2003 .... 200 mm (7.78 inches)
CRF100F .... 207 mm (8.15 inches)
Fork spring free length
XR80R
Standard .... 525.2 mm (20.68 inches)
Limit .... 514.7 mm (20.26 inches)
CRF80F
Standard .... 531.2 mm (20.91 inches)
Limit .... 520.7 mm (20.50 inches)
XR100R
1985 through 2000
Standard .... 566.0 mm (22.28 inches)
Limit .... 554.7 mm (21.84 inches)
2001 through 2003
Standard .... 548.0 mm (21.57 inches)
Limit .... 537.0 mm (21.14 inches)
CRF100F
Standard .... 546.0 mm (21.50 inches)
Limit .... 535.0 mm (21.06 inches)
Fork tube bend limit (1/2 indicator reading) .... 0.2 mm (0.008 inch)

Rear suspension

Rear shock absorber spring length
XR80R
Standard .... 136.0 mm (5.35 inches)
Limit .... 133.3 mm (5.27 inches)
CRF80F
Standard .... 137.0 mm (5.39 inches)
Limit .... 134.3 mm (5.29 inches)
XR100R
1985 through 2000
Standard .... 136.5 mm (5.37 inches)
Limit .... 133.8 mm (5.27 inches)

2001 through 2003	
Standard	140.4 mm (5.53 inches)
Limit	137.6 mm (5.42 inches)
CRF100F	
Standard	123.5 mm (4.86 inches)
Limit	121.0 mm (4.76 inches)
Suspension linkage bushing inside diameter	
Standard	18.000 to 18.052 mm (0.7087 to 0.7107 inch)
Limit	18.25 mm (0.718 inch)
Suspension linkage sleeve outside diameter	
Standard	17.941 to 17.968 mm (0.7063 to 0.7074 inch)
Limit	17.91 mm (0.705 inch)
Swingarm bushing inside diameter	
Standard	14.990 to 15.030 mm (0.5902 to 0.5971 inch)
Limit	15.20 mm (0.598 inch)
Swingarm pivot collar outside diameter	
Standard	14.966 to 14.984 mm (0.5892 to 0.5899 inch)
Limit	14.94 mm (0.588 inch)

Drive chain

Drive chain slider minimum thickness	6 mm (15/64 inch)
Drive chain length limit	
1985 through 1997	
XR80R (109 pins)	1412 mm (55-39/64 inches)
XR100R 9117 pins)	1516 mm (59-45/64 inches)
1998 and later (41 pins)	511 mm (20-7/64 inch)

Tightening torques

Handlebar bracket bolts	12 Nm (108 inch-lbs)
Front axle nut	See Chapter 6
Upper triple clamp bolts	
XR80R, XR100R	11 Nm (96 inch-lbs)
CRF80F, CRF100F	18 Nm (13 ft-lbs)
Lower triple clamp bolts	26 Nm (20 ft-lbs)
Damper rod bolt	
1985 through 1997	Not specified
1998 and later	20 Nm (14 ft-lbs)
Fork cap bolt	23 Nm (17 ft-lbs)
Steering stem bearing adjusting nut	See Chapter 1
Rear shock absorber upper mounting bolt	
1985 through 2000	34 Nm (25 ft-lbs)
2001 and later	44 Nm (33 ft-lbs)
Rear shock absorber lower mounting bolt	34 Nm (25 ft-lbs)
Suspension linkage bolts	44 Nm (33 ft-lbs)
Swingarm pivot bolt	
1998 through 2000	62 Nm (46 ft-lbs)
2001 and later	64 Nm (47 ft-lbs)
Engine sprocket bolts	
1985 through 1997	8 to 12 Nm (72 to 108 inch-lbs)
1998 and later	Not specified
Rear sprocket bolts/nuts	32 Nm (24 ft-lbs)

1   General information

The steering system on these models consists of a one-piece handlebar and a ball-bearing steering head attached to the front portion of the frame. The front suspension on 80 and 100 models consists of simple damper rod forks, which are not equipped with bushings. The front suspension on 50 and 70 models consists of telescopic forks with internal springs. The rear suspension on all models consists of a single shock absorber with concentric coil spring and swingarm. 80 and 100 models use Honda's Pro-Link suspension linkage. The suspension linkage produces a progressive rising rate effect, where the suspension stiffens as its travel increases. This allows a softer ride over small bumps in the terrain, together with firmer suspension control over large irregularities.

2   Handlebars - removal, inspection and installation

Refer to illustrations 2.3, 2.4, 2.6 and 2.7

1   The handlebars rest in a bracket on the upper triple clamp. If the handlebars must be removed for access to other components, such as the steering head bearings, simply remove the bolts and slip the handlebars off the bracket. It's not necessary to disconnect the throttle, clutch or brake cables, but it is a good idea to support the assembly with a piece of wire or rope to avoid unnecessary strain on the cables.

2   If the handlebars are to be removed completely, refer to Chapter 2 for the clutch lever removal procedure (except 50 models), Chapter 3 for the throttle housing removal procedure and Chapter 6 for the brake lever removal procedure.

3   On all except 50 models, remove the upper bracket bolts, lift off

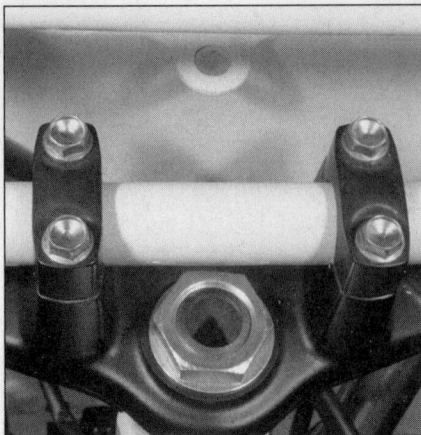

2.3 Remove the bolts and lift off the upper brackets

2.4 On 50 and 70 models, remove the handlebar nuts (arrows) from the underside of the triple clamp

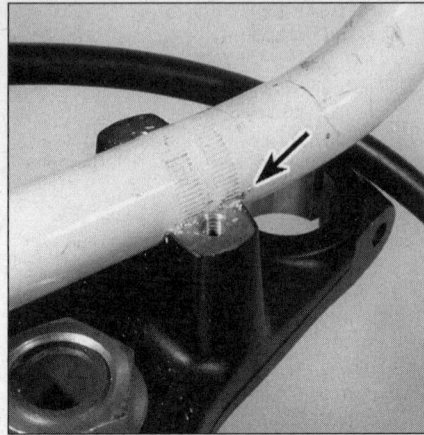

2.6 Align the punch mark in the handlebar (arrow) with the edge of the lower bracket

the brackets and remove the handlebars **(see illustration)**.

4   On 50 models, remove the handlebar mounting nuts from the underside of the upper triple clamp **(see illustration)**. Lift the handlebars off.

5   Check the handlebars and brackets for cracks and distortion and replace them if any problems are found.

6   On all except 50 models, place the handlebars in the lower brackets. Line up the punch mark on the handlebar with the parting line of the upper and lower brackets **(see illustration)**.

7   On all except 50 models, install the upper brackets with their punch marks facing forward **(see illustration)**. Tighten the front bolts, then the rear bolts, to the torque listed in this Chapter's Specifications. **Caution:** *If there's a gap between the upper and lower brackets at the rear after tightening the bolts, don't try to close it by tightening beyond the recommended torque. You'll only crack the brackets.*

8   On 50 models, install the handlebars in the upper triple clamp. Install the mounting nuts and tighten them to the torque listed in this Chapter's Specifications.

---

3   Front forks - removal and installation

---

1   Support the bike securely upright so it can't fall over during this procedure.

2   Refer to Chapter 6 and remove the front wheel.

70 through 100 models

Removal

Refer to illustration 3.3

3   If you plan to disassemble the forks, loosen the fork cap bolts now **(see illustration)**. This can be done later, but it will be easier while the forks are securely held in the triple clamps.

4   Unbolt the brake cable retainer from the left fork leg.

5   Loosen the upper and lower triple clamp bolts **(see illustration 3.3)**.

6   Lower the fork leg out of the triple clamps, twisting it if necessary.

Installation

7   Slide each fork leg into the lower triple clamp.

8   Slide the fork legs up, installing the tops of the tubes into the upper triple clamp. Position the forks so the top of each tube is flush with the top surface of the upper triple clamp.

9   Tighten the triple clamp bolts to the torque listed in this Chapter's Specifications.

10   The remainder of installation is the reverse of the removal steps.

50 models

Removal

Refer to illustrations 3.13a, 3.13b, 3.14a and 3.14b

11   The outer fork tubes are permanently attached to the upper triple

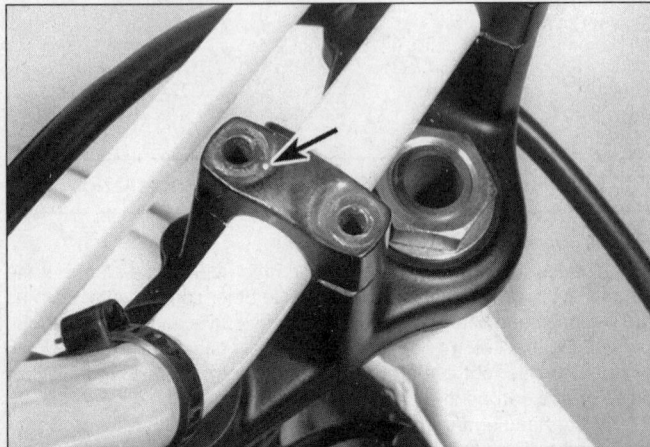

2.7 Install the upper brackets with their punch marks (arrow) facing forward

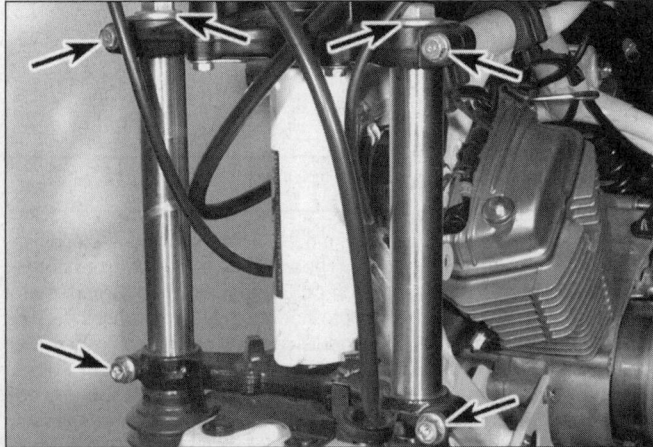

3.3 Loosen the fork cap bolts (upper arrows) while the forks are held in the triple clamps; loosen the triple clamp bolts (lower arrows) to remove the forks

3.13a Slide the rubber boot down the fork leg . . .

3.13b . . . and remove the snap-ring from its groove (arrow)

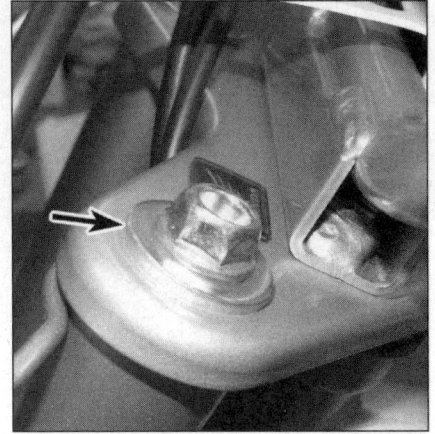

3.14a Remove the fork top bolt and washer . . .

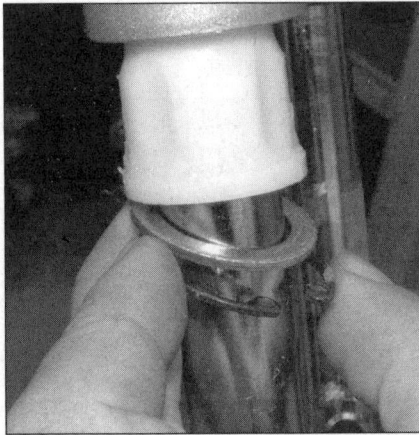

3.14b . . . and lower the fork assembly out of the outer fork tube

3.15 On installation, align the boss on the fork with the notch in the triple clamp (arrow)

4.2a On 1988 and later models, slide the fork gaiter out of its groove (arrow) and loosen the clamp at the top end to remove the gaiter

clamp. Removal of the forks involves removing the fork assembly from the outer tube.

12 If you're working on the left fork leg, loosen the brake adjusting nut and slip the cable out of the bracket on the fork leg (see Chapter 1 if necessary).

13 Slide the dust seal down the fork leg to expose the snap-ring, then remove the snap-ring **(see illustrations)**.

14 Remove the top bolt and washer from the upper end of the fork, then pull the fork assembly down and out of the outer fork tube **(see illustrations)**.

Installation

Refer to illustration 3.15

15 Installation is the reverse of the removal steps, with the following additions:

a) *Align the boss on the upper end of the fork leg with the notch in the upper triple clamp* **(see illustration)**.

b) *Tighten all fasteners to the torques listed in this Chapter's Specifications.*

4   Front forks - disassembly, inspection and reassembly

70 through 100 models

Disassembly

Refer to illustrations 4.2a through 4.2k

1   Remove the forks following the procedure in Section 3. Work on one fork at a time to prevent mixing up the parts.

2   To disassemble the forks, refer to the accompanying photo sequence **(see illustrations)**.

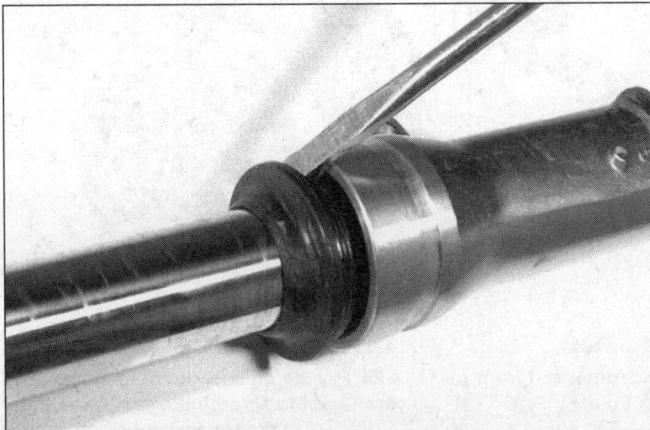

4.2b Pry the dust seal out of the outer fork tube

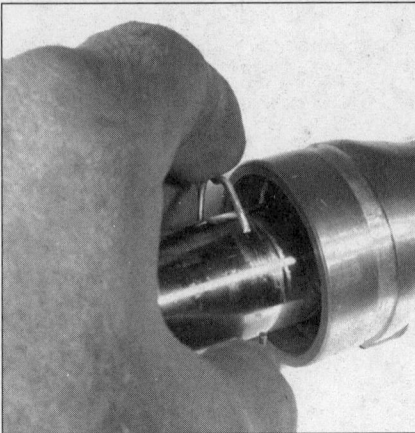

4.2c Pry the retaining ring out of its groove and slide it off the inner fork tube

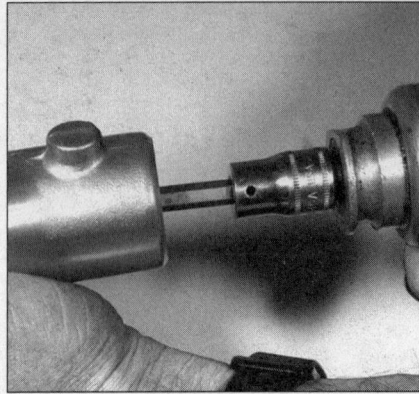

4.2d Loosen the Allen bolt in the bottom of the outer fork tube - an air wrench is the easiest way to do this if you have one, but if not, unscrew the bolt with an Allen wrench while the fork cap is still installed; the spring pressure will keep the damper rod from turning inside the fork

4.2e Remove the Allen bolt and its copper sealing washer; use a new washer on reassembly

4.2f Let the oil drain from the bottom of the fork; pump the inner fork tube up and down to expel the oil

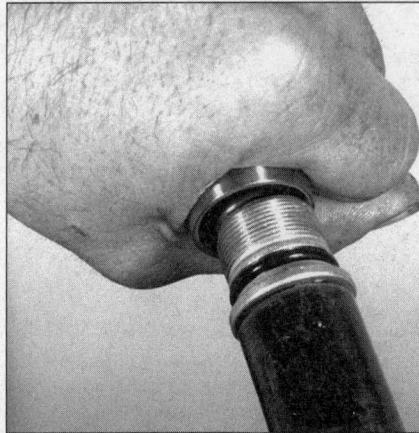

4.2g Unscrew the cap bolt and remove the O-ring - be careful of spring tension!

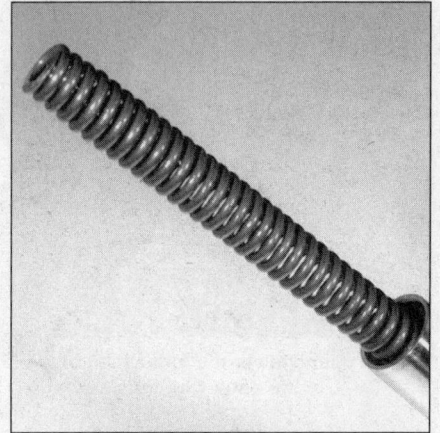

4.2h Pull the spring out of the fork; its narrow end faces into the fork tube on reassembly

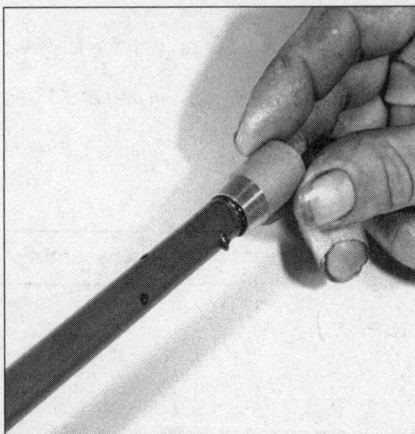

4.2i Take the oil lock piece off the end of the damper rod . . .

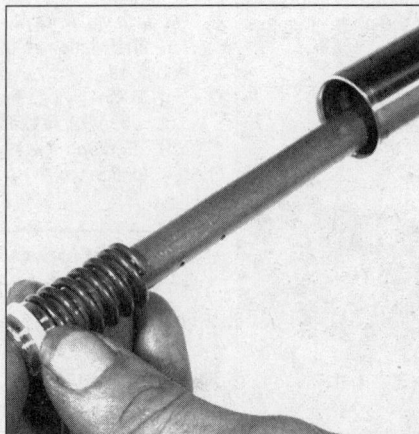

4.2j . . . and remove the damper rod from the inner fork tube

4.2k Pry the oil seal out of its bore; be careful not to scratch the seal's seating area in the fork tube

4.6 Replace the Teflon ring on the damper rod if it's worn or damaged

4.7 Place the damper rod in the inner fork tube so it protrudes from the bottom . . .

4.8 . . . then place the oil lock piece on the end of the damper rod and install the assembly in the outer fork tube

4.11 If you don't have a seal driver, a section of pipe can be used the same way the seal driver would be used - as a slide hammer (be sure to tape the ends of the pipe so the fork tube doesn't get scratch)

4.12 Make sure the retaining ring seats in its groove

Inspection

Refer to illustration 4.6

3   Clean all parts in solvent and blow them dry with compressed air, if available. Check the inner and outer fork tubes and the damper rod for score marks, scratches, flaking of the chrome and excessive or abnormal wear. Look for dents in the tubes and replace them if any are found. Check the fork seal seat for nicks, gouges and scratches. If damage is evident, leaks will occur around the seal-to-outer tube junction. Replace worn or defective parts with new ones.

4   Set the inner fork tube on a pair of V-blocks and check the runout with a dial indicator, comparing your measurement with the figure listed in this Chapter's Specifications. If you don't have the proper equipment, have the inner fork tube checked for runout at a dealer service department or other repair shop. **Warning:** *If the tube is bent, it should be replaced with a new one. Don't try to straighten it.*

5   Measure the overall length of the long spring and check it for cracks or other damage. Compare the length to the minimum length listed in this Chapter's Specifications. If it's defective or sagged, replace both fork springs with new ones. Never replace only one spring.

6   Check the Teflon ring on the damper rod for wear or damage and replace it if problems are found **(see illustration)**. **Note:** *Don't remove the ring from the damper rod unless you plan to replace it.*

Reassembly

Refer to illustrations 4.7, 4.8, 4.11, 4.12, 4.13 and 4.14

7   Place the rebound spring over the damper rod and slide the rod assembly into the inner fork tube until it protrudes from the lower end **(see illustration)**.

8   Place the oil lock piece on the base of the damper rod **(see illustration)**.

9   Insert the inner fork tube/damper rod assembly into the outer fork tube until the Allen-head bolt (with copper washer) can be threaded into the damper rod from the lower end of the outer tube **(see illustration 4.2e)**. **Note:** *Apply a non-permanent thread locking agent to the threads of the bolt. Keep the two tubes fairly horizontal so the oil lock piece doesn't fall off the damper rod inside the outer fork tube. Temporarily install the fork spring and cap to place tension on the damper rod so it won't spin inside the fork tube while you tighten the Allen bolt.*

10   Tighten the Allen bolt securely, then remove the fork cap and spring.

11   Lubricate the lips and outer diameter of the fork seal with the recommended fork oil (see this Chapter's Specifications). Slide the seal down the inner tube with the lips facing down. Drive the seal into position with a fork seal driver (Honda part no. 07747-0010100 and 07447-0010300 or 07947-1180001). If you don't have access to one of these, it is recommended that you take the fork to a Honda dealer or other repair shop for seal installation. You can also make a substitute tool from a piece of pipe **(see illustration)**. If you're very careful, the seal can be driven in with a hammer and drift punch. Work around the circumference of the seal, tapping gently on the outer edge of the seal until it's seated **(see illustration 4.2k)**. Be careful - if you distort the seal, you'll have to disassemble the fork and end up taking it to a dealer anyway!

12   Install the retaining ring, making sure it's completely seated in its groove **(see illustration)**.

4.13 Push the dust seal down until it seats in the outer fork tube

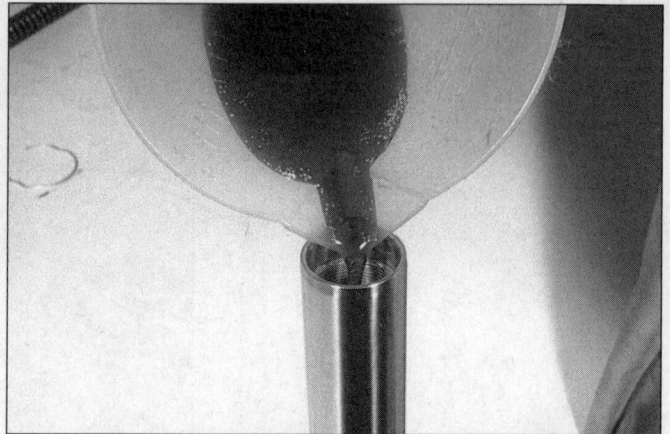
4.14 Pour the specified amount of oil into the fork

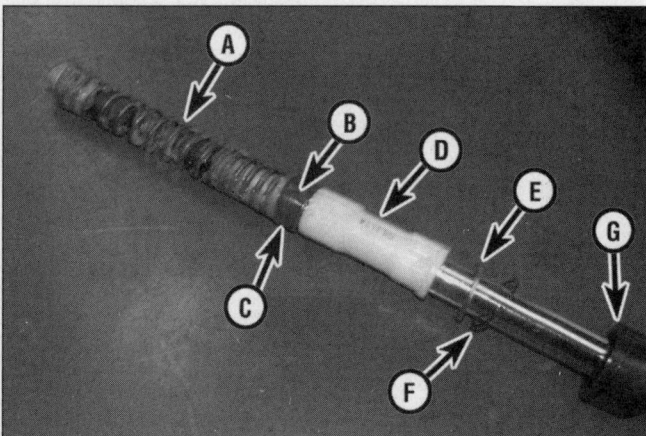
4.18 Fork assembly details (50 models)

a)	Spring and holder unit	e)	Back-up ring
b)	Retaining pin	f)	Snap-ring
c)	Slider piston	g)	Rubber boot
d)	Slider guide		

13   Install the dust seal, making sure it seats completely **(see illustration)**. If you're working on a 1988 or later model, pull the fork gaiter down into its groove on the outer fork tube and secure the upper end to the inner fork tube with the clamping band.

14   Compress the fork fully and add the recommended type and quantity of fork oil listed in this Chapter's Specifications **(see illustration)**. Measure the fork oil level from the top of the fork tube. If necessary, add or remove oil to bring it to the proper level.

15   Install the fork spring, with the small-diameter end facing down. Install the O-ring and fork cap.

16   Install the fork, following the procedure outlined in Section 3. Tighten the cap bolt after installation to the torque listed in this Chapter's Specifications.

50 models

Refer to illustration 4.18

17   Remove the forks following the procedure in Section 3. Remove one fork leg at a time to avoid mixing up the parts.

18   Drive the retaining pin out of the slider piston **(see illustration)**. Remove the spring assembly, slider guide, back-up ring, snap-ring and dust seal off of the fork leg.

19   Check all parts for wear and damage. Replace any worn or damaged parts. **Warning:** *Do not try to straighten a bent fork leg. Replace it with a new one.*

20   Installation is the reverse of the removal steps. The narrow side of

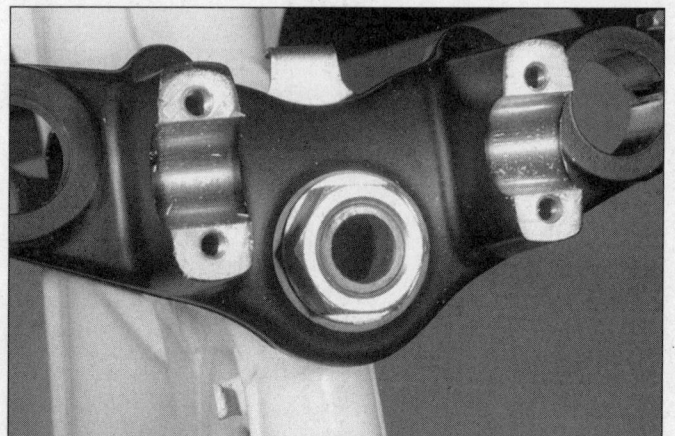
5.4 Loosen the steering stem nut

the slider piston faces away from the spring. Drive in the pin until it is flush with the slider piston surfaces.

5   Steering head bearings - replacement

Removal

Refer to illustrations 5.4, 5.6, 5.7, 5.8, 5.9 and 5.10

1   Remove the front wheel (see Chapter 6).

2   Remove the number plate and the front fender.

3   Refer to Section 2 and remove the handlebars.

4   Loosen the steering stem nut **(see illustration)**.

5   Refer to Section 3 and remove the front forks.

6   Remove the steering stem nut and washer, then lift the upper triple clamp off the steering stem **(see illustration)**.

7   Unscrew the steering stem bearing adjusting nut **(see illustration)**.

8   Place a container such as a cardboard box beneath the steering head, then lower the steering stem out of the head **(see illustration)**. The box will catch any bearing balls that fall out.

9   Remove any lower bearing balls that remain in the steering head **(see illustration)**. There are 21 balls in the lower bearing.

10   Lift the upper bearing race off the bearing and remove the bearing balls **(see illustration)**. There are 21 bearing balls in the upper bearing.

Inspection

Refer to illustrations 5.14a and 5.14b

11   Clean all the parts with solvent and dry them thoroughly, using compressed air, if available. Wipe the old grease out of the steering head and the bearing races.

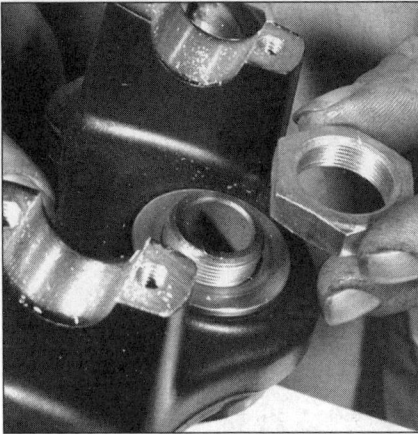

5.6 Remove the nut and washer and lift the upper triple clamp off the steering stem

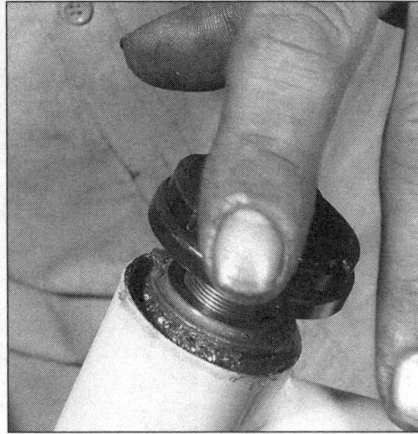

5.7 Remove the bearing adjusting nut

5.8 Place a box under the steering head to catch loose bearing balls, then lower the steering stem out of the head

5.9 Collect any bearing balls that remain in the steering head

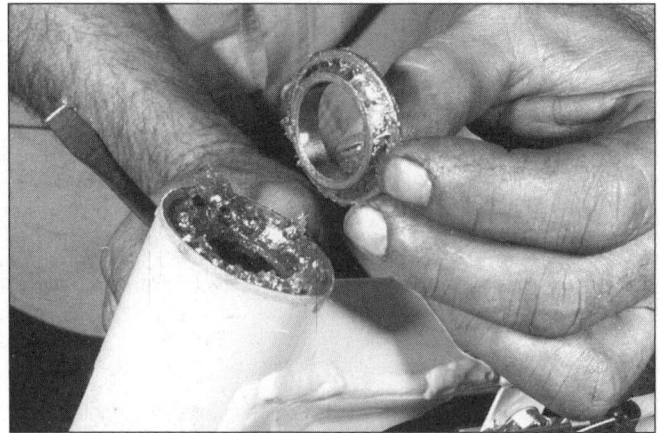

5.10 Lift the top race off the upper bearing and remove the upper bearing balls

12   Examine the races on the steering stem and in the steering head for cracks, dents and pits. If even the slightest amount of wear or damage is evident, the races should be replaced with new ones.
13   Check the ball bearings for wear. Replace any defective parts with new ones. If a new bearing is required, replace both of them as a set.
14   To remove the races, drive them out of the steering head with a brass drift (see illustration). A slide hammer with the proper internal-

jaw puller will also work. Since the races are an interference fit in the frame, installation will be easier if the new races are left overnight in a freezer. This will cause them to contract and slip into place in the frame with very little effort. When installing the races, coat them with oil and tap them gently into place with a bearing driver or a hammer and punch or a large socket (see illustration). Do not strike the bearing surface or the race will be damaged.

5.14a Drive out the bearing races with a hammer and brass drift

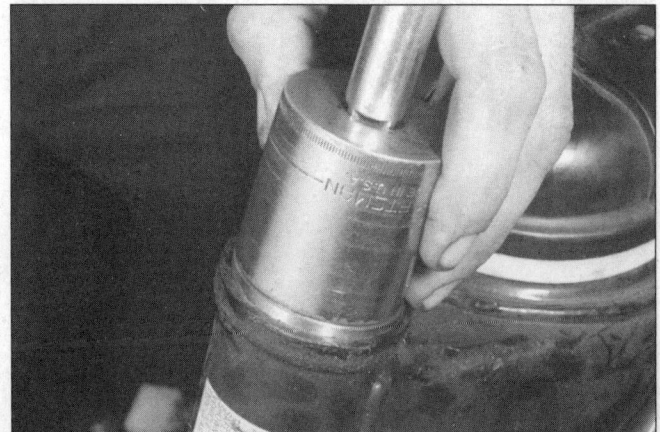

5.14b Drive in the bearing races with a bearing driver or socket the same diameter as the bearing race

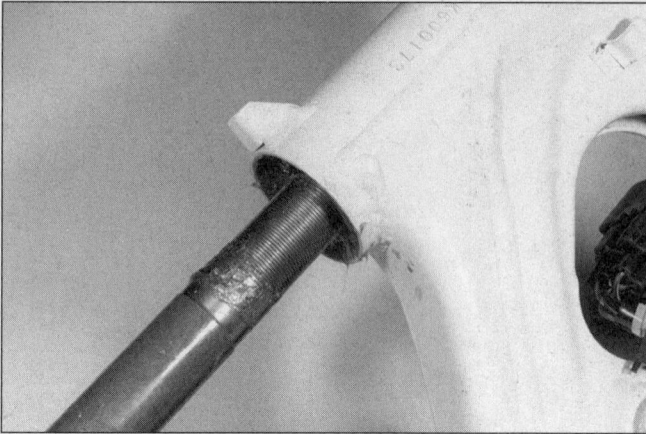

5.19 Slide the steering stem into the steering head, taking care not to dislodge any bearing balls

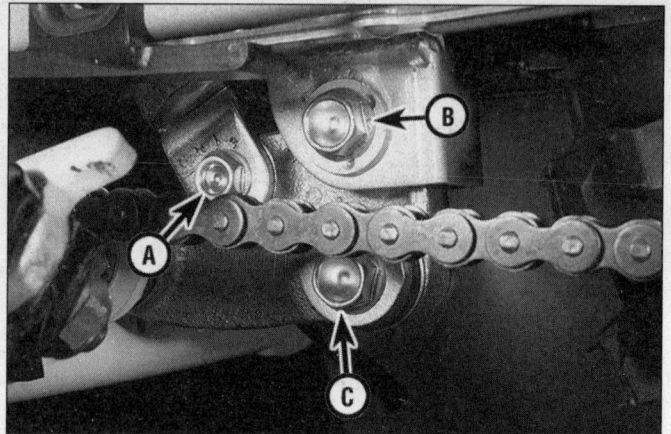

6.3 Remove the shock absorber lower mounting bolt and the shock arm-to-swingarm bolt

a) *Shock absorber lower mounting bolt*
b) *Shock arm-to-swingarm bolt*
c) *Shock arm-to-shock link bolt*

15   To remove the lower bearing bottom race from the steering stem, tap it evenly up the stem with a hammer and punch. Don't remove this race unless it, or the grease seal underneath it, must be replaced.
16   Check the grease seal under the lower bearing and replace it with a new one if necessary. Drive the new grease seal and lower bearing bottom race onto the steering stem with a hollow driver or piece of pipe.
17   Inspect the steering stem/lower triple clamp for cracks and other damage.

Installation
Refer to illustration 5.19
18   Coat the lower bearing race in the steering head with a thick layer of grease. On models with uncaged bearings, coat 21 bearing balls with grease and stick them to the lower race **(see illustration 5.9)**.
19   Carefully insert the steering stem/lower triple clamp into the steering head, making sure you don't displace any of the bearing balls **(see illustration)**.
20   Coat the upper bearing race in the steering head with a thick layer of grease. On models with uncaged bearings, coat 21 bearing balls with grease and stick them to the upper race, then install the upper bearing top race over the balls **(see illustration 5.10)**.
21   Install the bearing adjusting nut and tighten it to the correct setting (see Chapter 1).

22   Turn the lower triple clamp back and forth. It should turn easily, without binding and without looseness.
23   Install the upper triple clamp on the steering stem. Install the washer and nut, tightening the nut to the torque listed in this Chapter's Specifications.
24   The remainder of installation is the reverse of the removal steps.
25   After all parts are installed, recheck the steering head bearing adjustment and correct it if necessary (see Chapter 1).

6   Rear shock absorber - removal, inspection and installation

80 and 100 models
Refer to illustrations 6.3, 6.4a and 6.4b
1   Support the bike securely so it can't be knocked over during this procedure.
2   Remove the left side cover.
3   Unbolt the shock arm from the swingarm and remove the shock absorber's lower mounting bolt **(see illustration)**.
4   Remove the upper mounting bolt and lower the shock away from the bike **(see illustrations)**.

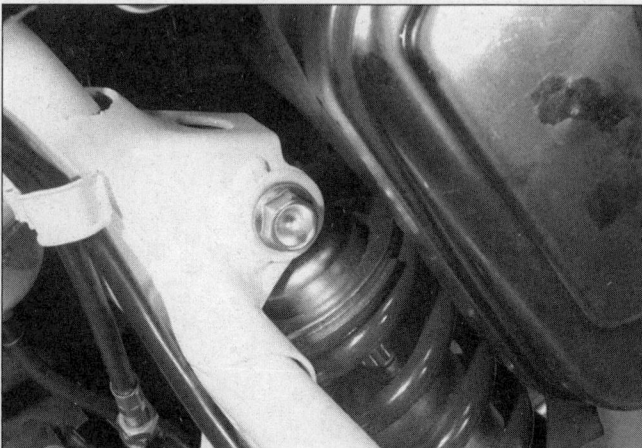

6.4a Remove the upper mounting bolt . . .

6.4b . . . and lower the shock through the swingarm

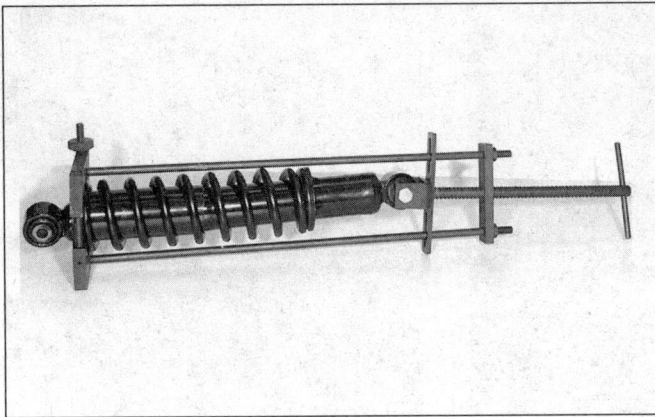

6.6   Use a spring compressor to remove the coil spring; don't use a makeshift substitute, as the spring is powerful and may cause injury if it gets loose

6.13 On 50 and 70 models, remove the bolts (arrows) and take the shock off

Inspection

Refer to illustration 6.6

5   Check the shock absorber for damage and oil leaks. If these can be seen, remove the coil spring and replace the damper unit.
6   Removal of the coil spring requires a spring compressor **(see illustration)**. These can be rented, but it might be more practical to take the shock absorber to a Honda dealer to have the spring removed and installed. **Warning:** *The spring is powerful and may cause injury if it flies out. Don't use a makeshift tool to compress the spring.*
7   Compress the spring and unscrew the lower joint from the shock. Remove the spring seat, rubber bumper and coil spring.
8   Measure the free length of the spring. If it's sagged to less than the value listed in this Chapter's Specifications, replace it with a new one.
9   Assembly is the reverse of the disassembly steps. Tighten the lower joint securely.

Installation

10   Installation is the reverse of the removal steps, with the following addition: Tighten the upper mounting bolt, lower mounting bolt and shock arm-to-swingarm bolt to the torques listed in this Chapter's Specifications.

50 and 70 models

Refer to illustration 6.13

11   Support the bike securely so it can't be knocked over during this procedure.
12   Remove the seat (see Chapter 7).
13   Remove the mounting bolts and nuts and lift the shock off the bike **(see illustration)**.
14   Installation is the reverse of the removal steps. Tighten the nuts and bolts to the torque listed in this Chapter's Specifications.

7   Rear suspension linkage (80 and 100 models) - removal, check and installation

Refer to illustrations 7.3 and 7.4

1   Support the bike securely so it can't be knocked over during this procedure.
2   Unbolt the shock arm from the swingarm and remove the shock absorber's lower mounting bolt **(see illustration 6.3)**.
3   Unbolt the shock arm from the shock link and take it out **(see illustration)**.
4   Unbolt the shock link from the frame and remove it **(see illustration)**.

Inspection

Refer to illustration 7.5

5   Remove the dust covers and push the sleeves out of the shock link and shock arm **(see illustration)**.
6   Clean all parts thoroughly with solvent and dry them with compressed air, if available. Check all parts for scoring, damage or heavy corrosion and replace them as necessary. Measure the outside diameter of the sleeves and the inside diameter of the bushings and compare them to the values listed in this Chapter's Specifications. Replace sleeves worn beyond the limit. If bushings are excessively worn, the shock arm or shock links will have to be replaced.

Installation

7   Apply a thin coat of moly-based grease to the bushings and sleeves and install them in the bushings.
8   Installation is the reverse of the removal steps. Tighten the bolts to

7.3 Unbolt the shock arm from the shock link and take it out

7.4 Unbolt the shock link from the frame

7.5 Suspension linkage components

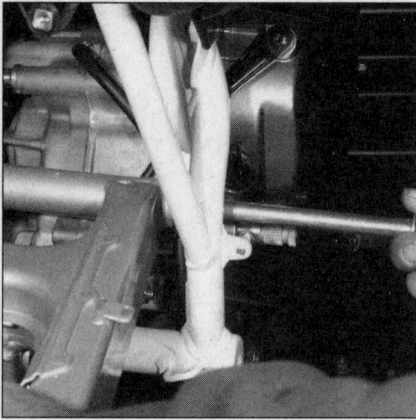

9.4a Unscrew the swingarm pivot bolt, support the swingarm and pull the bolt out

9.4b Remove the nut from the opposite end of the swingarm pivot bolt (arrow) and pull it out

10.2 Pull the dust covers off the swingarm

the torques listed in this Chapter's Specifications in the following order:
a) Shock link to frame
b) Shock link to shock arm
c) Shock arm to shock absorber lower end
d) Shock arm to swingarm

8 Swingarm bushings - check

1   Refer to Chapter 6 and remove the rear wheel, then refer to Section 6 and remove the rear shock absorber.
2   Grasp the rear of the swingarm with one hand and place your other hand at the junction of the swingarm and frame. Try to move the rear of the swingarm from side-to-side. Any wear (play) in the bushings should be felt as movement between the swingarm and the frame at the front. The swingarm will actually be felt to move forward and backward at the front (not from side-to-side). If any play is noted, the bushings should be replaced with new ones (see Section 10).
3   Next, move the swingarm up and down through its full travel. It should move freely, without any binding or rough spots. If it doesn't move freely, refer to Section 10 for servicing procedures.

9 Swingarm - removal and installation

Refer to illustrations 9.4a and 9.4b
1   Refer to Section 11 and disconnect the drive chain.
2   Remove the rear wheel and unhook the brake pedal return spring

from the swingarm (see Chapter 6).
3   Remove the shock absorber (see Section 6) and shock linkage (see Section 7).
4   Support the swingarm from below, then unscrew its pivot bolt from the frame and pull it out **(see illustrations)**.
5   Refer to Section 11 and check the chain guard and sliders for wear or damage. Replace them as necessary.
6   Installation is the reverse of the removal steps, with the following additions:
a) Tighten the swingarm pivot bolt to the torque listed in this Chapter's Specifications.
b) Refer to Chapter 1 and adjust the drive chain and rear brake pedal.
c) On 80 and 100 models, lubricate the swingarm bushings through the grease fittings (see Chapter 1).

10 Swingarm bushings (80 and 100 models) - replacement

Refer to illustrations 10.2, 10.3, 10.5a and 10.5b
1   Refer to Section 9 and remove the swingarm.
2   Pull the dust covers off the swingarm **(see illustration)**.
3   Pull the pivot collar out of the swingarm **(see illustration)**.
4   Measure the collar outside diameter and the bushing inside diameter. Replace the collar or bushings if they're worn beyond the limits listed in this Chapter's Specifications.
5   Remove the bushings with a slide hammer and blind hole puller **(see illustration)**. Tap in new ones with a bearing driver or a piece of pipe the same diameter as the bushing **(see illustration)**.

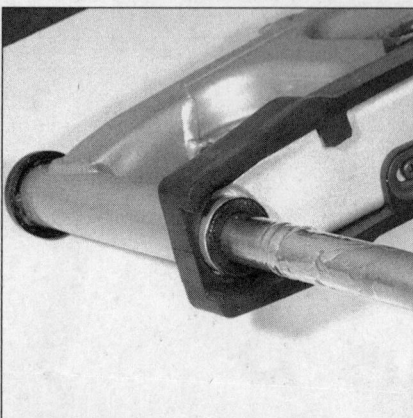

10.3 Slide the pivot collar out

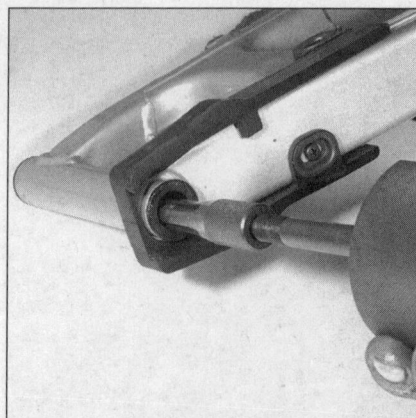

10.5a Remove the bushings with a slide hammer and blind hole puller attachment

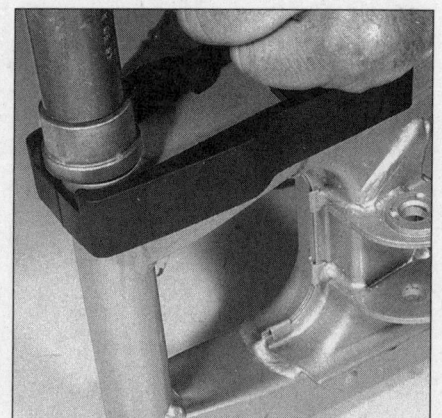

10.5b Drive in new bushings with a driver or piece of pipe the same diameter as the bushing

11.1 Remove the clip from the master link; its open end (arrow) faces rearward when the chain is on the top run

11.3 Pull the master link out of the chain

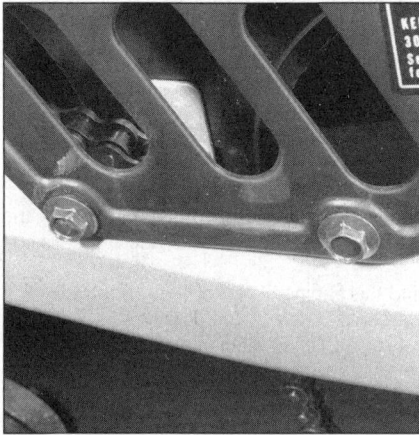

11.5a Inspect the chain guard . . .

11.5b . . . the slider on the frame . . .

11.5c . . . and the slider on the swingarm (this is the 80/100 design)

6   Coat the bushings and collar with moly-based grease and slip the collar into the swingarm. Install the dust covers.

11 Drive chain - removal, cleaning, inspection and installation

Removal
Refer to illustrations 11.1, 11.3, 11.5a, 11.5b, 11.5c and 11.5d

1   Turn the rear wheel to place the drive chain master link where it's easily accessible **(see illustration)**.
2   Remove the left-side engine cover **(see illustration 6.1a or 6.1b in Chapter 4)**.
3   Remove the clip and pull the master link out of the chain **(see illustration)**.
4   Lift the chain off the engine sprocket and remove it from the bike.
5   Check the chain guards on the swingarm and frame for wear or damage and replace them as necessary **(see illustrations)**.

Cleaning and inspection
6   Soak the chain in a high flash point solvent for approximately five or six minutes. Use a brush to work the solvent into the spaces between the links and plates.
7   Wipe the chain dry, then check it carefully for worn or damaged links. Replace the chain if wear or damage is found at any point.
8   Stretch the chain taut and measure its length. Compare the measured length to the value listed in this Chapter's Specifications

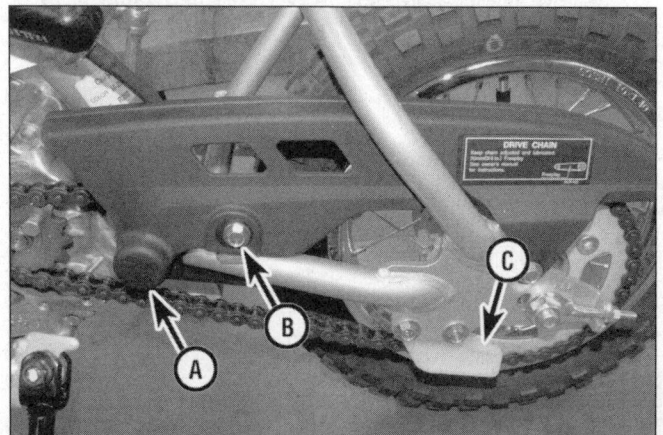

11.5d Here are the chain guard and sliders on 50/70 models

a)   Chain guard
b)   Front slider (hidden)
c)   Rear slider

and replace the chain if it's beyond the limit. If the chain needs to be replaced, refer to Section 12 and check the sprockets. If they're worn, replace them also. If a new chain is installed on worn sprockets, it will wear out quickly.
9   Lubricate the chain with SAE 80 or 90 gear oil (see Chapter 1).

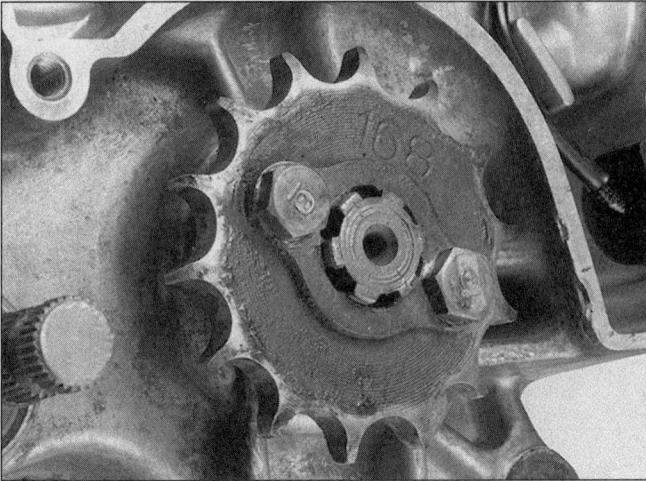

12.6 Remove the bolts and lift off the retainer to remove the engine sprocket

12.7 If the seal behind the engine sprocket has been leaking, pry it out and install a new one

Installation

10   Installation is the reverse of the removal steps, with the following additions:

a) *Install the master link clip so its opening faces the back of the motorcycle when the master link is in the upper chain run* **(see illustration 11.1)**.

b) *Refer to Chapter 1 and adjust the chain.*

12 Sprockets - check and replacement

Refer to illustrations 12.6 and 12.7

1   Support the bike securely so it can't be knocked over during this procedure.

2   Whenever the sprockets are inspected, the chain should be inspected also and replaced if it's worn. Installing a worn chain on new sprockets will cause them to wear quickly.

3   Remove the left-side engine cover **(see illustration 6.1a or 6.1b in Chapter 4)**. Check the teeth on the engine sprocket and rear sprocket for wear.

4   If the sprockets are worn, remove the chain (see Section 11) and the rear wheel (see Chapter 6).

5   Unbolt the sprocket from the rear wheel hub.

6   To remove the engine sprocket, remove two bolts and lift off the retainer plate **(see illustration)**. Lift the sprocket off the transmission shaft.

7   Inspect the seal behind the engine sprocket **(see illustration)**. If it has been leaking, pry it out (taking care not to scratch the seal bore) and tap in a new seal with a socket the same diameter as the seal.

8   Installation is the reverse of the removal steps, with the following additions:

a) *Tighten the sprocket bolts to the torques listed in this Chapter's Specifications.*

b) *Install the master link clip so its opening faces the back of the motorcycle when the master link is in the upper chain run* **(see illustration 11.1)**.

c) *Refer to Chapter 1 and adjust the chain.*

Chapter 6
Brakes, wheels and tires

Contents

Specifications

Brakes

Brake lining minimum thickness	See Chapter 1
Brake pedal height	See Chapter 1
Drum diameter (front and rear)	
70 through 100 models	
Standard	95 mm (3.74 inches)
Wear limit	96 mm (3.78 inches)*
50 models	
Standard	80 mm (3.1 inches)
Limit	80.5 mm(3.17 inches)*

*Refer to marks cast into the drum (they supersede information printed here)

Wheels and tires

Tire pressures	See Chapter 1
Tire tread depth	See Chapter 1
Axle runout limit	0.2 mm (0.008 inch)

Torque specifications

Axle nut (front and rear)	
80 and 100 models	62 Nm (46 ft-lbs)
70 models	59 Nm (43 ft-lbs)
50 models	47 Nm (35 ft-lbs)
Brake pedal pivot bolt	
XR80R, XR100R	39 Nm (29 ft-lbs)
CRF80F, CRF100F	55 Nm (41 ft-lbs)*
50 and 70 models	Not applicable

*Upper footpeg mounting bolt.

2.2 Unscrew the axle nut

2.3a Loosen the cable adjuster nuts . . .

1   General information

The vehicles covered by this manual are equipped with mechanical drum brakes on the front and rear wheels. The front brake is actuated by a lever on the right handlebar. The rear brake is actuated by a pedal on the right side of the vehicle. The lever is connected to the front brake assembly by a cable; the pedal is connected to the rear brake assembly by a rod.

All models are equipped with spoked steel wheels. **Caution:** *Brake components rarely require disassembly. Do not disassemble the brakes unless absolutely necessary.*

2   Wheels - inspection, removal and installation

Removal

Front wheel

Refer to illustrations 2.2, 2.3a and 2.3b

1   Support the bike from below with a jack beneath the engine or on a motorcycle stand. Securely prop the bike upright so it can't fall over

when the wheel is removed.

2   Hold the axle with a wrench and remove the axle nut **(see illustration)**.

3   Loosen the brake cable adjuster at the wheel until the cable can be slipped out of the brake arm **(see illustrations)**.

4   Support the wheel and pull the axle out.

5   Lower the wheel away from the motorcycle and take it out.

Rear wheel

Refer to illustrations 2.7, 2.9 and 2.10

6   Support the bike from below with a jack beneath the swingarm or on a motorcycle stand. Securely prop the bike upright so it can't fall over when the wheel is removed.

7   Remove the rear brake adjuster wingnut from the brake rod (see Chapter 1). Pull the rod out of its pivot and remove the pivot from the brake arm **(see illustration)**.

8   Rotate the wheel until the master link is accessible, then loosen the chain and disconnect the master link (see Chapters 1 and 5).

9   Hold the axle with a wrench and remove the axle nut **(see illustration)**.

10   Support the wheel and pull the axle out **(see illustration)**.

11   Lower the wheel away from the motorcycle and take it out.

2.3b . . . pull the cable housing down and slide the cable out of its bracket

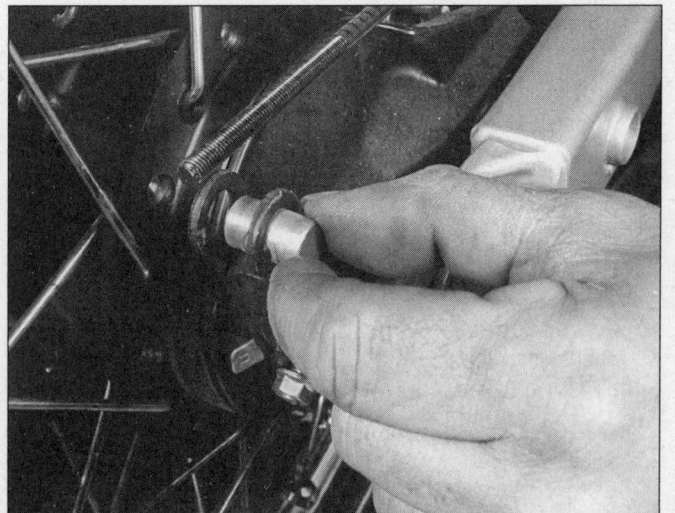

2.7 Remove the brake rod pivot from the brake arm

2.9 Unscrew the axle nut

2.10 Support the wheel and pull the axle out

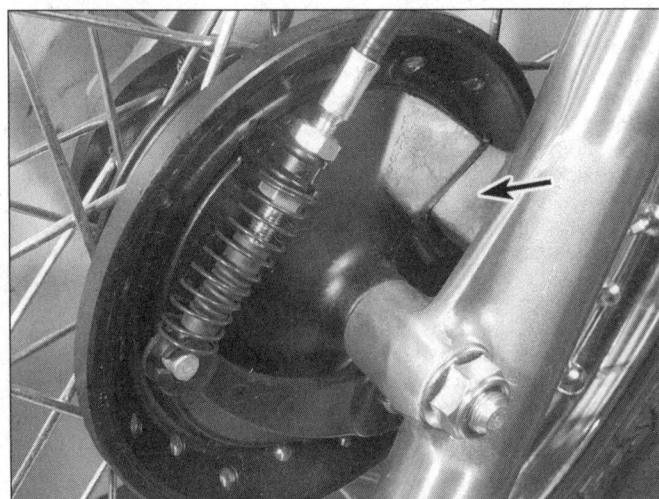

2.17a Make sure the fork protrusion fits into the notch in the brake panel (arrow)

2.17b Make sure the collar is in position in the left side of the hub

Inspection

12   Clean the wheels thoroughly to remove mud and dirt that may interfere with the inspection procedure or mask defects. Make a general check of the wheels and tires as described in Chapter 1.

13   The wheels should be visually inspected for dents, flat spots on the rim, bent spokes and other damage.

14   Individual spokes can be replaced. If other damage is evident, the wheel will have to be replaced with a new one. Never attempt to repair a damaged wheel.

15   Before installing the wheel, check the axle for straightness. If the axle is corroded, first remove the corrosion with fine emery cloth. Set the axle on V-blocks and check it for runout with a dial indicator. If the axle exceeds the maximum allowable runout limit listed in this Chapter's Specifications, it must be replaced.

16   Check the condition of the wheel bearings (see Section 4).

Installation

Refer to illustrations 2.17a, 2.17b and 2.17c

17   Installation is the reverse of the removal steps, with the following additions:

a) if you're installing a front wheel, make sure the fork protrusion fits into the notch in the brake panel (see illustration). Lubricate the barrel-shaped fitting at the end of the front brake cable with multi-purpose grease.

b) If you're installing a rear wheel, make sure the collar is in its proper position on the left side of the hub (see illustration). Also make sure the boss on the swingarm fits into the brake panel notch (see illustration).

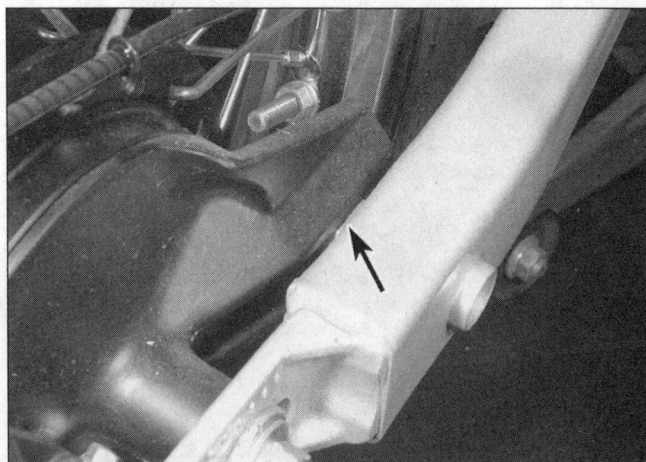

2.17c Make sure the swingarm protrusion fits into the notch in the brake panel (arrow)

3.2 Lift the brake panel out of the drum (rear brake shown; front similar)

3.3 The maximum inside diameter is cast inside the brake drum

c) Tighten the axle nut to the torque listed in this Chapter's Specifications.

d) Refer to Chapter 1 and adjust the brake.

3 Brake drum and shoes - removal, inspection and installation

Warning: *The dust created by the brake system may contain asbestos, which is harmful to your health (Honda hasn't used asbestos in brake parts for a number of years, but aftermarket parts may contain it). Never blow it out with compressed air and don't inhale any of it. An approved filtering mask should be worn when working on the brakes.*

Removal

Refer to illustration 3.2

1   Remove the wheel (see Section 2).

2   Lift the brake panel out of the wheel **(see illustration)**.

Inspection

Refer to illustrations 3.3, 3.6, 3.9, 3.10, 3.11, 3.12a and 3.12b

3   Check the brake drum for wear or damage. Measure the diameter at several points with a drum micrometer (or have this done by a Honda dealer or other qualified repair shop). If the measurements are uneven (indicating that the drum is out-of-round) or if there are scratches deep enough to snag a fingernail, replace the drum. The drum must also be replaced if the diameter is greater than that cast inside the drum **(see illustration)**. Honda recommends against resurfacing brake drums.

4   Check the linings for wear, damage and signs of contamination from road dirt or water. If the linings are visibly defective, replace them.

5   Measure the thickness of the lining material (just the lining material, not the metal backing) and compare with the value listed in the Chapter 1 Specifications. Replace the shoes if the material is worn to the minimum or less.

6   To remove the shoes, fold them toward each other to release the spring tension and lift them off the brake panel **(see illustration)**.

7   Check the ends of the shoes where they contact the brake cam and anchor pin. Replace the shoes if there's visible wear.

8   Check the brake cam and anchor pin for wear and damage. The brake cam can be replaced separately; the brake panel must be replaced if the anchor pin is unserviceable.

9   Look for alignment marks on the brake arm and anchor pin **(see illustration)**. Make your own if they aren't visible.

10 Remove the pinch bolt and nut and pull the brake arm off the cam **(see illustration)**.

11 Lift off the thrust washer (1985 through 1987 models) or wear indicator (1988 and later models) **(see illustration)**. Pull the brake cam out

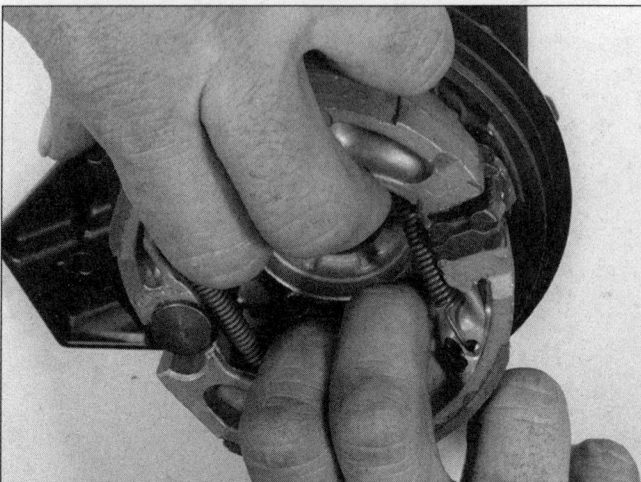

3.6 Spread the shoes and fold them into a V to release the spring tension

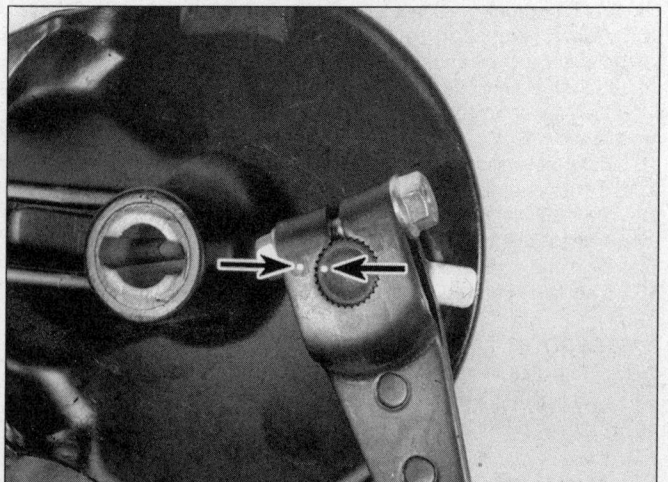

3.9 Look for alignment marks on the brake arm and cam (arrows); make your own marks if you can't see any

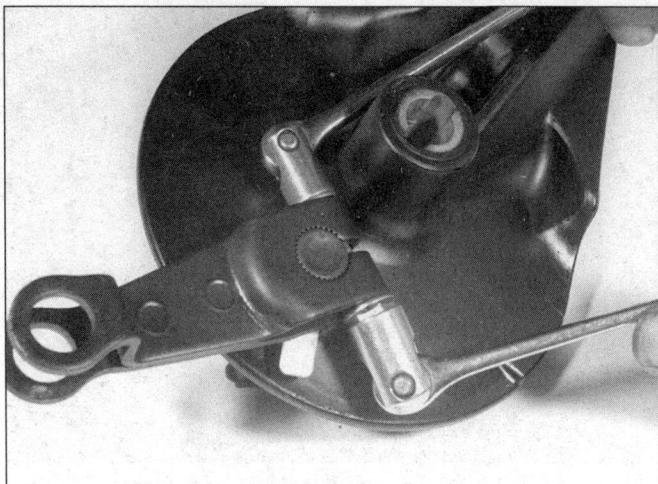

3.10 Remove the pinch bolt and nut and take the brake arm off the cam

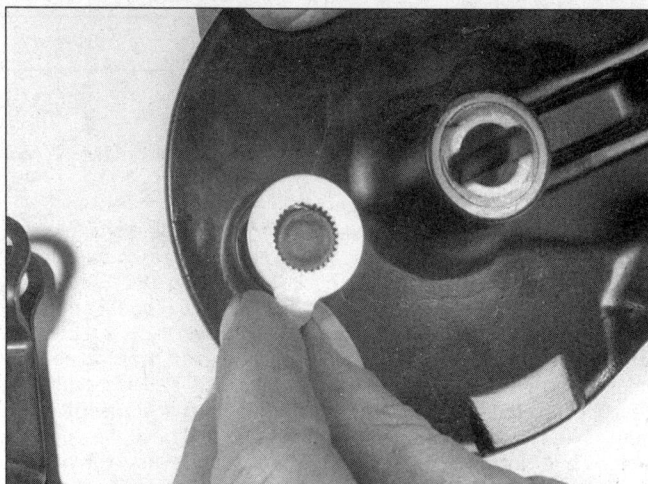

3.11 Remove the thrust washer (early models) or wear indicator (later models); the wide spline on the wear indicator fits into a wide groove in the brake cam

3.12a Replace the brake cam seal if it's worn or damaged

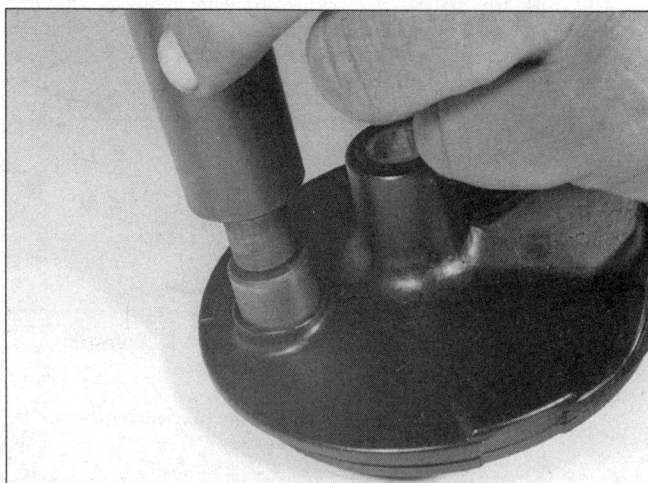

3.12b Pry out the old seal, then press a new one in with a socket the same diameter as the seal

of the brake panel.

12   Check the brake cam dust seal for wear and damage (see illustration). To replace it, pry it out of the brake panel and tap in a new one using a socket or seal driver the same diameter as the seal (see illustration).

Installation

Refer to illustration 3.16

13   Apply high-temperature brake grease to the brake cam, the anchor pin and the ends of the springs.

14   Install the cam through the dust seal. Install the thrust washer (1985 through 1987 models) or wear indicator (1988 and later models) (see illustration 3.11). If you're installing a wear indicator, align its wide groove with the wide spline in the cam.

15   Install the brake arm on the cam, aligning the punch marks. Tighten the nut and bolt to the torque listed in this Chapter's Specifications.

16   Hook the ends of the springs to the shoes. Position the shoes in a V on the brake panel, then fold them down into position (see illustration 3.6). Make sure the ends of the shoes fit correctly on the cam and the anchor pin (see illustration).

17   The remainder of installation is the reverse of the removal steps.

3.16 The assembled brakes should look like this

4   Wheel bearing replacement

Refer to illustrations 4.4a, 4.4b, 4.4c and 4.6

1   Refer to Section 2 and remove the wheel.
2   If you're working on a rear wheel, pull the seal collar out of the seal **(see illustration 2.17b)**.
3   Pry the seal out of the left side of the wheel.
4   Because the openings in the centers of the wheel bearings are narrow, it isn't possible to insert a drift through one bearing and tap out the opposite bearing. The Honda special tool (part no. 07746-0050100) has a notch that hooks over the bearing inner race **(see illustration)**. You can make an equivalent tool by grinding a notch in a piece of metal rod. To use the tool, place it in the bearing, hook it over the bearing inner race, then drive against the tool from the other side with a drift and hammer **(see illustration)**. Take out the bearing spacer **(see illustration)**, then insert the drift from the other side and drive the opposite bearing out. **Note:** *Once the bearings have been removed, they must be replaced with new ones since they're almost certain to be damaged during removal.*
5   Pack the new bearings with multi-purpose grease. Work the grease into the spaces between the bearing balls. Hold the outer race and rotate the bearing inner race as you pack it to distribute the grease.
6   Place the new left bearing on the hub with its sealed side out. Position the hub on a workbench or similar surface. Tap the bearing into position with a bearing driver or socket the same diameter as the bearing outer race **(see illustration)**.

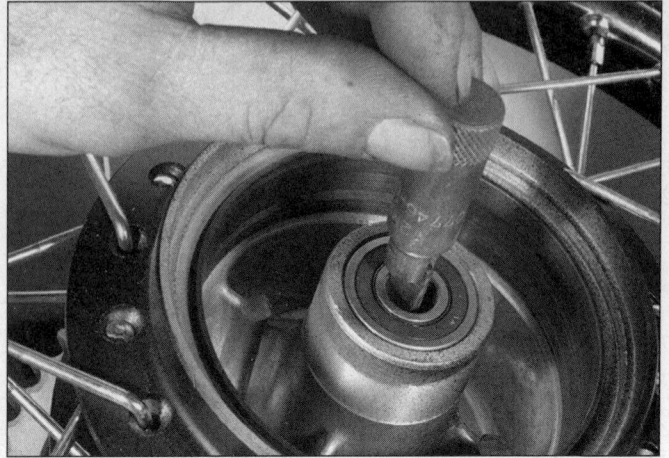

4.4a This Honda special tool is used to remove the wheel bearings . . .

7   Install the spacer, then turn the wheel over and install the right bearing in the same manner.
8   Tap a new seal into the left side of the wheel with a seal driver or a socket the same diameter as the seal. If you're working on a rear wheel, install the collar in the seal **(see illustration 2.17b)**.

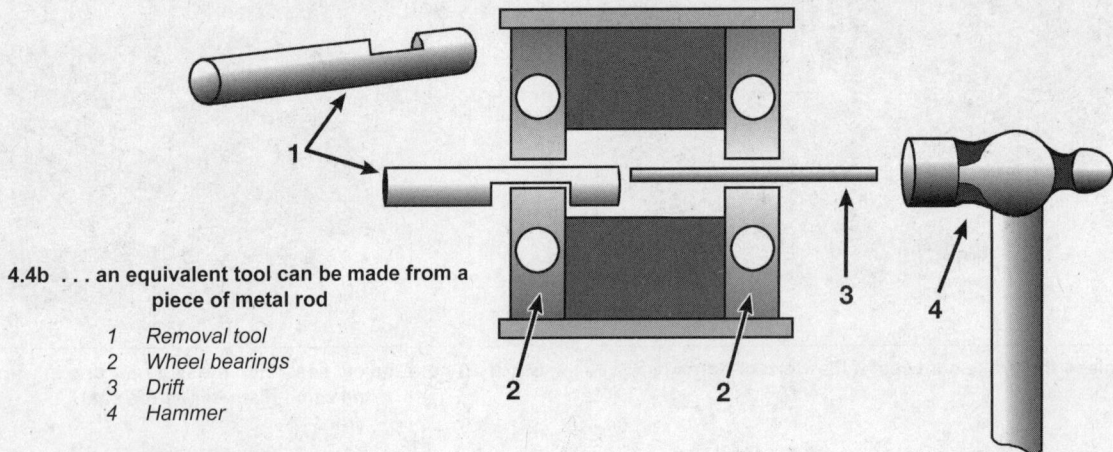

4.4b . . . an equivalent tool can be made from a piece of metal rod

1 *Removal tool*
2 *Wheel bearings*
3 *Drift*
4 *Hammer*

2218-6-4.4B HAYNES

4.4c Lift the spacer out of the hub

4.6 Install the bearings with their sealed sides facing out

5.3 Unbolt the brake cable retainer from the fork

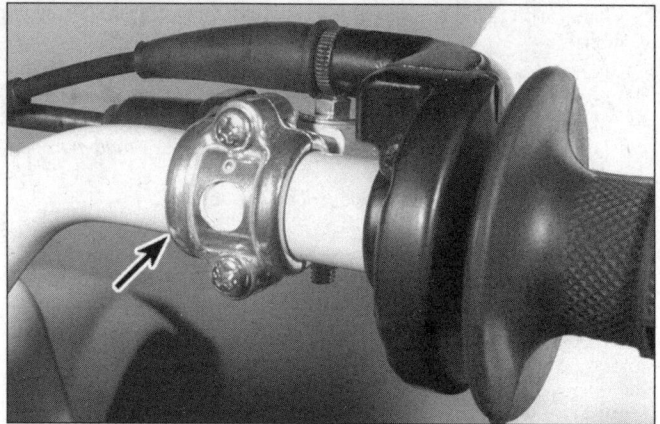
5.4 Remove the clamp screws to detach the brake lever from the handlebar; on installation, line up the parting line of the clamp halves with the punch mark on the handlebar (arrow)

5.7a Unhook the pedal return spring and remove the pivot nut (arrows)

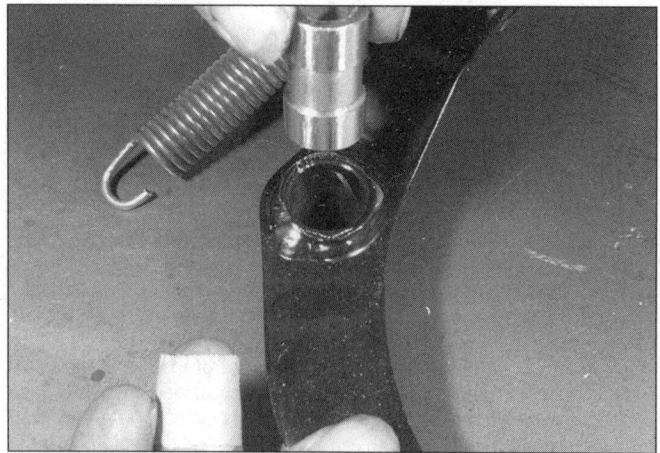
5.7b Slip the pivot bushing out of the pedal and check it for wear and damage

5   Brake cable, lever, rod and pedal - removal and installation

Front brake cable and lever
Refer to illustrations 5.3 and 5.4

1   Loosen the cable adjuster at the wheel all the way, then detach the cable from the brake arm and its bracket on the brake panel **(see illustrations 2.3a and 2.3b)**.
2   Loosen the handlebar adjuster all the way (see Chapter 1), then rotate the cable and slip its end fitting out of the lever.
3   Unbolt the cable retainer from the left front fork and take the cable off the bike **(see illustration)**.
4   To remove the lever, remove its clamp screws and take it off the handlebar **(see illustration)**.
5   Installation is the reverse of the removal steps, with the following additions:
 a) *Apply multi-purpose grease to the cable end fittings.*
 b) *Refer to Chapter 1 and adjust the front brake.*

Rear brake rod and pedal
Refer to illustrations 5.7a, 5.7b and 5.8

6   Remove the rear brake adjuster wingnut from the brake rod (see Chapter 1). Pull the rod out of its pivot and remove the pivot from the brake arm **(see illustration 2.7)**.
7   If you're working on an 80 or 100 model, unhook the brake pedal spring from the swingarm **(see illustration)**. Remove the pedal nut,

take the pedal off its shaft and remove the pedal pivot **(see illustration)**.
8   If you're working on a 50 or 70 model, unhook the brake pedal spring from the frame **(see illustration)**. Remove the cotter pin and washer and slip the pedal off its shaft.

5.8 Brake pedal and linkage details (50 and 70 models)

a) *Brake rod adjusting nut*   c) *Pedal return spring*
b) *Brake pedal pivot*

9   Installation is the reverse of the removal steps, with the following additions:

a) *If you're working on a 50 or 70 model, use a new cotter pin on the pedal pivot. On all models, use a new cotter pin if you separate the rod from the pedal.*

b) *Lubricate the rod end fittings and pedal shaft with multi-purpose grease.*

c) *Adjust brake pedal play as described in Chapter 1.*

6   Tires - removal and installation

1   To properly remove and install tires, you will need at least two motorcycle tire irons, some water, some talcum powder and a tire pressure gauge.

2   Begin by removing the wheel from the motorcycle. If the tire is going to be re-used, mark it next to the valve stem, wheel balance weight or rim lock.

3   Deflate the tire by removing the valve stem core. When it is fully deflated, push the bead of the tire away from the rim on both sides. In some extreme cases, this can only be accomplished with a bead breaking tool, but most often it can be carried out with tire irons. Riding on a deflated tire to break the bead is not recommended, as damage to the rim and tire will occur.

4   Dismounting a tire is easier when the tire is warm, so an indoor tire change is recommended in cold climates. The rubber gets very stiff and is difficult to manipulate when cold.

5   Place the wheel on a thick pad or old blanket. This will help keep the wheel and tire from slipping around.

6   Once the bead is completely free of the rim, lubricate the inside edge of the rim and the tire bead with a solution of water only. Honda recommends against the use of soap or other tire mounting lubricants, as the tire may shift on the rim. Remove the locknut and push the tire valve through the rim.

7   Insert one of the tire irons under the bead of the tire at the valve stem and lift the bead up over the rim. This should be fairly easy. Take care not to pinch the tube as this is done. If it is difficult to pry the bead up, make sure that the rest of the bead opposite the valve stem is in the dropped center section of the rim.

8   Hold the tire iron down with the bead over the rim, then move about 1 or 2 inches to either side and insert the second tire iron. Be careful not to cut or slice the bead or the tire may split when inflated. Also, take care not to catch or pinch the inner tube as the second tire iron is levered over. For this reason, tire irons are recommended over screwdrivers or other implements.

9   With a small section of the bead up over the rim, one of the levers can be removed and reinserted 1 or 2 inches farther around the rim until about 1/4 of the tire bead is above the rim edge. Make sure that the rest of the bead is in the dropped center of the rim. At this point, the bead can usually be pulled up over the rim by hand.

10   Once all of the first bead is over the rim, the inner tube can be withdrawn from the tire and rim. Push in on the valve stem, lift up on the tire next to the stem, reach inside the tire and carefully pull out the tube. It is usually not necessary to completely remove the tire from the rim to repair the inner tube. It is sometimes recommended though, because checking for foreign objects in the tire is difficult while it is still mounted on the rim.

11   To remove the tire completely, make sure the bead is broken all the way around on the remaining edge, then stand the tire and wheel up on the tread and grab the wheel with one hand. Push the tire down over the same edge of the rim while pulling the rim away from the tire. If the bead is correctly positioned in the dropped center of the rim, the tire should roll off and separate from the rim very easily. If tire irons

are used to work this last bead over the rim, the outer edge of the rim may be marred. If a tire iron is necessary, be sure to pad the rim as described earlier.

12   Refer to Section 7 for inner tube repair procedures.

13   Mounting a tire is basically the reverse of removal. Some tires have a balance mark and/or directional arrows molded into the tire sidewall. Look for these marks so that the tire can be installed properly. The dot should be aligned with the valve stem.

14   If the tire was not removed completely to repair or replace the inner tube, the tube should be inflated just enough to make it round. Carefully lift up the tire edge and install the tube with the valve stem next to the hole in the rim. Once the tube is in place, push the valve stem through the rim and start the locknut on the stem.

15   Lubricate the tire bead, then push it over the rim edge and into the dropped center section opposite the inner tube valve stem. Work around each side of the rim, carefully pushing the bead over the rim. The last section may have to be levered on with tire irons. If so, take care not to pinch the inner tube as this is done.

16   Once the bead is over the rim edge, check to see that the inner tube valve stem and the rim lock are pointing to the center of the hub. If they're angled slightly in either direction, rotate the tire on the rim to straighten it out. Run the locknut the rest of the way onto the stem and rim lock but don't tighten them completely.

17   Inflate the tube to 1-1/2 times the pressure listed in the Chapter 1 Specifications. **Warning:** *Do not overinflate the tube or the tire may burst, causing serious injury.* Check to make sure the guidelines on the tire sidewalls are the same distance from the rim around the circumference of the tire.

18   After the tire bead is correctly seated on the rim, allow the tire to deflate. Replace the valve core and inflate the tube to the recommended pressure, then tighten the valve stem locknut securely and tighten the cap. Tighten the locknut on the rim locknut to the torque listed in the Chapter 1 Specifications.

7   Tubes - repair

1   Tire tube repair requires a patching kit that's usually available from motorcycle dealers, accessory stores or auto parts stores. Be sure to follow the directions supplied with the kit to ensure a safe repair. Patching should be done only when a new tube is unavailable. Replace the tube as soon as possible. Sudden deflation can cause loss of control and an accident.

2   To repair a tube, remove it from the tire, inflate and immerse it in a sink or tub full of water to pinpoint the leak. Mark the position of the leak, then deflate the tube. Dry it off and thoroughly clean the area around the puncture.

3   Most tire patching kits have a buffer to rough up the area around the hole for proper adhesion of the patch. Roughen an area slightly larger than the patch, then apply a thin coat of the patching cement to the roughened area. Allow the cement to dry until tacky, then apply the patch.

4   It may be necessary to remove a protective covering from the top surface of the patch after it has been attached to the tube. Keep in mind that tubes made from synthetic rubber may require a special patch and adhesive if a satisfactory bond is to be achieved.

5   Before replacing the tube, check the inside of the tire to make sure the object that caused the puncture is not still inside. Also check the outside of the tire, particularly the tread area, to make sure nothing is projecting through the tire that may cause another puncture. Check the rim for sharp edges or damage. Make sure the rubber trim band is in good condition and properly installed before inserting the tube.

TIRE CHANGING SEQUENCE - TUBED TIRES

1 Deflate tire. After pushing tire beads away from rim flanges push tire bead into well of rim at point opposite valve. Insert tire lever adjacent to valve and work bead over edge of rim.

2 Use two levers to work bead over edge of rim. Note use of rim protectors

3 Remove inner tube from tire

4 When first bead is clear, remove tire as shown

5 When fitting, partially inflate inner tube and insert in tire

6 Work first bead over rim and feed valve through hole in rim. Partially screw on retaining nut to hold valve in place.

7 Check that inner tube is positioned correctly and work second bead over rim using tire levers. Start at a point opposite valve.

8 Work final area of bead over rim while pushing valve inwards to ensure that inner tube is not trapped

Notes

Chapter 7
Frame and bodywork

Contents

Specifications

Tightening torques

Seat mounting bolts...	10 to 14 Nm (25 to 33 ft-lbs)
Footpeg and sidestand bracket bolts	35 to 45 Nm (25 to 33 ft-lbs)
Seat mounting bolts (1985 through 1997 models)	10 to 14 Nm (72 to 108 inch-lbs)
Seat mounting nuts (1998 and later)..	Not specified
Footpeg mounting bolts	
XR80R, XR100R...	39 Nm (29 ft-lbs)
CRF80F, CRF100F	55 Nm (41 ft-lbs)
50 and 70 models	Not specified

1 General information

This Chapter covers the procedures necessary to remove and install the fenders and other body parts. Since many service and repair operations on these motorcycles require removal of the fenders and/or other body parts, the procedures are grouped here and referred to from other Chapters.

In the case of damage to the fenders or other body parts, it is usu-

2.2 Remove the seat mounting bolt on each side . . .

ally necessary to remove the broken component and replace it with a new (or used) one. The material that the fenders and other plastic body parts are composed of doesn't lend itself to conventional repair techniques. There are, however, some shops that specialize in "plastic welding", so it would be advantageous to check around before throwing the damaged part away.

Note: *When attempting to remove any body panel, first study the panel closely, noting any fasteners and associated fittings, to be sure of returning everything to its correct place on installation. In some cases, the aid of an assistant will be required when removing panels, to help avoid damaging the paint. Once the visible fasteners have been removed, try to lift off the panel as described but DO NOT FORCE the panel - if it will not release, check that all fasteners have been removed and try again. Where a panel engages another by means of lugs and grommets, be careful not to break the lugs or damage the bodywork. Remember that a few moments of patience at this stage will save you a lot of money in replacing broken panels!*

2 Seat - removal and installation

70 through 100 models

Refer to illustrations 2.2 and 2.3

1   Remove the side covers (see Section 4).

2   Remove the mounting bolt on each side of the seat **(see illustration)**. If you're working on an XR70R, remove the two mounting bolts at the rear of the seat under the fender.

2.3 . . . and disengage the seat from the frame bracket and the screw on the fuel tank (arrows)

2.5a Remove the screw (arrow) (one on each side of the bike) . . .

2.5b . . . and pull up the center post of the trim clip, then pull the trim clip out of the cover (one on each side of the bike)

2.6 Side cover and rear fender details (CRF50F; XR50R similar)

a) Seat bolts
b) Side cover tabs
c) Fender screw (one of three)

2.7 Engage the tabs (upper arrows) with the hooks (lower arrows) when installing the seat

3   Lift the back end of the seat. Pull it back and down to disengage the front end from the frame and fuel tank and lift it off **(see illustration)**.
4   Installation is the reverse of removal.

50 models
Refer to illustrations 2.5a, 2.5b, 2.6 and 2.7
5   Remove the trim clip and screw from each side cover at the front of the bike **(see illustrations)**.
6   Remove the bolts at the rear of the seat under the fender **(see illustration)**.
7   Pull the seat straight back to disengage its mounting tabs and lift it off **(see illustration)**.
8   Installation is the reverse of the removal steps.

3   Footpegs and sidestand bracket - removal and installation

Refer to illustrations 3.2a, 3.2b and 3.3
1   Support the bike securely so it can't be knocked over during this procedure.
2   Remove the footpeg bracket bolts **(see illustrations)**. On 80 and 100 models, the bolts on the left side also secure the sidestand bracket. Separate the footpeg from the motorcycle.
3   To remove the footpeg from the bracket, note how the spring is fitted

(see illustration). Remove the cotter pin, washer, pivot pin and spring.
4   Installation is the reverse of removal. On 80 and 100 models, tighten the bolts to the torque listed in this Chapter's Specifications.

4   Side covers - removal and installation

70 through 100 models
Refer to illustrations 4.1a and 4.1b
1   Remove the side cover bolts **(see illustration)**. Pull the cover free of the grommets and take it off the motorcycle **(see illustration)**.
2   Installation is the reverse of removal. Tighten the bolts securely, but don't overtighten them and strip the threads.

50 models
3   Remove the seat (see Section 2).
4   Disengage the retaining tabs and free the side covers from the seat and rear fender **(see illustration 2.6)**.
5   Installation is the reverse of the removal steps.

5   Front fender - removal and installation

Refer to illustration 5.2
1   Remove the front wheel (see Chapter 6).

3.2a The kickstand pivots on the left footpeg bracket (right arrow); remove the bracket mounting bolts (left arrows) to detach the bracket from the frame

3.2b The 50/70 footpeg bracket is secured by four bolts (arrows) (two bolts hidden)

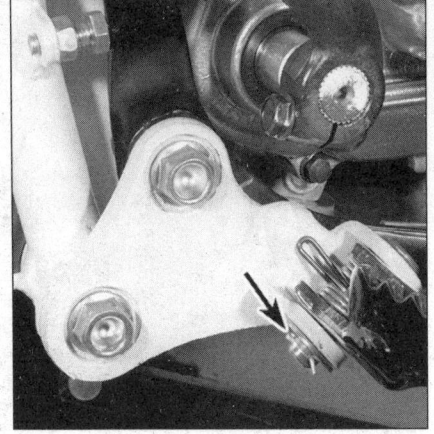

3.3 Remove the cotter pin, washer and pivot pin (arrow) to detach the footpeg from the bracket

4.1a Remove the side cover mounting bolt . . .

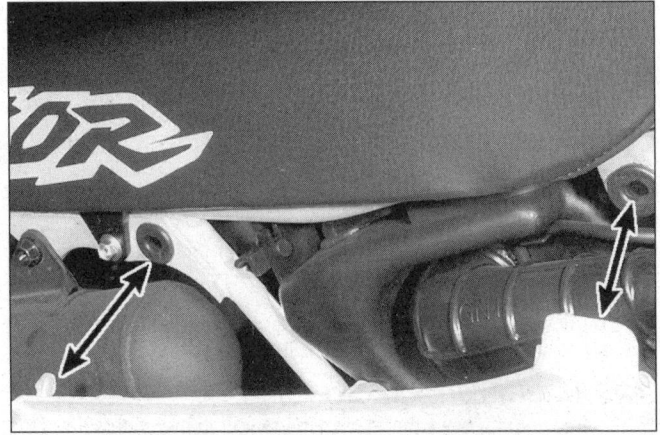

4.1b . . . and carefully pull the lugs free of the grommets (arrows)

2   Remove the fender nuts and bolt (see illustration). Lower the fender clear of its bracket and take it out.

3   Installation is the reverse of removal. Be sure to reinstall the grommets in their correct locations. Tighten the nuts and bolts securely, but don't overtighten them and strip the threads.

6   Number plate - removal and installation

Refer to illustration 6.1

1   Remove the number plate screw and tie (see illustration). Lift the number plate off.

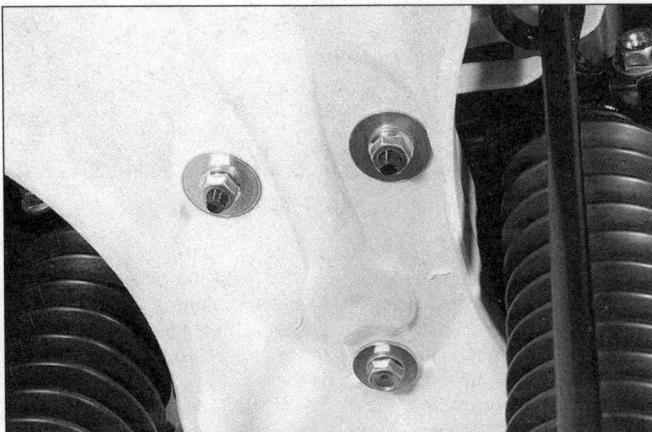

5.2 The front fender nuts and bolts are accessible from below

6.1 Unhook the strap (upper arrow) and remove the screw (lower arrow) to detach the number plate

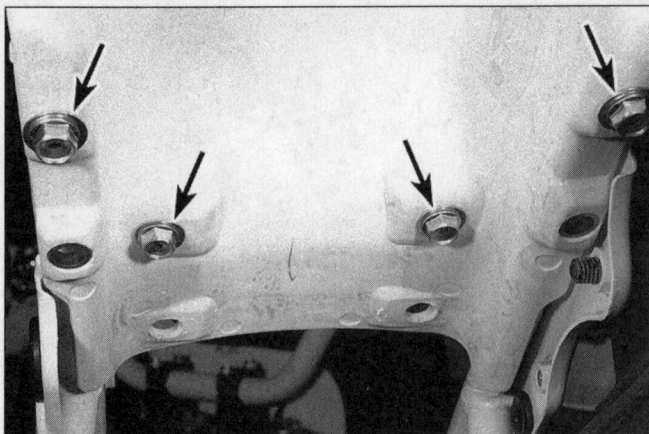

7.2 The rear fender bolts are accessible from below

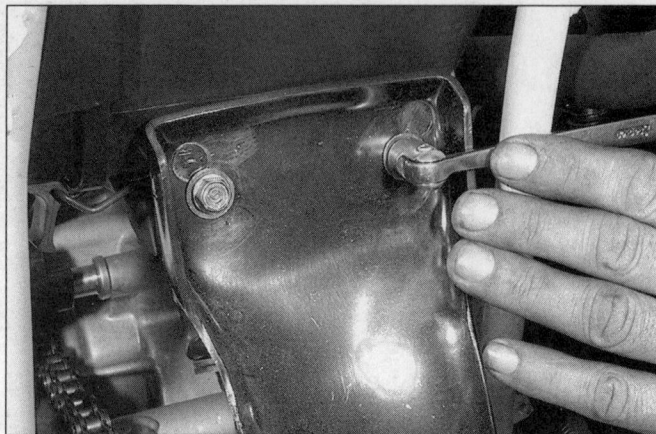

7.3 Remove two bolts to detach the inner fender

2   Installation is the reverse of removal. Tighten the screw securely, but don't overtighten it and strip the threads.

7   Rear fender - removal and installation

1   Remove the seat and side covers (see Sections 2 and 4).

80 and 100 models

Refer to illustrations 7.2 and 7.3
2   Remove the fender mounting bolts (and grommets if equipped) and take the fender off **(see illustration)**.
3   If necessary, unbolt the inner fender and lift it off **(see illustration)**.

XR70R

4   Remove the three nuts that secure the fender to the underside of the seat, then separate the fender from the seat.

XR50R, CRF50F and CRF70F

5   Remove the screws that secure the fender to the underside of the seat **(see illustration 2.6)**.

All models

6   Installation is the reverse of the removal steps. Tighten all fasteners securely, but don't overtighten them and strip the threads.

8   Skid plate (80 and 100 models) - removal and installation

Refer to illustrations 8.2 and 8.3
1   Support the bike securely so it can't be knocked over during this procedure.
2   Remove the two lower bolts and one through-bolt **(see illustration)**. Lower the skid plate away from the motorcycle.
3   Installation is the reverse of removal. Tighten the bolts securely, but don't overtighten them and strip the threads **(see illustration)**.

9   Frame - general information, inspection and repair

1   All models use a diamond-type frame made of steel. In this design, the engine serves as the lower front portion of the frame.
2   The frame shouldn't require attention unless accident damage has occurred. In most cases, frame replacement is the only satisfactory remedy for such damage. A few frame specialists have the jigs and other equipment necessary for straightening the frame to the required standard of accuracy, but even then there is no simple way of assessing to what extent the frame may have been overstressed.

8.2 Remove the skid plate bolts at the rear . . .

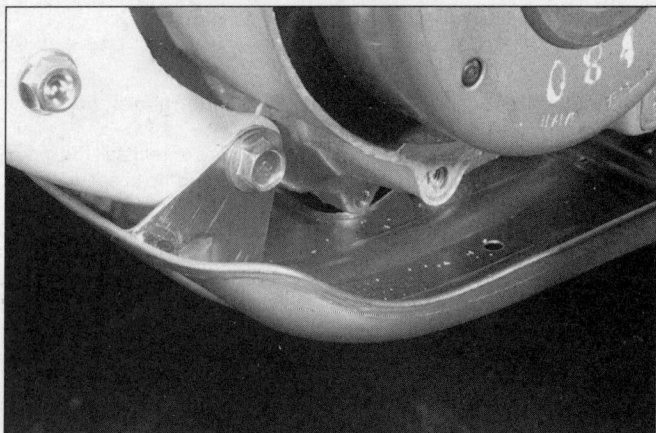

8.3 . . . and at the front

3   After the motorcycle has accumulated a lot of miles, the frame should be examined closely for signs of cracking or splitting at the welded joints. Corrosion can also cause weakness at these joints. Loose engine mount bolts can cause ovaling or fracturing to the mounting bolt holes. Minor damage can often be repaired by welding, depending on the nature and extent of the damage.
4   Remember that a frame that is out of alignment will cause handling problems. If misalignment is suspected as the result of an accident, it will be necessary to strip the machine completely so the frame can be thoroughly checked.

Prior to troubleshooting a circuit, make sure the insulation is in good condition and that there are no broken terminals or loose wires. When unplugging a connector, don't pull on the wires - pull only on the connector housings themselves.

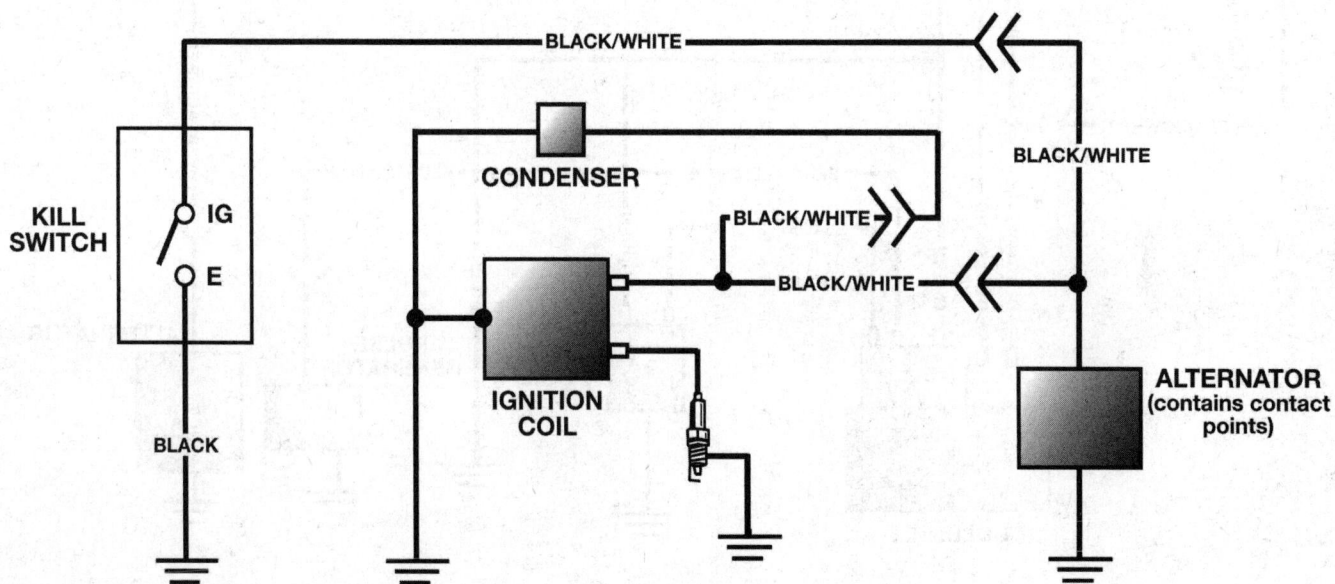

BLACK/WHITE

CONDENSER

BLACK/WHITE

BLACK/WHITE

BLACK/WHITE

KILL SWITCH

IG

E

IGNITION COIL

ALTERNATOR
(contains contact points)

BLACK

2218-WD-A HAYNES

Wiring diagram - models with breaker point ignition

**IGNITION
SWITCH
(2001 and later models)**

IG   E

BLACK/WHITE

GREEN

BLACK/WHITE

GREEN

IG

E

**KILL
SWITCH**

BLACK

BLACK/WHITE

BLACK/WHITE

BLACK/RED

GREEN

BLUE/YELLOW

BLACK/YELLOW

BLUE/YELLOW

GREEN

GREEN

BLACK/RED

**IGNITION
COIL**

**PULSE
GENERATOR**

ALTERNATOR

CDI UNIT

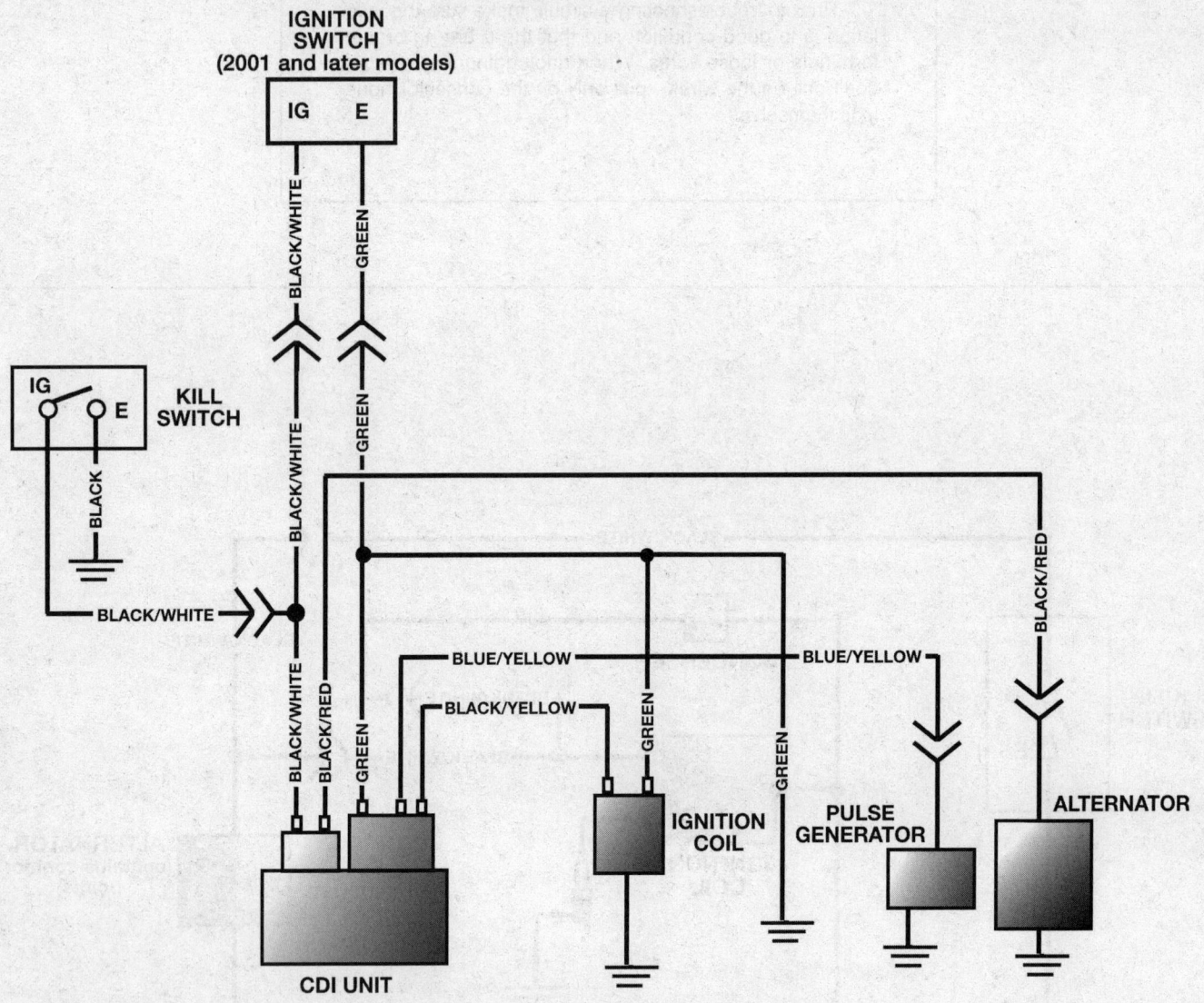

2218-WD-B HAYNES

Wiring diagram - models with CDI ignition

Conversion factors

Length (distance)
Inches (in)	X	25.4	= Millimeters (mm)	X 0.0394	= Inches (in)
Feet (ft)	X	0.305	= Meters (m)	X 3.281	= Feet (ft)
Miles	X	1.609	= Kilometers (km)	X 0.621	= Miles

Volume (capacity)
Cubic inches (cu in; in³)	X	16.387	= Cubic centimeters (cc; cm³)	X 0.061	= Cubic inches (cu in; in³)
Imperial pints (Imp pt)	X	0.568	= Liters (l)	X 1.76	= Imperial pints (Imp pt)
Imperial quarts (Imp qt)	X	1.137	= Liters (l)	X 0.88	= Imperial quarts (Imp qt)
Imperial quarts (Imp qt)	X	1.201	= US quarts (US qt)	X 0.833	= Imperial quarts (Imp qt)
US quarts (US qt)	X	0.946	= Liters (l)	X 1.057	= US quarts (US qt)
Imperial gallons (Imp gal)	X	4.546	= Liters (l)	X 0.22	= Imperial gallons (Imp gal)
Imperial gallons (Imp gal)	X	1.201	= US gallons (US gal)	X 0.833	= Imperial gallons (Imp gal)
US gallons (US gal)	X	3.785	= Liters (l)	X 0.264	= US gallons (US gal)

Mass (weight)
Ounces (oz)	X	28.35	= Grams (g)	X 0.035	= Ounces (oz)
Pounds (lb)	X	0.454	= Kilograms (kg)	X 2.205	= Pounds (lb)

Force
Ounces-force (ozf; oz)	X	0.278	= Newtons (N)	X 3.6	= Ounces-force (ozf; oz)
Pounds-force (lbf; lb)	X	4.448	= Newtons (N)	X 0.225	= Pounds-force (lbf; lb)
Newtons (N)	X	0.1	= Kilograms-force (kgf; kg)	X 9.81	= Newtons (N)

Pressure
Pounds-force per square inch (psi; lbf/in²; lb/in²)	X	0.070	= Kilograms-force per square centimeter (kgf/cm²; kg/cm²)	X 14.223	= Pounds-force per square inch (psi; lbf/in²; lb/in²)
Pounds-force per square inch (psi; lbf/in²; lb/in²)	X	0.068	= Atmospheres (atm)	X 14.696	= Pounds-force per square inch (psi; lbf/in²; lb/in²)
Pounds-force per square inch (psi; lbf/in²; lb/in²)	X	0.069	= Bars	X 14.5	= Pounds-force per square inch (psi; lbf/in²; lb/in²)
Pounds-force per square inch (psi; lbf/in²; lb/in²)	X	6.895	= Kilopascals (kPa)	X 0.145	= Pounds-force per square inch (psi; lbf/in²; lb/in²)
Kilopascals (kPa)	X	0.01	= Kilograms-force per square centimeter (kgf/cm²; kg/cm²)	X 98.1	= Kilopascals (kPa)

Torque (moment of force)
Pounds-force inches (lbf in; lb in)	X	1.152	= Kilograms-force centimeter (kgf cm; kg cm)	X 0.868	= Pounds-force inches (lbf in; lb in)
Pounds-force inches (lbf in; lb in)	X	0.113	= Newton meters (Nm)	X 8.85	= Pounds-force inches (lbf in; lb in)
Pounds-force inches (lbf in; lb in)	X	0.083	= Pounds-force feet (lbf ft; lb ft)	X 12	= Pounds-force inches (lbf in; lb in)
Pounds-force feet (lbf ft; lb ft)	X	0.138	= Kilograms-force meters (kgf m; kg m)	X 7.233	= Pounds-force feet (lbf ft; lb ft)
Pounds-force feet (lbf ft; lb ft)	X	1.356	= Newton meters (Nm)	X 0.738	= Pounds-force feet (lbf ft; lb ft)
Newton meters (Nm)	X	0.102	= Kilograms-force meters (kgf m; kg m)	X 9.804	= Newton meters (Nm)

Vacuum
Inches mercury (in. Hg)	X	3.377	= Kilopascals (kPa)	X 0.2961	= Inches mercury
Inches mercury (in. Hg)	X	25.4	= Millimeters mercury (mm Hg)	X 0.0394	= Inches mercury

Power
Horsepower (hp)	X	745.7	= Watts (W)	X 0.0013	= Horsepower (hp)

Velocity (speed)
Miles per hour (miles/hr; mph)	X	1.609	= Kilometers per hour (km/hr; kph)	X 0.621	= Miles per hour (miles/hr; mph)

Fuel consumption*
Miles per gallon, Imperial (mpg)	X	0.354	= Kilometers per liter (km/l)	X 2.825	= Miles per gallon, Imperial (mpg)
Miles per gallon, US (mpg)	X	0.425	= Kilometers per liter (km/l)	X 2.352	= Miles per gallon, US (mpg)

Temperature
Degrees Fahrenheit = (°C x 1.8) + 32

Degrees Celsius (Degrees Centigrade; °C) = (°F - 32) x 0.56

*It is common practice to convert from miles per gallon (mpg) to liters/100 kilometers (l/100km), where mpg (Imperial) x l/100 km = 282 and mpg (US) x l/100 km = 235

DECIMALS to MILLIMETERS

Decimal	mm	Decimal	mm
0.001	0.0254	0.500	12.7000
0.002	0.0508	0.510	12.9540
0.003	0.0762	0.520	13.2080
0.004	0.1016	0.530	13.4620
0.005	0.1270	0.540	13.7160
0.006	0.1524	0.550	13.9700
0.007	0.1778	0.560	14.2240
0.008	0.2032	0.570	14.4780
0.009	0.2286	0.580	14.7320
		0.590	14.9860
0.010	0.2540		
0.020	0.5080		
0.030	0.7620		
0.040	1.0160	0.600	15.2400
0.050	1.2700	0.610	15.4940
0.060	1.5240	0.620	15.7480
0.070	1.7780	0.630	16.0020
0.080	2.0320	0.640	16.2560
0.090	2.2860	0.650	16.5100
		0.660	16.7640
0.100	2.5400	0.670	17.0180
0.110	2.7940	0.680	17.2720
0.120	3.0480	0.690	17.5260
0.130	3.3020		
0.140	3.5560		
0.150	3.8100		
0.160	4.0640	0.700	17.7800
0.170	4.3180	0.710	18.0340
0.180	4.5720	0.720	18.2880
0.190	4.8260	0.730	18.5420
		0.740	18.7960
0.200	5.0800	0.750	19.0500
0.210	5.3340	0.760	19.3040
0.220	5.5880	0.770	19.5580
0.230	5.8420	0.780	19.8120
0.240	6.0960	0.790	20.0660
0.250	6.3500		
0.260	6.6040		
0.270	6.8580	0.800	20.3200
0.280	7.1120	0.810	20.5740
0.290	7.3660	0.820	21.8280
		0.830	21.0820
0.300	7.6200	0.840	21.3360
0.310	7.8740	0.850	21.5900
0.320	8.1280	0.860	21.8440
0.330	8.3820	0.870	22.0980
0.340	8.6360	0.880	22.3520
0.350	8.8900	0.890	22.6060
0.360	9.1440		
0.370	9.3980		
0.380	9.6520		
0.390	9.9060	0.900	22.8600
0.400	10.1600	0.910	23.1140
0.410	10.4140	0.920	23.3680
0.420	10.6680	0.930	23.6220
0.430	10.9220	0.940	23.8760
0.440	11.1760	0.950	24.1300
0.450	11.4300	0.960	24.3840
0.460	11.6840	0.970	24.6380
0.470	11.9380	0.980	24.8920
0.480	12.1920	0.990	25.1460
0.490	12.4460	1.000	25.4000

FRACTIONS to DECIMALS to MILLIMETERS

Fraction	Decimal	mm	Fraction	Decimal	mm
1/64	0.0156	0.3969	33/64	0.5156	13.0969
1/32	0.0312	0.7938	17/32	0.5312	13.4938
3/64	0.0469	1.1906	35/64	0.5469	13.8906
1/16	0.0625	1.5875	9/16	0.5625	14.2875
5/64	0.0781	1.9844	37/64	0.5781	14.6844
3/32	0.0938	2.3812	19/32	0.5938	15.0812
7/64	0.1094	2.7781	39/64	0.6094	15.4781
1/8	0.1250	3.1750	5/8	0.6250	15.8750
9/64	0.1406	3.5719	41/64	0.6406	16.2719
5/32	0.1562	3.9688	21/32	0.6562	16.6688
11/64	0.1719	4.3656	43/64	0.6719	17.0656
3/16	0.1875	4.7625	11/16	0.6875	17.4625
13/64	0.2031	5.1594	45/64	0.7031	17.8594
7/32	0.2188	5.5562	23/32	0.7188	18.2562
15/64	0.2344	5.9531	47/64	0.7344	18.6531
1/4	0.2500	6.3500	3/4	0.7500	19.0500
17/64	0.2656	6.7469	49/64	0.7656	19.4469
9/32	0.2812	7.1438	25/32	0.7812	19.8438
19/64	0.2969	7.5406	51/64	0.7969	20.2406
5/16	0.3125	7.9375	13/16	0.8125	20.6375
21/64	0.3281	8.3344	53/64	0.8281	21.0344
11/32	0.3438	8.7312	27/32	0.8438	21.4312
23/64	0.3594	9.1281	55/64	0.8594	21.8281
3/8	0.3750	9.5250	7/8	0.8750	22.2250
25/64	0.3906	9.9219	57/64	0.8906	22.6219
13/32	0.4062	10.3188	29/32	0.9062	23.0188
27/64	0.4219	10.7156	59/64	0.9219	23.4156
7/16	0.4375	11.1125	15/16	0.9375	23.8125
29/64	0.4531	11.5094	61/64	0.9531	24.2094
15/32	0.4688	11.9062	31/32	0.9688	24.6062
31/64	0.4844	12.3031	63/64	0.9844	25.0031
1/2	0.5000	12.7000	1	1.0000	25.4000

Index